T0158804

Sea and Shore Stories,
And The
Nuclear Boogeyman
Life's Experiences and Lessons

Ebe Chandler McCabe, Jr.

 iUniverse®

SEA AND SHORE STORIES, AND THE NUCLEAR BOOGEYMAN
LIFE'S EXPERIENCES AND LESSONS

iUniverse books may be ordered through booksellers or by contacting:

iUniverse
1663 Liberty Drive
Bloomington, IN 47403
www.iuniverse.com
1-800-Authors (1-800-288-4677)

ISBN: 978-1-5320-0257-1 (sc)
ISBN: 978-1-5320-0258-8 (hc)
ISBN: 978-1-5320-0256-4 (e)

Library of Congress Control Number: 2016913621

Print information available on the last page.

iUniverse rev. date: 11/01/2016

For

This book was written for my cultural and genetic descendants, with the hope that they will consider my views as their own mature. Foremost in mind during the writing were the following young men:

Keith Chandler (KC) McCabe, II, my older grandson. He went to college on a scholarship, graduated with a civil engineering degree in 2015, and quickly gained employment in his chosen field. The maturity, work ethic, and sensibility he has so far demonstrated augur well for a continued successful life as a valuable contributing citizen of excellent character.

Christopher (Fofer) Michael Palmer, my younger grandson. I met him the day he was born. Then, when medical difficulties inhibited his mother's contribution to his development, I gained the privilege of teaching him to walk and talk. He has become an excellent student with musical as well as academic proficiency. His parents and I look forward to seeing his fine character and capabilities continue to make him into a special human being.

Acknowledgements

That this book is as intelligible as it is to those without scientific or engineering expertise is largely due to the perceptive comments of Mrs. Eliot Ann Marshall. Also, her constructive, enabling support was a major contributing factor to completing the book.

That the organization of this book has been substantively improved over its original form is largely due to heeding the comments of Mr. Fritz Marston.

Contributors

I couldn't have written this book without the contributions of a multitude of nurturing people and organizations. The following deserve particular mention.

My parents and family. They taught and set an example of honesty and integrity.

My Educators. They opened my mind to knowledge.

The U.S. Government. It gave me the opportunity to get an education that I couldn't afford.

The U.S. Naval Academy. In addition to guiding and administering my college education, it honed honorable values and force fed me much needed discipline.

My Naval Academy classmates. They have remained an ongoing invaluable example of the best aspects of mankind.

Active and Reserve Navy personnel. They taught and set an example of skill and integrity.

Conventional and nuclear submariners. They set an exceptionally high standard and example of excellence.

Our Finest Generation. I observed some of these admirable Americans as they were completing their naval careers. They were still examples of the exceptional competence that produced the outstanding World War II performance of our submarine force.

My civilian subordinates, contemporaries, and bosses who set a further fine example of competence and integrity.

Preface

This book began when my stepdaughter asked me to write down my Navy experiences for my grandsons. The scope grew to cover other matters.

Experiences are history. And, because human nature hasn't changed, history repeats itself. So this book also is about today and tomorrow, and your life as well as mine.

Skepticism is a core aspect of my views. It grew as I did.

Earning a living led me to reject the "liberal" view that we are owed one and the "conservative" view that we must stand completely on our own. Seeking the reality between those extremes meant trying to cast off my ideologies.

What I've learned cannot help readers to change anyone but themselves. In that respect, we all need safeguards against our own natural hate, greed, and complacency.

My views aren't endorsed by any organization or entity. They aren't original either. *(There's nothing new under the sun.)* But they do reflect available public information.

I've had no access to any classified National Security Information for over 20 years. For highly classified material, it's been at least twice that long.

Individuals I've known have been separated from events by curtailing the use of names. Locating related events near each other even if chronology wasn't served added to that.

An explanation of some military terms is appended.

Contents

Part I

Fledgling Years

I-1 The Beginning

Early Days

I was born in 1933, during the Great Depression that cost my father his job as a surveyor. He became a milkman. In 1937, we moved to New York City, where Dad was a fruit inspector. But that was still city life, and after six years we moved to Dad's rural home town, where he was well known and respected.

Internationally, war was being used to advance national interests. Japan had invaded Manchuria (Northeast China) and set up a puppet state there in 1931. Italy invaded Abyssinia in 1935, and Japan made a full scale invasion of China in 1937. Germany started World War II by invading Poland in September 1939. U.S. anti-war sentiment was strong (especially among Republicans). Nonetheless, in September 1940, President Franklin Delano Roosevelt (FDR) traded 50 mothballed U.S. destroyers to England for 99-year leases of strategic bases. Then, in October 1940, the first peacetime draft of U.S. citizens began. And the Lend-Lease Act was passed in March 1941 to support England, Russia and China with war materials.

Winston Churchill had been England's First Lord of the Admiralty in World War I. He was involved in the Gallipoli defeat and proposed the disastrous naval attack on the Dardanelles. In 1935, he was out of office and unpopular. But he adamantly opposed appeasing Germany, declaring:

With Germany arming at breakneck speed, England lost in a Pacifist dream, France corrupt and torn by dissension, America remote and indifferent...do you not tremble for your children?

3

England continued its appeasement.

International tension escalated on October 31, 1941 when the USS Reuben James (DD-245), a 21 year old destroyer, was torpedoed by a German submarine (U-Boat U-552). The James was escorting a Europe-bound convoy of war materials. She sank with a loss of 115 sailors. There were 44 survivors.

World War II

England's Prime Minister, Neville Chamberlain, had described his 1938 meeting with Adolph Hitler as meaning "peace for our time." After Germany invaded Poland in September 1939 and England declared war on Germany, the calls for Chamberlain's resignation increased. That happened on May 10, 1941, when Germany invaded Holland, Belgium, and the Netherlands.

Winston Churchill was named prime minister. He became England's greatest war leader and perhaps the greatest 20th Century world leader. His strategic lapses were overcome by sage counsel and dwarfed by oratorical eloquence, bulldog tenacity, understanding of human nature, and intellect. (Quotes showing his wisdom, wit, and mastery of the English language are an entertainment still.) The posture he so compellingly fostered is very evident in the following parts of two different speeches he made shortly after becoming prime minister:

> *We shall defend our island, whatever the cost may be, we shall fight on the beaches, we shall fight on the landing grounds, we shall fight in the fields and in the streets, we shall fight in the hills; we shall never surrender.*

> *But if we fail, then the whole world, including the United States, including all that we have known and cared for, will sink into the abyss of a new dark age made more sinister, and perhaps more protracted, by the lights of perverted science. Let us therefore brace ourselves to our duties, and so bear ourselves, that if the British*

*Empire and its Commonwealth last for a thousand years,
men will still say, This was their finest hour.*

On December 7, 1941, 37 days after the Reuben James sank, Japan attacked an un-alert Pearl Harbor. The next day, FDR gave his historic *Day of Infamy* speech. (We heard it on the tall Philco radio console in our living room.) America's fearful mood turned into hope, confidence, and determination. Congress declared war on Japan the same day. Isolationist and anti-war sentiment went into hiding. Our military enlistment centers were clogged with volunteers. Many more were drafted.

Four days later, Germany declared war on the USA. We declared war on Germany and Italy before that day was out.

FDR still is maligned for his socialism. It has even been alleged that he knew the Japanese would attack Pearl Harbor and did nothing because he wanted to go to war. But that proves only the maliciousness of partisan politics.

I recently replayed the *Day of Infamy* speech on the internet (seeing it for the first time). It stirred me again. And, while I believe that the war saved America from the economic woes that FDR worsened, I also have unbounded admiration for the wartime strength and leadership this physical cripple provided.

FDR's and Churchill's broadcasts molded our (the Allies) attitude and insistence on unconditional surrender of our foes (the Axis). That and the courage of the men who fought that war (often called Our Finest Generation) are reminders of my early years.

FDR died on April 12, 1945, early in his fourth term. Our new president, Harry S. Truman, made a nervous initial address to the nation, and a neighbor said he was just a haberdasher. My father said that everything would be fine because "the job makes the man." (It doesn't.) But Truman had a good start. Hostilities with Germany ended within a month.

Truman didn't know about the atomic bomb until he became president. But he had one dropped on Hiroshima in an attempt to induce Japan to surrender. Japan didn't, and our only other atomic bomb was dropped on Nagasaki. Japan capitulated. America was exultant. The death toll had ceased and our "boys" would be coming home.

A radio announcement of the war's end (I think by Gabriel Heater) described the wonderful new clearness of the skies. I went outside, couldn't see anything different, and had to have my parents explain that statement to me.

Home Town Years

When we left New York City, I was a scrawny, buck-toothed city kid who had mashed a few noses over being ridiculed about my teeth. Dad gently tried to foster a less combative stick-up-for-yourself approach. Mom encouraged me to read and praised all indications of mental prowess. I was fascinated by the town library's trove of *The Bobbsey Twins* series and by the musty piles of my uncle's books, which gave me the sagas of *Beowulf,* of *Charlemagne,* and of *Roland.* But the world of books produced oblivion to everything else, so my parents' focused on getting me outdoors and playing in the fresh air.

Our town had not even one traffic light. Its white and black residents were separate. That was brought home to me when an adult white male called me aside. He said that, while it was OK for younger children of different races to play together, I had passed that age and needed to stop playing with colored children. (I also had been called a "nigger-lover" by another white kid.) My father said there would be less trouble if I followed that advice. But, its racism notwithstanding, I still see that community as it was when I grew up as more supportive and caring than many in America today. That's because the separation that we decry and legally restrict seems to be increasing, unfair group discrimination against non-members is common, and only a few of us are free of ethnic prejudice.

My great-grandfather was important to this part of my life. A community legend, he started going to sea at the age of 12, educated himself, earned a Master's License, brought his ship safely through a storm that washed her Captain overboard, and became a Captain from then on. He became wealthy as a skipper of seagoing salvage tugs. His small size was compensated for by his lightning-quick, fierce fighting skill. That was accompanied by an indomitable character and a volcanic temper. But his word was his bond and he had a deeply caring, benevolent nature. Nobody confronted him. Old men gossiping at local haunts told tales of his exploits.

My father adored my great-grandfather and had the same values but not the fierceness. Still, giving up on anything was abhorrent to Dad, who was fond of saying: It's not how many times you fall off the horse that counts; it's how many times you get back on. And he extolled education, saying things like: the man who knows how will always have a job, the man who knows why will always be the boss. He also frequently stated: They can take your job away from you, but they can't take away your education. My father also took advantage of my dislike of farm work to press his agenda. I once said, while he and I were cleaning manure out of a chicken house, that there had to be better ways to make a living. Dad responded that, if I wanted a better life, I had better get an education.

My mother also put a high value on education and both Dad and Mom considered all work honorable. Earning one's way was their key to being independent. They even reprimanded me for complaining about a summer job that put me knee-deep in week-old garbage in the back of the dump truck used to haul it away.

When I was 13 years old, braces corrected my buck teeth. (They were removed early because we couldn't afford to finish the treatment.)

Harry S. Truman

Being president, and using the atomic bomb, made Harry S. Truman a center of attention. Elitists even attacked him for mispronouncing words. I empathized with him because my pronunciation of words learned from books was often demeaned. Also, I admired his defense of his daughter Margaret. When a music critic panned her singing voice, *Give 'em Hell Harry* called the review poppycock, stated that he hoped to meet the critic and that, when that happened, the man would need a new nose, beefsteak for black eyes, and perhaps a supporter below.

Truman also was known for his presidential motto that "The buck stops here" and the statement that "If you can't stand the heat, get out of the kitchen." Unpopular for the cronyism and corruption in his administration (things I wasn't then aware of), and for desegregating the armed forces by executive order, he was expected to lose the 1948 election. But he made an aggressive "whistle-stop" train campaign and won. He then happily posed with the prematurely issued Chicago Tribune newspaper front page headline stating "DEWEY BEATS TRUMAN."

When North Korea invaded South Korea in 1950, Truman started the Korean War as a "Police Action." Then, when General MacArthur, one of America's best generals ever, "imperiously" advocated attacking China, Truman fired him. But the prolonged war, the MacArthur firing, integration of the military, and political corruption made Truman too unpopular to run for re-election. Unrepentant, he retired to his home in Independence, Missouri.

If ever a medal for political correctness is issued, it won't bear Harry S. Truman's name. But he is still lauded for never using his high position for personal profit. He also remains a great example of tenacity and of facing issues squarely. And, despite the cronyism and corruption in his administration, some have rated him as one of America's better presidents.

The regard I had for President Truman nosedived when researching this book revealed his pardon of Ex-Congressman Ernest J. May. (That's discussed later.)

Military Leanings

My gravitation toward the Military began with my father's boyhood desire to go to West Point. He didn't realize that dream, but touted the Military Academy's virtues. That was made easier by the accolades showered on famous West Pointers like General Eisenhower and General MacArthur.

Dad's high regard for West Point probably played a big part in my becoming an avid Army football fan. My heroes were Doc Blanchard (Mr. Inside), Glenn Davis (Mr. Outside), and Arnold Tucker (Quarterback). All three of them are in the College Football Hall of Fame. Under their legendary coach, Red Blaik, their football team went 27-0-1 while they were on the squad. Blanchard and Davis were three-time All-Americans. Tucker also garnered that honor his senior year, giving Army an All-American backfield. Blanchard became the first college junior to win the Heisman Trophy, and Davis won it the next year.

WWII brought glory years to Service Academy football by bringing top athletes to West Point and Annapolis. In 1943, Navy had the #4 ranking and beat #11 Army. The next two years, #1 Army beat #2 Navy. Then, in 1946, Army was undefeated but had a 0-0 tie with Notre Dame. Some rated Notre Dame #1, others gave the nod to Army. After the war, the service academies' football rankings dropped, but I remained a die-hard Army fan.

The Academy Appointment

In his effort to get me into West Point, Dad approached U.S. Senator John Williams. They had attended the same one-room school and Dad still called him Johnny. I met the Senator when he came to one of our high school basketball games to see his nephew play. He was complimentary but later told Dad that he had to appoint the best Republican boy and we were Democrats.

My father then turned to Senator J. Allen Frear, a Democrat. Dad's brother had been his fraternity brother at college, and approached him. The Senator said he would be glad to appoint me if I got the best grade on the civil service exam he gave. But, because he had four cadets at West Point, he had only an appointment to Annapolis. I took the exam, finished fourth of about 25 candidates, and had a chance to get in as a qualified alternate. But I failed the physical because of an uneven bite. After a year at college, I tried again, and the Senator had appointments to both academies. I got the highest grade and chose Annapolis. (It had rejected me. And the townspeople respected seagoing and disparaged sleeping in foxholes.)

When the next physical came around, I had worn braces for another year. They involved a metal collar around each tooth, wires attached to each collar and regularly tightened, and elastic bands providing tension between the upper and lower braces. The time constraint made for vigorous tightening of the braces, and they were a constant pain. These braces also had to come off before the work was done. But they produced an acceptable bite, and I was told that I had passed the physical.

Several weeks later, Senator Frear phoned and asked why I hadn't requested a physical re-exam. I said they told me I had passed. He said that they failed me for poor eyesight and replaced me with a football player. Two days later, I passed the re-exam he arranged, and entered the Naval Academy as scheduled. (At my 50th class reunion, I said that I still remembered the 20-20 line on the eye chart. A classmate grinned and correctly stated that it was D-E-F-P-O-T-E-C.)

I-2 The Naval Academy

Plebe Summer started the Academy's plebe (freshman) year. The upper classes were on cruises, but there were enough assigned to whip us into shape. We learned to march, spit-shine shoes, salute, roll neckerchiefs, etc. We also got "fried" (assigned demerits and extra duty) and had no time off the grounds.

There also was a whaleboat race day. The heavy whaleboats had heavy oars, and each race was gut-wrenching. The boat I was in won its first race. We soon raced again, against another winner, and were handily beaten. So we joined the other defeated crews ashore and watched the rest of the races—a classic case of the agony of unrewarded victory competing with the relative comfort of defeat. I still wonder about that.

One of the first things we had to correct was "Irish Pennants," the thread ends that hadn't been removed from our new uniforms. I had no idea about the term's origin, but the derogatory connotation was obvious. Later, I concluded that the most likely origin was the initial poverty of early Irish immigrants. The only clothes they had were home-made. When they became able to buy manufactured clothing, they wore it untrimmed as evidence of their newfound prosperity. The derisive term Irish Pennant resulted. And, even if that wasn't the source, the term is an example of ethnic derogation.

We also soon heard about the first black midshipman. He had reportedly died of exposure, tied to a spider buoy in the harbor. But my naval career also began with very clear instruction that the Navy was integrated, and racial and religious discrimination were prohibited. There indeed was no apparent discrimination by most of us. Our common difficulties militated against prejudice, and the racism that remained was covert.

We also learned the roll of being the on-duty midshipman officer's messenger, assigned to run and get the name of a midshipman being fried. I had that duty one day and followed along toward a group of midshipmen assembled in ranks. One stood out because, in that long line of carefully spit-shined black shoes, his were heavy, tan boondocks. He was, of course, fried for being out of uniform. But he reportedly was fried so often that he marched extra duty before and after each day's assigned tasks. At the end of one of his extra-long days, he supposedly was even found to have put his heavy Garand M1 rifle up in a tree so it would be readily available for his next morning's extra duty. (Those were operable guns.) This individual wasn't unique in finding the transition to Service Academy life difficult. Almost all of us had to accept substantial change. Those who didn't had to seek careers more suited to their talents.

Plebe Year

Academic year soon started. Plebes were inspected at meal formations, and sat at a seated attention ("braced up") during meals. We got last choice of food—but had plenty to eat. And we ate "square" meals by taking the food from the plate, raising the utensil vertically to mouth level, and carrying it horizontally to the mouth. The utensil was returned via the square route for the next bite. And professional questions were meted out to be looked up. One might be asked, for example, the length, tonnage, and armament of a specific warship. Sometimes, the plebes had a turn to ask professional questions back. If one stumped the upper classmen, the asking plebe might be granted "Carry On" (relaxing) for the rest of that meal. Earning a Carry On wasn't easy because the first classmen (seniors) were in their fourth year of this ritual and were hard to stump. The only question that earned me a Carry On was the meaning of the Russian aircraft MIG designation. (It's the names of the designers, Mikoyan and Gurevich.)

Another facet of plebe year was the "Come Around"—reporting to a first classman in his room. That could be for having displeased him, or because he wanted to give instruction, or just because he felt like it. So one marched down the center of the corridor, squarely turned each corner, reported as ordered, and was interrogated or instructed or ridiculed as the first classman and his room-mate(s) wished. An offensive statement or attitude might be the cause for a rebuke or the assignment of a task to be completed and reported at another Come Around. Or the offending plebe might be ordered to "Sit on the Little Green Bench," an imaginary stool. (It didn't take me long to fall off.) This onerous process was far better than getting fried, which any upperclassman could find a reason for doing if he wished. But, as we learned the ropes, as the upperclassmen had before us, the penalties tapered off.

Reef Points, a booklet of Navy and Naval Academy lore, contained information that we had to regurgitate on demand. Some of it was juvenile, like being asked *How is the Cow?* and having to answer: "*Sir, she walks, she talks, she is full of chalk. The lacteal fluid extracted from the female of the bovine species is highly prolific to the nth degree.*" And some of it was wise, like the poem *The Laws of the Navy*, written by RADM Ronald A. Hopwood of Britain's Royal Navy, and first published in 1896. I remember its first verse as:

> *Now these are the Laws of the Navy,*
> *Unwritten and varied they be;*
> *And he who is wise will observe them,*
> *Going down in his ship to the sea.*

That poem provides still sound wisdom about succeeding. Its messages include: speaking ill of one's seniors can devastate one's own chances of success, leave (vacation) is necessary to restore the abilities of the hard-working, a deserved promotion may not come, reprimands should not be given in anger, etc.

Despite their wisdom, the *Laws of the Navy* are tendentiously orientated toward describing a perfect officer in a perfect Navy. That's very clear in the wording that states:

> *Every law is as naught beside this one -*
> *Thou shall not criticise but obey!*

The Nuremberg Impact

The obedience mandate limit, as taught at the Naval Academy, was that anyone who carries out an unlawful order is as responsible as the individual who issues it. The basis for that was the Nuremberg War Trials, where the defense of obedience to orders was rejected. Those trials began in November 1945 and, on October 1, 1946, sentenced 11 Nazis to death. Ten of them were hanged on October 16, 1946. The 11th (Goering) had committed suicide the previous night.

The Nuremberg Trials have been heavily criticized as the unprincipled application of ex post facto law and as "Victor's Justice." They certainly were victor's justice; whether they were unprincipled or unjust depends on how one views the 40[+] million deaths caused by the Nazis.

Under the Nuremberg Principles, those who commit militarily unnecessary acts (murder, ill-treatment, deportation, slave labor, etc.) are responsible for those acts. That puts officials in the position of being either being held accountable for carrying out ordered but illegal acts (if and when the ax falls) or being punished for not carrying them out (if the ordering official/organization remains in power). The choice is easier if severe acts are involved. When lesser unlawful acts are ordered, however, those ordered to commit them face retribution for disobedience or the sacrifice of their principles. In one form or another, everyone faces this issue.

Admiral Doenitz is an example of the precedent set for the military at the Nuremberg Trials. He had commanded Germany's U-boats, and then the German Navy, and was Hitler's successor (for 20 days). Among the crimes Doenitz was charged with was conducting unrestricted submarine warfare and failing to rescue survivors of attacked ships. But, as Admiral Nimitz (our Pacific Fleet Commander) testified, the U.S. had conducted unrestricted submarine warfare in the Pacific from the start of the war. (Many military men believed that Doenitz did no more than his duty.) Doenitz was found not guilty of conducting unrestricted submarine warfare, except for the case of neutral vessels. No sentence was imposed for that. His 10 year sentence was imposed (and served) for planning, initiating, and waging a war of aggression, and for crimes against the laws of war.

Officer Staff

Officers on the Academy staff typically were excellent role models. One, in particular, sometimes took time to discuss items of mutual interest with us. We asked him what funding cuts do to the ability to defend the country. He said that the peacetime defense budget was always slighted and, when war came, a lot of servicemen died as a result. I now see that as inevitable, with modern weapons raising the death toll.

One staff officer was known for frying midshipmen right and left. He was avoided when possible, and his nickname reflected poorly on the maturity of the Brigade of Midshipmen. But some midshipmen who had considerable contact with the man spoke highly of him. And he provided realistic preparation for duty with seniors who behaved much like he did.

Our instructors included both civilians and officers. Most of our officer instructors were Navy Lieutenants or Marine Captains. (That's the same rank.) One of them, a Marine, described the Marines' effectiveness as being like the Army capturing an island in a month while losing 400 men a day and the Marines capturing it in a week while losing 800 men a day. That's what he felt Marine Gung Ho (esprit de corps) achieved.

As no doubt exists everywhere, we felt that some instructors were unfair. One of those once assigned a homework problem that no one in the class could do. We asked him to show us how. He wrote the formula that we knew on the blackboard, and said that we only had to make the various substitutions. But he wouldn't identify them. We had to teach ourselves that course.

One Midshipman Company had an Army Officer as a Company Officer. He was Captain George Patton IV, the son of infamous World War II Major General George S. Patton, Jr. Reportedly, Captain Patton loaned one of his father's military history books to a midshipman. It contained his father's marginal notes about battles, with a typical comment being "No Guts." And the reputation of the father made us apprehensive about the son. My only encounter with him was when I had to go past him to get to a seat for a lecture, and stepped on one toe of his shoes, destroying its spit-shine. His comment was a sharp *That's alright, Mister, I walk on them too.* But that was his only reaction. And our apprehension may have been misplaced. This second Major General George S. Patton was known for having great concern for his men as well as for being a spit and polish soldier.

The Academy also stressed "Duty, Honor, Country." That mantra grew stronger in us over the years.

Attrition

Many plebes got a hefty dose of demerits. Some exceeded the limit and were discharged. But it was rare for an upper classman to exceed the limit. Still, the rules were always there, and a serious infraction during any year could result in a "Class A" offense. Some of these could alone be cause for discharge. The others could put an offender who already had a lot of demerits over the limit. And even a midshipman with a good conduct record was put in a precarious position by one.

Academic failure (failing any course) was a more frequent cause for discharge. But there was the alternative, in some cases, of becoming a "Turnback." That meant repeating the entire year and graduating with the next class. There was also the possibility for a re-examination, but that seemed even rarer than turning back.

Some Midshipmen resigned. One of my plebe summer roommates did that because he missed his home and girlfriend badly. Another classmate, an Admiral's son, resigned early in our first academic year. A basic factor in these and many other discharges, including some academic ones, was unhappiness with the way of life that the Academy involved and presaged.

Our class started with about 1200 midshipmen and graduated about 850. (The numbers I remember are 1198 and 849.) That's about a 71% graduation rate. A statement bandied about at the start of Plebe Summer was that, if we looked at the person to the right and the one to the left of us in ranks, we could expect that one of us three wouldn't graduate. But I recently saw, on the Complete College America website, that only 60.6% of full-time college students now graduate in eight years. So our graduation rate was significantly higher than today's norm, perhaps because of higher entrance requirements and closer supervision.

Loyalty

Not bilging (putting in a difficult position) a classmate became ingrained in us. That went beyond not "ratting" to not causing harm, to giving help, and to giving a heads up about adversity in the wind. My roommate and I were an example of mutual support between midshipmen. Like everyone else's, our room was routinely inspected, with the midshipman In Charge of Room getting the demerits for the infractions found. The duty of being In Charge of Room was supposed to be rotated weekly. But my roommate accrued demerits readily, and the In Charge of Room tag above our door remained under my name for almost all of our last two years. We also supported each other academically. I helped him in scientific courses and had the benefit of his proficiency in Bull (English, History, and Government). That far outweighed the few demerits it cost me to be In Charge of Room.

It's also was dogma that one did not report the improper actions of a senior. The penalty for that, ostracism, was unofficial. A classmate who crossed that line was so treated. Except for his room-mate, other midshipman carefully avoided him. His fiancé was a major factor in his sticking it out and graduating. But I suspect that repercussions of that experience affected him until he died. Unfair as such discrimination can be, it has a rational side: ratting on one's seniors can destroy the working relationship. The dilemma is: what misbehavior is so serious that violating a taboo is necessary despite the inevitable retaliation? "Whistleblowing" and the Nuremberg Principles are closely related to this issue, which has no easy answer.

Academics

There was fierce academic competition at the top of each class. One competitor, when the daily quiz from the previous class was returned, checked his grade (typically a perfect 4.0) and asked those nearby theirs. That provided an incentive for others to focus more on classes with him—just to be able to occasionally show a better grade. So he made them better students.

The top competitors had counterparts near the bottom of the class. There, the academically less skilled struggled to avoid failing a course and getting kicked out. To them, the mantra *Two Five and Survive* had real meaning (2.5 was the passing grade). The midshipman with the lowest grade for four years was the class Anchor Man, and a relatively high proportion of Anchor Men advanced to the rank of Admiral. Their success still seems to me to be due to unflappability and exceptionally hard work.

Steam (Marine Engineering) was boring. Studying the touted M-Type Boiler and its saturated and superheated steam tube nests was especially painful. But the nadir of Steam's appeal was the training movie *The Magic of Steam*. When showed right after the noon meal, it could put an entire class asleep in a few minutes. And it was shown repeatedly. That made courses in subjects like thermodynamics relatively palatable. Our final exam in that was a big surprise. It straightforwardly covered the course with no tricky questions. I expected a high grade and got a 3.96, losing points for mislabeling a heat cycle diagram. And there were so many high grades that the integrity of the exam was expected to be questioned. If it was, we didn't hear about it.

I never saw another Academy exam that straightforward. And the only time I came close to a very high class standing was in the course on the nautical Rules of the Road. I didn't miss any quiz questions until the last and most heavily weighted question on the final exam. That dropped my course standing to about 250. But I came away with a lasting appreciation for the "General Prudential Rule." I remember its essence as: *In obeying and construing these rules, due regard shall be had for the dangers of navigation and collision, including special circumstances such as the limitations of the craft involved, and necessary action taken to avoid immediate danger."* A lot of other arenas could benefit from such an explicit *do whatcha gotta to be safe* mandate.

Quizzes at the Academy were typically "multiple guess" ones with the "most correct" answer being chosen. Sometimes several or all of the answers were partially correct. That difficulty could be compounded by the adding of "All of the above" or "None of the above" after the other answers. And semantics could make matters unduly complex. Divining the intent of the quiz author could help, and a handy generalization was that Answers B and C were the most often correct ones. If one of those could be ruled out, the other was the best choice when in doubt about the rest. So we got unknown answers "right" more than by random choice.

The ongoing struggle, in every class, with the daily quiz did have an occasional lighter moment. I remember a question that had Choices A, B, and C followed by Choice D, All of the above. That was followed by Choice E, None of the above. A midshipman plaintively asked the instructor: *Sir, in Question___, does None of the above include All of the above?* I remember the laughter that elicited but not the instructor's reply, which most likely was the common one: *No talking during the quiz.*

Physical Challenges

A notable physical challenge was the Obstacle Course. I didn't do very well at it, but it wasn't all that hard to get through.

Swimming was a tougher challenge for me. On my first try at jumping off a high board and swimming underwater across the Olympic-sized pool (to simulate swimming under burning oil), a grab-assing classmate fell into the pool and on me. I broke the surface before touching the pool edge. On two retries, I ran out of breath and didn't make it. But the make-up test went well.

My toughest non-academic challenge was swimming a half-mile wearing a light cotton uniform. When the time limit was up, I was about 10 yards past the finish line.

We also had to get past the Dilbert Dunker, an airplane fuselage segment containing a single-seat, open cockpit. Installed in a swimming pool, Dilbert rolled down rails at about a 45° angle. When it hit the pool, it flipped over, putting its occupant upside down and under water. We were supposed to look at and unbuckle the seatbelt, swim down and away from the Dunker, and surface. I missed my Dunker session due to being sick and did a makeup. The midshipman ahead of me was determined but tense. When Dilbert flipped over, he unbuckled himself, swam straight down, turned, and swam back into the cockpit, jamming himself in. The Dunker was retrieved, putting him upside down behind the seat with his legs flailing. He was gingerly removed. (His eventual triumph over Dilbert had to be a jubilant moment.)

When my turn came and Dilbert flipped, I couldn't see my seat belt because of air bubbles. It took a seeming eternity to find and release the belt buckle. But I avoided my predecessor's mistake.

The final semester at Annapolis had a memorable course—golf. It was termed a "carryover" sport. Those who had played before had a lot of fun. Those who, like me, had never played found it challenging. I finally learned to hit the ball, but not very well. The last golf class involved actual play on the Academy golf course, for which we had to provide our own golf balls. I had enough cash to buy three used balls and made it almost all the way to the first green before losing them all. Later, I concluded that, on an Ensign's pay of $222 a month, I couldn't afford golf balls, let alone golf clubs. I never became a golfer and take solace in a definition of golf as a game whose aim is to put a miniature ball into a minute hole with an instrument ill-suited to the purpose (a description falsely attributed to Winston Churchill).

Service academy graduates may lack some of the political and social savvy that a civilian career path provides. But Annapolis taught high standards, overcoming adversity, and sound use of power. I'd be offended if it didn't still teach organizational and self-discipline, responsibility, obedience, respect for seniors and subordinates, tenacity, loyalty, hard work, and helping others.

Seagoing Training

Our first at-sea training was on our two-month Youngster (sophomore) Cruise, immediately following Plebe Year. I was on the USS Missouri (BB-63), a 45,000 ton Iowa Class battleship. Its main battery was nine 16"/50 guns. {16" gun barrel diameter, 50 calibers (50X16=800") long}. We were told that each 16" shell cost $5000, "the price of a Cadillac." But the most impressive part of the ship was an in-deck brass plaque commemorating the signing of the WWII unconditional surrender by the Japanese.

During Youngster Cruise gun firing exercises, I was a 5"/38 gun loader. The shells came up to us in an ammo hoist running from the next deck below. It was a dual hoist that cycled so that, when a round was at the top, the other side was at the bottom for loading of the next round. When the round at the top was removed, the hoist cycled to raise the next round up. The design of the shells was such that their detonators weren't armed until after they left the gun barrel. Nonetheless, the training very strongly emphasized that the hoist cycled faster than a dropped round would fall, that partially removing a round would cycle the hoist, and putting the partially removed round back would result in the round free falling about 16' to the bottom of the hoist and landing on its nose at the hoist bottom. We learned to firmly grip a raised round, pull it from the hoist, and load the shell. An exception was a foreign midshipman. (After graduating, he served in his own nation's Navy.) Until he was assigned another gun firing station, he was a case of "no speaka da English." That succeeded because no one ratted and he played that role well.

Our main task was preparing the ship for decommissioning. Holystoning wooden decks was the toughest part. For that, a stick inserted in an indentation in a wide side of a boiler insulation brick was used to vigorously rub the brick against the wooden decking to make it gleam. That wore down the deck planking and had been banned since 1931. But nobody told us that.

Scrubbing out bilges was a close second to holystoning. And the glee the ship's crew took in sitting on their duffs and telling future officers what to clean next was hardly endearing.

During the cruise, there was a thorough weekly inspection of the ship. For one of those, a dirty trash can was assigned to me and another midshipman. We kept it moving to ensure that the trash can remained unseen by the Inspection Party.

Shortly after the beginning of Youngster academic year, an announcement was made stating that, though the cruise on the Missouri had been demanding, we would be pleased to know that she was the cleanest ship to ever begin decommissioning. But, for me at least, Youngster Cruise was a lesson in the undesirable aspects of serving in the (chicken-s..t) Big Ship Navy.

The next summer's cruise was a big improvement. I was aboard the USS Antietam (CVS-36), a 27,100 ton Essex Class aircraft carrier. One experience was a flight in an F3D Skyknight fighter jet in which there were side-by-side seats for the pilot and the passenger. The pilot pointed out the ejection "tunnel" leading aft between the seats and said that, if he ordered it, to bail out very fast or find myself alone in the plane. The flight went smoothly, with some aerobatics. Then, when we were preparing to land, the tiny-looking landing deck didn't seem to appreciably increase in size until we were close to the landing, which also went very smoothly. (I'm still awed by the skill of carrier pilots.)

One of the first things we learned about aircraft carriers was that the elevator for taking planes to and from the flight deck had an alarm that went off just before it started lowering. Once it sounded, getting on the elevator was forbidden because it lowered so fast that anyone who tried to get on would free fall to the next deck, a potentially fatal drop. And the wires that attached the planes to the catapults had been known to, when they went over the bow after a launch, decapitate sailors who too soon got too close to the retrieval station under the bow. Also, returning aircraft in trouble could produce fiery crashes.

Antietam also carried two-engined S2F antisubmarine aircraft. The arresting wire tension had to be set high to halt them. On this cruise, that destroyed an F4U Corsair, a high speed, propeller-driven, gull-winged fighter known as an "Ensign-Killer" because it took so much skill to fly it. When this Corsair's tail hook contacted the arresting wire, which was still set for an S2F, the plane broke in two behind the cockpit. Its forward part, and the pilot, went over the canted (angled) landing deck into the water. The plane-guard destroyer picked up the unhurt pilot. He was returned to the carrier by highline. For that, the destroyer came alongside at about 30 yards distance and matched the carrier's course and speed. A light line was heaved across and used to haul in a heavier one and then the highline. One end of that was secured on the carrier, the other end was tended on the destroyer by sailors who pulled it in as the ships rolled toward each other and let it out as they rolled apart. A semi-enclosed seat beneath a pulley on the highline carried the pilot. Other sailors hauled him to the carrier using the line attached to the seat assembly.

I was one of the midshipmen who also experienced highline transfer—to spend time on a destroyer. That was pleasant and I hoped for a destroyer assignment upon graduation.

My other summer cruise was an amphibious warfare one. We spent a lot of time in a big room containing a big, simulated sea area, where little ship models were pushed around to simulate an amphibious invasion. That was so boring that the instructors periodically set off firecracker-like "explosions" to keep us awake. But we gained an appreciation of the incredible complexity of loading an invasion fleet so that all the ammunition, rations, jeeps, tanks, etc. went ashore in the right order.

Orders to Duty

When we chose our first officer duty assignments, those who graduated with distinction (a 3.4 or higher overall grade) chose first. The rest drew lots. My overall grade was 3.394⁺ and I drew about halfway in the class. (A 3.395 would have been rounded off to 3.4.) There were a goodly number of Air Force billets (there was then no Air Force Academy). Navy Air also had a goodly number, but my 20/30 eyesight didn't qualify me for pilot training. The Marines had a small allotment, the Engineering Duty specialty a tiny one, and the rest of the choices were on ships with officer vacancies. Pearl Harbor was the most desired duty station. San Diego was next. When my turn came, those choices were gone and I picked a destroyer based in Norfolk, Virginia.

Carryover

While I'm thankful for my Annapolis education, I didn't enjoy it much. But the only negative I've carried forth has been the preference I see as being given to athletes. Not only did that almost prevent me from attending, it has involved persistent, oxymoronic post-graduation solicitations to academically prepare "well-qualified" candidates to enter the Academy. Those finally stopped when I said that I'd increase my contributions to the Disabled American Veterans before supporting Navy football.

My aversion to special preparation of athletes doesn't mean that athletes who graduate are unworthy. Doc Blanchard was an Air Force pilot who was commended for bravery and retired as a Colonel. And Roger Staubach and David Robinson became top professional athletes and admirable role models. But many civilian college football players reportedly don't earn degrees. And the few who make it to the National Football League reportedly get paid an average of $2 million a year, but about 78% of them are broke three years after their playing days end.

That my disagreement with preference for athletes hasn't affected my view of the Navy was again proved to me by the emotions aroused when I heard the Brigade of Midshipmen sing *Navy Blue and Gold after* the 2015 Army-Navy football game.

Part II

Naval Officer Duty

II-1 Fletcher Class Destroyers

Getting Started

Upon graduating, we got an unheard of 60-day leave. After about 30 days of hanging out at the beach and driving around in my first car, I was asked to report to my first duty station early. The reason stated was my becoming better able to contribute during training at Guantanamo Bay (Gitmo) and be more ready for a six-month deployment to the Mediterranean. Boredom with the beach made me as glad to oblige as I was reluctant to start off on the wrong foot. So, early in July of 1957, I reported to my first ship. She was a 376.5' long, 2050 ton Fletcher Class destroyer armed with five 5"/38 naval guns in five single mounts, two quad 40 mm mounts, a five 21" torpedo mount, and one depth charge rack on the starboard side of the stern. According to Wikipedia, the Fletchers were designed in 1939, 175 of them were built from 1942-44 and this highly successful class served in the U.S. Navy into the 1960s.

My first assignment was in the Gunnery Department as First Lieutenant, the supervisor of the Deck Force (Boatswain's Mates and Seamen). That pleased me. I had no desire to become part of the Engineering Department. And my next step, Gunnery Officer, kept me where I preferred to be.

Shortly after I reported, the amplidyne (motor-generator) drive on a 40 mm gun mount failed. The sailor dispatched to pick up a replacement returned from the Supply Center empty-handed. He said that the Center had the part but were at their "minimum stocking level" and couldn't issue it. An inoperable gun mount meant submitting a Casualty Report on our lowered readiness. And because I wasn't yet embroiled in ongoing activities, the Captain ordered me to go and get the part.

At the Supply Center, the issuing clerk told me that the minimum stocking level was required in order to have enough parts to support the fleet. Pointing out that I came from the fleet and needed the support was unavailing. So I went to his supervisor, and his, and his, etc. When I reached a Supply Corps Commander (the same rank as an Army Lieutenant Colonel), he asked me how far I intended to take this. I said to the Center's Commanding Officer. The Commander authorized issue of the part. I don't know what else he did, but we didn't have such a problem again.

My next unusual task was harder. One of the ship's sailors had contracted a venereal disease (VD) and been treated and cured. That had recurred every time the ship returned to Norfolk, but hadn't happened anywhere else. So the Captain ordered that he and his wife be counseled. Protesting that the sailor didn't work for me was unavailing. The buck had been passed to me.

The sailor's job performance was good and he had been advanced in rate several times. Misbehavior had caused him to be busted (demoted) several times too. But that wasn't unusual, and he had worked his way back up again.

I thought about the VD training I had attended. Only one session had any pleasant aspect. It was given at the Naval Academy shortly before our Youngster Cruise. The Medical Officer conducting it had lightened things up by stating that orange juice was a cure for VD. He waited for the expected question about whether it was taken before or after and said neither—but instead of. That was no help, and neither was anything else I could recall. So I boned up on the health risks of uncured or recurrent VD, and decided to present those with the focus on getting the sailor and his wife cured and aware of the long-term consequences of recurrence. Then I arranged to have the sailor bring his wife aboard.

The abashed couple had no questions and was obviously as glad as I was when our session was over. We heard no more about VD in that family, so the effort appeared successful. (If a more senior officer—like the XO—had taken on this job, success would have been better assured.)

The Captain

One of the first things I learned from the crew was how significant an act that humanizes an officer can be. The Captain had, reportedly, on the bridge at sea, calmly remarked that his balls itched, unbuckled his belt, lowered his trousers, and scratched his crotch. And the crew was still chuckling about it. It was a delighted *"Did you hear what the Old Man did?"* reaction. I suspected that the Captain had deliberately staged that little display. But I never had the temerity to ask.

The Captain's job was physically demanding. He was on the bridge for every significant evolution, and those were frequent. That's why, in addition to the Captain's Cabin down in Officer's Country, naval ships that are large enough have a Captain's Sea Cabin just behind the bridge, better enabling the Captain to get to the bridge and oversee evolutions quickly. But intense operations took a significant toll that could make even light-sleeping Captains hard to wake up.

Great emphasis was placed on keeping the Captain informed about all shipping encountered. Because there were a lot of ships heading to and from Norfolk and the Chesapeake Bay, nearby operations could involve numerous calls to the Captain after daily exercises were over.

A 1948 Naval Academy graduate, Donald R. Morris, reputedly at the top of his class in English, History, and Government but fourth from the bottom in Marine Engineering, wrote a relevant fictional book, *Warm Bodies*. It opened with a discussion of the problem with keeping the Captain informed.

As I recall his work, Morris described being on his first ship after graduation, an LST (Landing Ship Tank). He was standing a night watch as a Junior Officer of the Deck (JOOD). The OOD was a grizzled old Lieutenant. Morris noted a radar contact, well astern and slowly dropping back, and asked about informing the Captain. The OOD demurred until Morris became insistent, and then said OK (to teach him a lesson). On this LST, communication between the bridge and the Captain's Sea Cabin was by voice tube. So the OOD took a set of parallel rulers (used for plotting courses on navigation charts), banged loudly on the voice tube until the Captain sleepily asked what was up, and then yelled loudly into the voice tube: *Piss*

Call, You Old Son-Of-A-Bitch! After a prolonged silence, the Captain finally said: *Very Well, call me if it gets any closer.*

We identified with Morris' book. When an officer guffawed loudly in his stateroom, it was a good bet that he was reading *Warm Bodies.*

Scuttlebutt

A scuttlebutt is a shipboard water fountain—akin to a business office water cooler. Both are known for the dissemination of unofficial information, and scuttlebutt is a term for Navy gossip. Much of it is baseless and much more is profane but, despite the party line about ignoring it, scuttlebutt is a barometer of the crew's outlook and morale.

The corrosion that required so much deck force work gained more attention from me when I heard scuttlebutt stating that a seaman had stuck a paint scraper (a hand tool) through the side of the hull of another Fletcher class destroyer. Reputedly, she had been sent to the shipyard for hull repairs. But the scuttlebutt wasn't confirmed.

Boatswain's Mates

It didn't take long for me to come to appreciate my Boatswain's Mates and the plight of their rating. The number of BMCs (Chief Boatswain's Mates) wasn't dropping as fast as the number of BMC billets. That produced an advancement backlog of lower rated BMs. That wasn't career enhancing, but it meant that a lot of lower rated BMs were very capable.

That capability was fortunate for me because the only BMC assigned to the ship worked for the Executive Officer (second-in-command) as the Ship's Master at Arms. We had no First Class Boatswain's Mates (BM1s) either. But our three BM2s (Boatswain's Mates Second Class) were very capable. One was the LPO (Leading Petty Officer) of the First Division (Forward part of the Deck Force). A second was the LPO of the Second Division (Aft part of the Deck Force). These could handle any task the Deck Force was given.

The third BM2 was a fan of the "old" Navy. He felt that the UCMJ (Uniform Code of Military Justice) coddled sailors and was inferior to its predecessor, the "Rocks and Shoals." As an example, he described having gotten seasick on his first at-sea experience. The remedy applied by his supervisor was to "kick my ass from one end of the ship to the other," make him clean up the vomit, and he had never been seasick again. This BM also had a simple assessment of the root cause of difficulties: *Salt water and sailors will f**k up anything.*

Boatswains Mates and seamen made up the Deck Force, which performed tasks like boat coxswain duties, raising and lowering the ship's boat, anchoring, rigging for refueling and replenishment, highline transfer, handling the mooring lines, and maintaining the ship's exterior. Keeping the ship's topside looking good was ongoing and arduous. My LPOs pointed out the main problem as being insistence on an unblemished haze gray appearance without applying the best primer, red lead, and waiting for it to dry three days before applying haze gray top coats. That "wash down with paint" solution was short-lasting and made the total workload bigger. So, with some difficulty, I got permission to follow the painting recommendations. But after a day of noticeably standing out from the other ships because of highly visible, drying red lead primer, we were told to put a coat of haze gray on it. That made us look just like all the other ships. (Standing out in an unappealing way is avoided everywhere.)

A ready supply of paint was kept in the Paint Locker. It was kept locked and the keys tended to remain in a pocket of the last sailor tasked with getting some paint. When no one remembered who that was, the word was passed on the General Announcing System for "The Man with the Keys to the Paint Locker, Lay Up to Same." Then the Captain would chew me out because access to a space containing flammable material was unduly difficult. But I was unable to change the environment and knew that would happen again.

Tight Money Consequences

Not long after I reported for duty, the Engineers came to me to borrow rags because they were running out of the ones used to wipe up grease and oil in the engineering spaces. The rags were to be repaid when the next quarterly allotment came through and they bought more. That sounded fair, so I went to check on the supply kept by the Boatswain's Mates. There I heard that this was an old ploy, repeatedly played out with the Engineering Department not paying back what they had borrowed. So I refused to loan the rags. Shortly thereafter I was called in for a session with the XO. He asked how the Engineers could do without these supplies. My response was that we too had a hard time making our supplies last and couldn't afford to give them away, and brashly suggested that they use their old underwear. And, perhaps because the deck force's rags were used on polishing and cleaning tasks that, if not done, showed on the ship's exterior, that's what happened.

The Engineering Department had a very tough job, and I was ambivalent about my stance. I also watched with misgivings as they operated an aging steam plant with scant funds. Inability to steam as ordered could not only mean not keeping up with the other ships, it could put a ship dead in the water and at the non-existent mercy of the sea. But the ship answered all bells (steamed as ordered) despite its mechanical problems. One that I noted during my First Lieutenant's weekly inspection was that the boiler safety valves were wired shut, a big no-no. But the alternative was steam leakage that would further erode the valve seats, make the leakage worse, and increase scarce boiler-grade water usage. Valve replacement wasn't affordable, but the engineers' competence kept the ship steaming. It helped that their Department Head was well liked by his department as well as good at his job. (I felt that it was a loss to the Navy when he left it. He made religion his life's work, and earned the title of "Father.")

Crew Size

The ship didn't have enough sailors to man all its weapons. That was a result of the ship's "allowance" of about 250 being well below her "complement" of about 330 crew members. The example of short-staffing that sticks most in my mind is the one fire control technician we had. He was an FT2 (a Fire Control Technician, Second Class).

I remember him most for the time he worked for over a day without sleep to fix a fire control system failure. Then, after he succeeded and collapsed in his bunk, I had to wake him in a little over an hour because of another failure. He dragged himself out and tackled the new problem without complaint. That he did such tasks repeatedly, and professionally, made him and others of his ilk treasures.

I gained a deeper appreciation for the difference between the peacetime and wartime Navy about 20 years ago, when I went to a ship's reunion. There I met our destroyer's first Commanding Officer and talked with officers who had served on the ship during World War II. They told me about ferrying officials to the USS Missouri (BB-63) for the signing of the surrender in Tokyo Bay. And a wartime Gunnery Officer aboard the destroyer and I swapped stories. He was astounded to hear about the ship's allowance, and especially about having only one FT. I was astounded to hear that he had a dozen fire control technicians, with three of them being Chief Petty Officers. Also, the number of wartime crew members had far exceeded the complement of the ship when I was on it, making the much smaller post-war allowance a puny figure indeed. But, when he was the Gunnery Officer, World War II was in its late stages, and the full resources of the country had been devoted to it for several years.

Short-staffing lessens the Navy's fighting readiness and makes a Navy career less attractive. And the "Can Do" attitude can stretch a fighting force too thin. During my destroyer duty, I didn't appreciate the expertise of the Navy's senior officers whose job it was to keep the fleet functioning. Now, my 20-20 hindsight sees that they stretched fragile rubber bands close to their limits without breaking many.

Crew Character

Along with sailors who worked their tails off, we had a few personnel problems. One was the yeoman who handled the ship's correspondence, reports and service records. Helpful, an excellent typist, and thoroughly knowledgeable, he also had a reputation with the crew: a ship's wag commented that we could always tell when he was returning from liberty because the shore patrol wagon was bouncing up and down so much when it came down the pier to return him. That was typical overstatement, but this yeoman did get into trouble when the ship's reports weren't reaching their destination. The XO then discovered about a year's worth of reports, all neatly typed, properly signed, in correctly addressed envelopes, and stuffed in the overhead of the Yeoman's Shack. We soon had a replacement yeoman. No more problems surfaced, so he must have worked out well. But I don't remember him at all. (What isn't surprising is that it took so long to learn that our reports weren't going anywhere—and what that indicates about their value.)

Seasickness on the first day at sea was not unusual for many crew members, especially if the ship went toward Cape Hatteras, where rough seas were common. We hid that if we could. One such day, during the evening meal, I was silently congratulating myself for being at the table. But, after I leaned toward someone in order to better hear and be heard, I turned my head back to where the steward was holding a serving plate of greasy pork right in front of my face. One look, and one whiff, made me bolt from the wardroom to endure my only episode of seasickness.

To staff the fleet, the Navy took in some enlistees with little education. One of those was in my deck force. His reading and communication skills were seriously lacking. The other sailors understood his speech, but the only word I heard him enunciate clearly was Mother-F...ing, which he used regularly. And, because advancement in the Navy depended on examination grades, his military future was as a non-rated seaman. But he was a hard worker, and painting and chipping paint require a lot of work but not literacy. His LPO told me that the young man's goal was to be a boat coxswain and he had an aptitude for that. So we trained him to be one. Everything went well until he departed from his prescribed route, went into shallow water, and bent the motor whaleboat shaft and screw when they hit bottom. The XO investigated and found the coxswain solely responsible. Feeling guilty for not having specifically emphasized the shallow water hazard (it was outside the prescribed route), I told the XO that better management by me could have prevented this occurrence. But the XO said that this was the proper outcome because the young man had no future in the service. He also ordered that the sailor not be used as a coxswain again.

Former crew members of the destroyer I served on hold regular reunions. And they put together an excellent roster of their locations. I tried to find former my former FT2 on it, but he hadn't been located. But, through the crew's organization, a former BM2 (Boatswain's Mate, Second Class) on the ship telephoned me, and we swapped life stories. He had been my Second Division Leading Petty Officer (LPO), and he and the First Division LPO kept me out of a lot of the trouble my youth and inexperience invited. I asked him if he knew what had happened to his First Division counterpart, and he said that he too had heard that he had died, but didn't know why. In his own case, he said that he had been promoted to BM1 but there had been virtually no promotions to Chief Boatswain's Mate for so many years that he got out of the Navy. Then he went into hock to buy a bulldozer, rented it out, and ended up owning 20 of those machines. I said that didn't surprise me at all because his competence, and that of the BM2 in charge of the First Division, had made me trust them completely. What did surprise me is how much he appreciated hearing that. I also was delighted when our discussion showed that he had become a pillar of his church and community.

We also talked extensively about the First Division's LPO, a light-skinned man of color with extremely high personal standards and pride. I recalled the time that we had refueled at sea, topped off all the fuel tanks, and told the tanker to stop pumping. They tardily did that. Fuel oil overflowed into the passageway outside the XO's stateroom, and then into it, where he was sleeping. The XO, awakened by the commotion, sat up, put his feet into about six inches of fuel oil, turned on his lights, and saw his white buck dress uniform shoes floating in the black pool his feet were in. He aimed his verbal ire at the tanker's crew, who couldn't hear the insults. And, within a day, there was a newly installed cofferdam under his newly resized door, ensuring that a future overflow would reach his stateroom last. The First Division LPO, insulted because of the overflow despite having done everything right, oversaw the oil cleanup and then took his white hat, which had one tiny oil spot on it, and heaved it over the side because that stain couldn't be removed. (He was, in addition to his high professional competence, the most immaculately groomed member of the crew in both dress and working uniforms.)

Early during my destroyer tour, Intra-crew crew animosity was evident. There was an incident of fuel oil contamination of a fire main, with the associated hazard and the mess created when it was opened for topside cleanup being blamed on the Engineers. That was followed by an "accidental" dropping of a full five-gallon paint can by the Deck Force from the main deck about 20 feet down into the engineering spaces, with the cleanup of that mess being similarly difficult. And, on liberty, fights between the Engineering and Deck Ratings were frequent. But, as the next section states, that issue was resolved at Guantanamo Bay.

Guantanamo Bay

The ship's first major training evolution during my tour was at the Guantanamo Bay (Gitmo) training facility. That intensive training was accompanied by a major improvement in intra-crew respect when another ship's crew baited ours (or vice versa). A brawl started and our Engineering and Deck Ratings fought together against a common foe. And, for the rest of my time on the ship, our crew stood by each other.

At Gitmo, we practiced the use of all the ship's weapons that we were able to man. The firing was intensive and exhausting, but we learned a lot about our capabilities. We also fired a torpedo (our only torpedo firing exercise or drill when I was aboard). I manned the Torpedo Firing Director, a rudimentary fire control computer, and the Chief Torpedoman (TMC) did the firing. The torpedo veered left and sank after running for a while. U.S. destroyer-fired torpedoes hadn't been a significant World War II weapon, and there was little or no expectation (other than my own) that this one would run properly. The five torpedoes just sat there, supposedly ready but not expected to perform. I now think of this torpedo's failure as an example of a self-fulfilling prophesy.

At the time, Cuba was in its pre-Castro period, and noted for corruption and prostitution. A step taken to try to improve the overall picture was a party at the Officer's Club for local young ladies from good families. It was a nice party, and several of us bachelor officers made arrangements to subsequently go on a joint date with some of them. And we did, packed tightly in a car, do just that. We went to a night club built high on the side of a cliff—a very attractive place with a magnificent view. The ladies had a stereotypical view of American men and American culture that one of them expressed as "John Wayne, Bang-Bang." But they were delightful company, and we enjoyed the evening so much that we started back later than planned. My date was the daughter of a merchant. We stopped at her home, a two story, flat roofed building that looked as if it occupied an entire block. Atop the roof, about six male members of her family were awaiting her return. My date, though there had been no misbehavior other than her late return, scurried hurriedly and fearfully into the house. I wasted no time getting back in the car, and we promptly left. Realizing that we had offended an Old World culture, I didn't expect any further contact with that young lady. That became inevitable when rebels blew the night club we went to off the side of the cliff, ending those Officers' Club parties and liberty off the naval base. I still wonder what happened to those Cuban good families when Castro took over.

The Mediterranean Tour

We soon deployed to the "Med" for a six-month tour with Admiral "Cat" Brown's Sixth Fleet. The sea crossing involved "cross-connected" propulsion shaft and boiler operation (operating both screws from the steam generated by one boiler). That limited our speed and maneuverability but was fuel-efficient, and we made the trip without refueling.

One particular image of that ocean passage remains with me. I already knew that the greenish-brownish hue of the shallow, near shore ocean turns into a clear, lovely blue beyond the Continental Shelf. (That's the source of the term blue water sailor.) While we were in the deep mid-Atlantic, our destroyer was sent off from the other ships and steamed alone for a while. During that time, at about mid-morning, I walked to the stern of the ship, and gaped in awe. There was no other ship in view. The sky was clear. Not a wave or ripple broke the complete flatness of the ocean. Its beautiful blue color was broken only by our long, straight, white wake that stretched to the horizon. Before or since, I've never seen the ocean come even close to being so calm and so quietly beautiful.

It was on this trip that I got my first really strong chewing out as a Commissioned Officer. Indirectly involved was knowledge that taking a misbehaving sailor to non-judicial punishment (Captain's Mast) was considered a mark of leadership failure.

At sea, the Boatswain's Mates and seamen often spent what spare time they had in the Boatswain's Locker, the uppermost below decks compartment in the ship's bow. It surged and dropped with wave action, giving the Deck Force a space where no one was likely to intrude. They were proud of staying there without getting seasick.

One choppy day, I entered the Boatswain's Locker and took time to get used to being quickly raised and dropped six feet. Then, while talking with the Boatswain's Mates, who were seated around a small table on which their coffee pot precariously rested, I heard a clinking sound from the pot, picked it up, looked inside, and found a half-full bottle of whiskey. The shamefaced look all around told me that they all knew what the coffee pot held.

I expressed my disapproval in terms they knew well, took the bottle and headed aft, and quickly became acutely aware of the problem of being seen carrying a half-full whisky bottle. When I got to the hatch to the foc'sle (forecastle), I saw what I thought was a solution, opened the hatch scuttle, stuck my upper body out, and heaved the bottle over the side. Just about the time I finished shutting the scuttle, the word "Ensign McCabe, Report to the Captain on the Bridge!" was passed on the General Announcing System.

When I encountered the Captain's intimidating glare and demand for an explanation, I recounted what had happened and stated that I had wanted to handle the matter myself rather than put the sailors on report. The Captain summarily dismissed me. A few hours later, the XO called me in and pointed out that I had destroyed the evidence. But we both knew that, because there was no drunkenness involved, informal handling was better than official action—at least on this ship. So I got a well-deserved royal chewing out for the incredible stupidity of where I threw the whiskey bottle from but not for the throwing. (If I had taken the coffee pot, with the whiskey bottle in it, and had the senior petty officer at the scene accompany me to the main deck just aft of Officer's Quarters, and given him the choice of dropping it over the side or accompanying me to the XO's stateroom with it, things would have worked out much more smoothly.)

During our deployment, we saw something of Izmir (Turkey), Gibraltar, Rhodes, the Red Sea and the Suez Canal, Aden, Djibouti (French Somaliland), and Piraeus (Greece). During port visits, it was necessary to walk past a bevy of Ladies of the Evening to get away from the pier area. After that had happened several times, one of the officers I was going on liberty with remarked that he was damned if that gauntlet's same members hadn't been on the pier at every port we had visited. So, since we didn't know what our next port would be until after we were back out at sea, the sex industry following the Fleet knew its movements better than we did.

The Med Tour provided good destroyer training. Ordinary steaming was done with fuel economy in mind, and we looked for a light brown haze coming from the smokestacks as a measure of fuel-air mixture efficiency. But when significant maneuvering took place, there was black smoke above and white water astern of the speeding destroyers. And *Black Smoke and White Water* was all an oncoming watchstander needed to hear to know what to expect on his watch.

A pilot was required in the Suez Canal. In its narrower parts, there was a danger of the ship's motion and propeller suction causing the water alongside to flow appreciably faster on the side nearest the embankment than it did on the other side. That produced a lower pressure in the water on that side (the Bernoulli Effect), and the higher pressure side pushed the ship toward the embankment. The natural reaction to being sucked in toward the embankment is to try to steer away from it. That puts the stern closer to the embankment, increases the Bernoulli Effect, and makes running into the side of the canal more likely. The solution is to put the helm over as if steering for the embankment. When the stern starts moving out, the rudder is put over the other way, pulling the bow out and countering the Bernoulli Effect. The Suez Canal Pilots were adept at this maneuver, which was so counter-intuitive that inexperienced ship's officers like me stared wide-eyed at what seemed to be exactly the wrong thing to do and seeing it work. (The Bernoulli Effect also causes airflow over the curved upper surface of an airplane wing to be faster than the airflow on the flat underside, with the pressure difference between the air on the lower and upper sides of the wing generating Lift to help keep the plane airborne.)

During a Mediterranean port visit, we hosted an African dignitary. He came aboard in colorful tribal dress. We had an honor guard for him and had assigned our cleanest looking sailors to it. I was the honor guard officer and we had practiced the procedure—a vital step because of our unfamiliarity with the process. But the visiting dignitary didn't know the procedure. And, as I finished my sword salute and was bringing the sword down (which involves the sword descending in an arc in a plane perpendicular to its holder's shoulders), he stepped forward. Leaning back and pulling my wrist quickly to my right side kept the sword from contacting the honoree. Nobody indicated that this near miss was unusual. But when the dignitary departed, we didn't repeat the saluting part but just piped him over the side with the honor guard at attention next to the gangplank. And that near incident was the only use of my sword in the line of duty.

We once were assigned to transfer exercise observers from another ship. The sea was choppy. As Boat Officer, I chose our best coxswain and picked two seamen to handle the falls (the block and tackle used to lower and raise the whaleboat.) We got away from the ship nicely. About a quarter of the way to the other destroyer, the waves were tossing us about. (Whaleboats' noted seaworthiness had been decreased significantly when motors were put in them.) I asked the coxswain if he thought we could turn around. He said maybe—if we could start on one wave and finish before the next one arrived. We agreed, precariously made the turn, and returned to our destroyer. While connecting to the lifting falls, a wave slammed us into the ship, cracking several ribs on the whaleboat. But we hooked up and were brought back aboard. The XO relieved my concern about not completing the transfer by telling me that the Captain hadn't realized that the sea was that rough and was glad that I had returned. There was no further attempt to transfer observers that day.

Another memory of the Mediterranean was getting underway from the port of Rhodes because of a storm. We rode it out on the lee side of the island, with one anchor out to a length of six times the water depth, and the other anchor underfoot (almost straight up and down) to curtail the swinging of the ship as the wind and sea pushed us around. As First Lieutenant, I had to oversee the anchoring. Doing that took up virtually all of my first sea duty Christmas.

Piraeus, Greece was memorable for the voluble affability of its people and for the good food at the restaurants. It was there that I first tasted Baked Alaska, a dessert that our stewards subsequently prepared for us on special occasions. (Baked Alaska is the name coined in 1876 by New York City's Delmonico Restaurant to describe a French dish consisting of meringue surrounding sponge cake surrounding ice cream, with the concoction heated in an oven until the meringue is firm.)

The Port of Aden I remember for being in a restaurant with other ship's officers. One disputed the bill. The discussion heated up and the room began to fill with angry-looking Arab men. We hastily paid the exorbitant bill and left.

Izmir, Turkey didn't leave a good impression. The ship's officer on shore patrol duty gave me a tour of the area in the van he was assigned. We went through a darkened community to an area he called the Compound, where outcast females reputedly lived and supported themselves through prostitution. We saw no one and I didn't leave the ship in Izmir any other time. My only other input about the place was scuttlebutt stating that an aircraft carrier sailor had made advances to a woman and been slashed by her friends/family. Reportedly, the sailor lived but required over 600 stitches to close the cuts.

A memory of the XO we had then comes from a time when we were steaming on a course that put a heavy sea abeam. Several of us were sitting in the wardroom and discussing the rolls we were taking—noting that we were alternating between extended periods of seeing all sky and then all sea through the portholes. Our pale, ex-Frogman (Seal) XO left, making a disgruntled comment that our talk could make anyone seasick.

We once moored in a barren-looking port in Africa. Soon afterwards, a solitary and very thin young man came down the pier. Over his arm was a basket of peanuts that he wanted to sell. That arm looked normal and unblemished down to where there was no hand but a seemingly smooth, rounded end. The word that he was a leper made the rounds, and he found no buyers. I still don't know whether leprosy (Hansen's disease) produces such a deformity.

Another memory of that port is watching a merchantman moor to a quay (pier parallel to the shoreline). That old tub put its starboard side nearest the quay, turned its bow away, backed down, and dropped its port anchor well away from the quay. It then used the kicking of the stern to port characteristic of backing down a single screw vessel, along with tension on the anchor chain, to neatly moor. Until then, I hadn't realized that rusty old tubs would have adept shiphandlers.

In one port, we were the only ship to moor and had to have a Senior Shore Patrol Officer. I was selected, with the Captain emphasizing that I had to make a report directly to the Sixth Fleet Commander, and to make sure that the crew didn't embarrass the ship. He also said that the venereal disease rate among the inhabitants was extremely high, that they were so impoverished that the men might prostitute their wives, and that I was to keep our crew away from that hazard. My shore patrolmen were French soldiers plus enough red Fez-wearing native militiamen to make up two jeep-loads of Shore Patrol. The soldiers had holstered pistols, the militiamen bolt action rifles. None of them spoke English, and I retained virtually none of my high school French. Concerned that my patrol might use too much force, I made no attempt to split up the jeeps, and we started out our two-jeep patrols with hand signals.

We soon got into an off-limits area, where I found most of my First and Second Division sailors already starting to explore—and they hadn't been on liberty for more than half an hour. I gathered them up and said they would be escorted back to the ship. They said that would be an insult and they would return, quickly, on their own. And so they did.

The senior soldier and I managed a communication about preventing the sailors from entering places where prostitution might take place. His statement was: *Ah, a la maison de femme!* I understood it and that's where our shore patrol efforts were concentrated. The area contained rows of individual single-story dwellings. We saw sailors go in front doors and sent in militiamen. They found no sailors. So we sent one militiaman around to the back door and another to the front. Carrying their rifles at Port Arms, they trapped the off limits sailors between them and marched them back to us.

When the sailors realized that getting caught off-limits meant loss of liberty, they avoided the area. They also didn't drink much (perhaps due to being intimidated by the armed Shore Patrol). The most embarrassing incident was one of the ship's officers eating some native food that gave him severe intestinal cramping. He headed for the nearest public toilet, but didn't get there before soiling his white service uniform.

On our last day in port, my shore patrol and I had a steak dinner together. That it was camel steak, very tough and stringy, surprised me but didn't perturb my guests. Feeding them didn't cost me much, and we parted amicably. The ship got underway, I submitted my report, and heard nothing back. (No news is good news.)

The Mediterranean deployment ended early for me. To prepare me to be the Gunnery Officer, I was assigned to DesLant (Destroyers, Atlantic) Afloat Gunnery School for training, and left the ship while she was moored in Cannes. Missing the reputedly great liberty there was disappointing. Moreover, I had the duty the day we moored, where we were the outermost ship in a nest of destroyers. That night, the swells were reaching into the harbor. We were secured to the nest by both our normal, manila mooring lines and by wire cables. Concerned because we were straining at the mooring lines, I kept a careful eye on them. Strands of wire in the mooring cabling started breaking and unraveling. And that alone is dangerous. So I woke the Captain and told him the situation. He discounted my concern at first, but soon realized that something had to be done quickly because it takes considerable time to light off a secured steam plant. I had the duty section and everyone else aboard rousted out and an expedited propulsion plant startup begun. This evolution was not something we had practiced, but we managed to get power up and move the ship to a safe anchorage. So my last night in the Mediterranean involved more than I expected.

Post-Med Activities

During division maneuvers after the Mediterranean Cruise, a Division Commander (DivCom) staffer periodically sent a "Radio Check." Each ship responded "Roger, Over" in alphabetical order of their call signs, and the DivCom staffer ending the check with "Roger, Out." After the day's activities ended, nighttime Radio Checks were initiated by a radioman who lisped. I recall one of his radio checks as follows (I made up the call signs):

Dingo Delta, This is Slushball Echo, Wadio Check, Over.
This is Boogeyman, Woger, Over.
This is Epidemic, Woger, Over.
This is Golfball, Woger, Over.
This is Mantlepiece, Woger, Over.
This is Slushball Echo, Woger, Out.

Except for the staged lisping, there was no hint of frivolity.

Another (probably false) voice radio tale flashed through the destroyer force. It reportedly occurred during a period of intense maneuvering, and went something like:

Boy, Am I F..ked Up!
Unknown Station, This is Papa Bear, Identify Yourself!
Papa Bear, this is Unknown Station, I'm Not That F..ked Up!

The second Engineering Officer during my shipboard tour was a former submarine machinist's mate who had earned a commission. During his early time on the ship, he was standing JOOD (Junior Officer of the Deck) watches, just as I was. I went to the bridge to relieve him one very dark night, and saw that a huge group of ships was engulfing our group. After explaining that the other ships were searching for a man overboard, he described our course and speed and other relevant information, and asked me if I were ready to relieve him. I said that I didn't understand what was going on, didn't think anyone else did either, and wasn't about to relieve the watch until we were clear of this mess. (I also wisecracked about getting a life preserver now in order to avoid the rush.) After the ships went their separate ways, I relieved him. He was happier to get off watch than anyone else I've ever seen.

The new Engineering Officer was very capable and industrious. He even tried, unsuccessfully, to get the boiler safety valves operating normally. But their being tied shut didn't stop the ship from reaching 38 knots during a speed test.

After the new Engineering Officer finished his OOD training, he became a non-watchstander on call 24 hours a day to address problems in the engineering spaces. Once, while we were steaming at night during local operations out of Norfolk, a dense fog arose. I was the OOD and heard another ship's foghorn that seemed to be coming from ahead. (In fog, there is no way to tell the direction or distance of a foghorn's source, because sound transmission in air is three dimensional and has unpredictable variations.) The virtually mandatory action in such a situation, regardless of whether there is a radar contact on the screen, is to stop the ship's engines. I did that. In a very short time, the Engineering Officer popped up on the bridge. He reminded me that the propulsion plant lineup wasn't suited to a Stop Bell. I pointed out the fog and the foghorn, and asked what he would do. He looked and listened, said it was better to back down than leave the engines stopped, and headed for the engineering spaces. So I backed down until there was slight sternway, stopped the engines again, and alternated between one-third ahead, stop, and one-third astern bells without gaining significant headway or sternway. No radar contact was gained, and our straining eyes detected no ship. Eventually, the other foghorn was silent for an appreciable period, and we resumed slow speed steaming. That was my only experience with a "phantom" foghorn.

Not long after the Med Cruise, a consequence of seagoing triggered a career change for me. I met an unusually lovely and personable young lady and set up a dinner date for the next Friday evening, after the ship returned from local operations. On Friday afternoon, a strong wind made the Captain decide (wisely) to anchor until it died down. While on anchor watch, I saw a submarine steam up to a pier, back down, tie up, put its brow over, and send its Liberty Party ashore. Several hours later, the wind died down and we tied up at our pier. I hied myself to the nearest phone and called my date. Her mother answered, said that my behavior was unacceptable, refused to let me speak to her daughter, and told me to never call back.

My sailors often griped about Norfolk's strong anti-Navy sentiment, saying that it hadn't been many years since signs stating

"Sailors and Dogs, Keep off the Grass" had been taken down. Family sentiment may have been a factor in my case, but I was more concerned about the daughter not doing the communicating. Fortunately, this occurrence showed our incompatibility before a relationship could develop. But the best result was the awakening of my latent desire to be a submariner. At the time, that required a year's at-sea experience as well as the OOD qualification I already had, and a submarine school class would begin shortly after I had a year aboard. So I submitted my request for submarine training.

My application wasn't acknowledged. The XO advised me to let things take their course. (A well-known statement about Navy processing was: "The wheels grind exceedingly slow but exceedingly fine.") But when I expressed my intent to call the Bureau of Naval Personnel about my request, he sat me down and told me that it hadn't left the ship. That, of course, was highly improper, but better than if it had been forwarded with a "Not Recommended" endorsement. The XO explained that I was badly needed on the ship, that I would be the next Gunnery Officer, and that the ship would highly recommend my acceptance for submarine training if my request were timed so that I had two years aboard. He said that, if the request had gone off stating that the ship couldn't afford to lose me, that wouldn't have carried any weight. (The Navy considers everyone expendable, so an expressed desire to keep me aboard would have made me a more desirable applicant.) So I submitted a timely second request.

When that request was approved, I was roundly congratulated. But my mother said that the son of a lady who lived near her had died when the submarine he was on was sunk during the war, and she forbid me from going into submarines. (I pointed out that I wasn't asking permission and she never brought that up again.) The only other objector was furious that anyone wanted to be on as barbaric a weapon as a submarine. I thought his was an isolated view until I concluded, years later, that a similar outlook contributes to discounting the value of submarines in warfare and/or to not using them to proper advantage.

After the Mediterranean deployment, when we were doing local ASW (Anti-Submarine Warfare) training operations off Norfolk, a seamanship lesson came as a surprise to me. We had a German

Naval Officer aboard, standing watch with me. He was a Lieutenant Junior Grade (Oberleutnant Zur See). I was either still an Ensign or a new LTJG (Lieutenant Junior Grade). He was a trainee/observer. I was the Officer of the Deck (OOD). It was early morning, before the day's exercises were to begin, and both the destroyer and the then surfaced submarine we were working with were lying to (engines stopped). Thinking that the post-war German Navy wasn't well-experienced, I didn't expect the German Officer to be knowledgeable. He dispelled that illusion by commenting that we were in an unsuitable position because the submarine was directly downwind of us. I didn't see a problem because of the distance we were apart, with both ships under power and able to maneuver. My trainee pointed out that the destroyer had a considerable above water structure while the submarine had very little. Consequently, the destroyer would be blown down toward the submarine and a loss of propulsion could unnecessarily cause the submarine to have to maneuver. If the submarine had been lulled into a feeling of safety, she might not see the problem soon enough to prevent development of an unsafe condition. So I put speed on for long enough to take position where the wind would blow us clear of the submarine if we lost power. And I used much of the rest of the time I had with that German Officer to learn from him. Without explicitly stating so, he taught defense-in-depth that provides as many barriers as can reasonably be raised against unsafe conditions, something I didn't receive formal training in until much later.

I was now the Special Sea Detail OOD (the Special Sea Detail was on watch for entering and leaving port). But the Captain was always right there, and at the Conn for getting underway and mooring. I was the OOD for at-sea refueling and replenishment as well. The Captain had the Conn then too, and my job was to order minute shaft turn (speed) changes to assure that we didn't surge too far forward or drop too far back, and thereby endanger the refueling or replenishment hook-ups.

I did get to conn the ship away from the pier once. And we did numerous man overboard drills, throwing a floating dummy (Oscar) overboard, putting the rudder over full to kick the stern away from the overboard side, shifting the rudder when course had changed 60°, reversing course so as to return down the same track we had come down (a maneuver called a Williamson Turn), and stopping so as to be dead in the water alongside Oscar. We all got fairly good at that. But I was sure that we all needed a lot more shiphandling training than we were getting.

> Note: A collision at sea or running aground ended the careers of the officers involved. Almost all such occurrences can be avoided by better preparation and alertness. Investigation labeled such matters as culpable faults. Cost and time constraints on related training didn't seem to be in the scope of review. That and "Can-Do" were part of the Navy way. But this is a human issue and not just a Navy one. You'll see it if you hear: *If you can't do it, we'll find someone who can.*

My development as a shiphandler suffered a setback when a new officer reported aboard. He was an accomplished shiphandler and a former merchant mariner with long sea experience. The Captain made him the Special Sea Detail OOD. My compensation was the value of his counsel.

One of the things more senior naval officers did (and no doubt still do) was visit the ships under their command and give the junior officers the chance to air their gripes. A Navy Captain did that on our destroyer. The gripes aired were undoubtedly the same ones heard in today's more modern Navy—it's an example of how, the more things change, the more they stay the same. In our case we got an enthusiastic pep talk about the new ship designs coming down the road to solve the Navy's problems. That he had to know that the problems wouldn't be solved, and that we had to live with today and not tomorrow, was not mentioned. But we appreciated his interest, which was the valuable part of the experience.

Aircraft Carrier Seamanship

Aircraft carrier seamanship was often derided by destroyer sailors. Being the ship on which the screening destroyers took station, it was important that carrier course and speed changes be known by the ships trying to match that course and speed. But carriers preoccupied with maintaining the best course and speed for air operations often changed them without telling the destroyers. That could make station keeping on an aircraft carrier difficult because the normal steaming lineup on a destroyer didn't provide a speed capability equal to a carrier's.

A maneuver used to permit the destroyers to limit their maximum speed to that achievable with two boilers online was the "slideback" method of stationing. That meant keeping the normal Task Force speed below the destroyer two-boiler operation maximum, with the carrier cranking up speed and changing course as necessary for air operations. With warning, the destroyers could estimate where their new station would be. Without warning, the destroyers could quickly be left behind and slow to catch up. Once, a destroyer protested repeated failures to give warning of course and speed changes. The carrier absurdly replied: *Maximum speed required of you is _____ knots using slideback method of stationing.*

The behavior of aircraft carriers even made the *Naval Institute Proceedings* magazine as a joke that went something like the following. An aircraft carrier Captain was in an Officer's Club with the Captains of the destroyers that had been screening his ship. He said that he understood that Turn Green meant to turn 45° to Starboard and Turn Red meant turn 45° to Port but didn't know the meaning of Turn White. They reluctantly revealed that it meant: *Watch Out, that big S.O.B. has gone the wrong way again!*

Carriers' necessary primary focus on safe air operations produced much frustration in the destroyer forces carefully trained in ship maneuvers and station-keeping. But no one can serve on a carrier task force without developing deep admiration for the courage and skill of the pilots.

Night Steaming

Fleet activities were heavy during the day, and the nights were often quiet steaming. That challenged the alertness of the bridge watch. Officers of the Deck moved around the bridge and Pilot House, listened and responded to occasional radio traffic, and checked the radar and the ship's position, but still had to fight the tendency to nod off. That challenge was harder for the Lookouts, who were stationed on the wings of the bridge and didn't have anything to do but peer at the unchanging seascape. We all knew the danger behind not being alert—sometimes understated as: *A collision at sea can ruin your entire day.* Still, virtually all officers and enlisted men, after tiring workdays, too often had to pick their drooping heads off their chests during dreary night watches, especially when the ocean was calm. So it was important to keep prodding ourselves awake and to periodically walk out to the bridge wings to engage the Lookouts' attention. I now see that as illustrative of the difference between literal requirements and reality. The requirement in this case, unremitting alertness, was buttressed by the penalty specified for sleeping on watch by the Uniform Code of Military Justice being Death or such other penalty as a court martial may direct. But the reality was that, if anyone fell asleep on watch, the entire watch was at fault. And, if a Lookout fell asleep, not only would there be no court martial, the person who would be held accountable was the Officer of the Deck. He wouldn't be court martialed (unless harm came to the ship or crew), but a perceived lack of trustworthiness could end his naval career.

The Crew's Food

Eventually, the sailors who stood bridge watches with me felt free to air their gripes. Their greatest complaint was the food in the General Mess. (Officers purchased their own food and ate in the Officer's Mess.) I pointed out that the dinner plate routinely sent to the OOD on the bridge tasted fine. My watchstanders alleged that what was sent to the bridge wasn't what they were getting. So I had my Messenger of the Watch remove the belt denoting his position, go to the Mess Hall, get a typical serving, and bring it to me. It tasted awful. I sent the tray to the Supply Officer in the Wardroom, with direction to inform him that this was what the crew was eating. (Political Correctness has never been my strong suit.) That produced a brief uptick in food quality. But, because a mark of surface ship Supply Officer Excellence was how much of the allotted money for food was not expended but turned back in, the General Mess food quality soon returned to its previous state.

The Court Martial

Destroyer duty also provided me with my only Navy Court Martial experience. A husky ship's sailor had come back to the ship drunk, made his way into the space containing the Main Battery fire control computer, and used the hard wooden handle on a wire brush to wreak damage. The computer remained operable, but he cracked the glass port directly above a disk and ball assembly essential to computer operability. The Captain convened a Special Court Martial, made up of ship's officers, to try him. I was the Prosecutor, and made the point that, with a little more effort, the accused could have removed a warship from service for an extended period. The Court Martial Panel asked a lot of questions of the accused, and found him guilty. The sentence included forfeiture of two-thirds pay for three months, three months at hard labor, and a bad conduct discharge. The Captain, as convening authority, rescinded the bad conduct discharge.

Judge Advocate General (JAG) review found the questioning by the Court Martial Panel excessive and inappropriate (despite Uniform Code of Military Justice authorization of questions by the Panel) but concluded that the Panel had focused on trying to find mitigating circumstances, and sustained the result. The sailor was shipped off to do his sentence. Overall, I felt that the disruption of ship's activities was unacceptable, that a trial of a crew member by a small ship's officers hazarded objectivity but hadn't produced unfairness in this case, that a trial by a JAG panel would be unlikely to produce a balanced or knowledgeable perspective, and that the whole process should be avoided if good order and discipline could be otherwise assured.

Gun Firing

While I was First Lieutenant, my battle station was amidships, at the 40 mm gun mounts. These were two mounts of four guns each, one set firing to starboard, the other to port. Having been the chief director operator of a 40 mm National Guard coastal artillery gun, the 40 mm mounts weren't a totally new experience. And I had already had the benefit of ammunition safety training given by a grizzled army sergeant. His message was: if it's possible for an accident to happen, it will, you just don't know when. He taught us to dig a deep pit near each gun so a misfired round could be dumped and cause no harm if it went off. We also learned to use the bore cleaning rod to bang on the nose of a misfired round until it popped out of the rear of the gun, hustling it over to and dropping it in the pit, and backing off hurriedly. Practical experience was gained by observing what happened when the gun next to us in the firing line had a misfire. Several guardsmen took the bore cleaning rod and rammed it down the muzzle repeatedly. There was a steady Thunk with each ram. What we heard was a predictable sequence of Thunk, Thunk, Thunk.... that ended up as Thunk, Thunk, Thu-Bang! as the next gun in line had a "cook-off" that fired a round just as the bore cleaning rod hit the jammed round in our gun. We initially thought that the misfired round had gone off, and the operator on the other side of my gun director took off running. He came back shame-faced and took a lot of ribbing. But I saw no 40 mm misfires detonate in the National Guard or, while I was First Lieutenant, on destroyer duty.

After I became a destroyer Gunnery Officer, we did have a 40 mm misfire. Our process was the same as the Army's. This round came out the breech and was tossed over the side. A few seconds later it went off. We heard the detonation but saw nothing. No damage was done. We went on with the exercise.

We also had 5" gun firing experiences. Once, our column of destroyers was steaming along for firing at an aircraft-towed target. The towing aircraft appeared and made its first run, coming from aft and up the starboard side. We were the last destroyer in line and the first to fire. As our forward guns were training right toward their firing position, one went off prematurely. The fired round cut the target sleeve towing cable fairly close to the plane, and the rest of the cable and the towed sleeve arced gracefully into the ocean. Without any communication, the towing aircraft banked right sharply, reversed course, and went home. There was no ado about that one-shot gunnery exercise.

Another disconcerting event occurred when an airborne target sleeve was being towed from ahead of our column of destroyers and down the starboard side of the column. When "Air Action Starboard" was ordered, the forward gun mounts trained right. After "Commence Firing" was ordered, Mount 51 ran away, and trained right significantly aft of the ship's beam. Mount 52 fired and burnt cork and expelled gases from its muzzle entered Mount 51 through the Gun Captains hooded station. I had ordered Cease Fire and looked for but couldn't see the Mount 51 Gun Captain. Neither mount was moving. Mount 51 didn't answer sound powered phone calls. I looked down to the bridge, the Captain looked up at me, and I said that I thought I had better go and look into Mount 51. The Captain agreed. So I went down to the main deck, and banged on the entry hatch to the Mount. There was no response. I opened the hatch. The gun crew members were at their firing stations, blackened with gunfire residue. No one was moving. No one was talking. But, in a few more minutes, the wide eyed stares returned to normal. The Mount was trained centerline and secured. And, except for their readily healed psyches, no one was injured. The Gun Mount was repaired and the same crew performed well in future exercises. (I never did find out if the firing cutout mechanisms that prevent firing into one's own ship would prevent one mount from firing into another, runaway mount.)

The South Atlantic Cruise

In the Summer and Fall of 1958, after a new Captain took command, we were made part of a Task Force. Its other ships were another destroyer, two destroyer escorts, two fleet oilers, an aircraft tender (a support/repair ship), an Essex class ASW (antisubmarine warfare) aircraft carrier, and a second aircraft tender that had been converted into a missile launching platform. The task force commander was aboard the carrier. But it was the missile launching platform that the task force was established to support.

Additional funds were provided to make the ships ready for this assignment. Our only information was that we had to be prepared for unusually heavy weather. So the Deck Force invested in new lifelines and ratlines (a term for sailing ship rope ladder lines, but to us meaning light lines strung netlike between the lifelines to prevent items and sailors from being washed overboard).

From Norfolk, we deployed to the far South Atlantic, down by the Falkland Islands. The voyage was pleasant most of the way. We crossed the equator, had the requisite Shellback ceremony, and saw the Southern Cross in the heavens on clear nights. (It's only visible south of the equator.)

As we neared our destination, we began to experience heavy weather. Once, while I was outside the pilot house and on the starboard wing of the bridge, the ship rolled about 60° to starboard. Wrapping my arms and legs around the compass repeater stanchion made sure I didn't get tossed off.

During much of that part of the voyage, no one was allowed on the main deck, and fore and aft travel was either inside or on the 01 Level (the only extensive deck above the main deck). We did have one instance of a sailor being washed from the 01 Level down to the main deck and being caught by the ratlines. He was fortuitously unhurt and scrambled back to the 01 Level before anyone else could react. After that, even the 01 Level was avoided during heavy seas. Those were monstrous to the smaller ships, and the wind howled fiercely as well. I once looked aft from the bridge and saw a wave above the top of the Number 2 (aftmost) smokestack, something I didn't think possible. (We were going up the side of one wave, the wave I saw over the stack was behind us.) Huge following seas were the most stomach churning. It took a lot of rudder to maintain course then, and the experience gave me a new perspective on the old naval wish for Fair Winds and Following Seas.

The wind and sea were sometimes fierce enough that the Oilers couldn't maintain the designated course. Also, except for the destroyers and the carrier, the task force was made up of single screw vessels. That meant having no backup propulsion source if a screw was lost, with an increased likelihood of wallowing in heavy seas or even foundering. But the carrier was relatively unaffected, probably without the need for its crew to spend more time holding on to the tableware than on eating.

The Task Force Commander's course selection soon became better suited to the less maneuverable ships. Even then, when the high winds and seas made their daily late afternoon appearance, it wasn't unusual to see the whole sonar dome of another destroyer when that ship's forward structure came completely out of the water. (Those domes were located well behind the bow, supposedly assuring that the water flow around them would be smooth.) But we slept well because the pounding made us so tired. All that was necessary was to take a position that permitted quickly grabbing and holding on tightly.

There was normal fleet maneuvering when the sea was calm. That soon taught us that the carrier seamanship so derided by the destroyer forces was far superior to that of ships with no such experience. I had the deck (OOD) watch when that point was forcibly rammed home. We were on plane guard station on the port beam of the carrier. My in-training OOD (the JOOD) had the conn (giving course and speed orders) while I observed. There were tactical radio circuits on the bridge, and I was monitoring those too. The Task Force Commander sent a long, involved administrative message over one of the tactical circuits, putting me in the position of copying down the message with a grease pencil. (It was improper to send an administrative message over a tactical circuit, and this message also was unsuited in length to voice radio transmissions.)

My attention to the administrative message was interrupted by a lookout yelling: *Mr. McCabe, Mr. McCabe!* Looking up, I saw the Missile Platform's bow dead ahead and said: I Have the Conn Right Full Rudder All Engines Ahead Full! Engineering promptly responded that they couldn't answer a full bell (in this steaming configuration). I replied: Give Me All You've Got! As the ship heeled over and we started to clear that 14,000 ton renegade, I passed the word on the 1MC: Captain To The Bridge! Before he arrived, I had put on left full rudder to make sure our fantail was clear. We never got to the point where action by both ships was necessary to avoid collision (*in extremis*). Had that happened, collision would have been inevitable because the Missile Platform charged through our station. When the Captain arrived, he calmly listened to my tale, smiled, and went back to the wardroom to finish lunch.

After the Captain left, I saw that my right hand was trembling, and stuck it in my pocket until that stopped. Then I had to consider the trainee who had the Conn when this evolution started. He had left the bridge and didn't return. When I was relieved as OOD, I went to see the XO and told him what had happened. He listened without comment. All that I heard back was that my former JOOD had been taken off the watch bill. I never saw him again.

A clue about what our Task Force was up to was the film badges (radiation dose measuring devices) we were all issued. Additional perspective came when we were directed to man the Main Battery Director (gun control station) and use it to measure the bearing and vertical angle to "Flashlight." That was when, on several occasions, no one was allowed topside and the completely dark night suddenly turned into daylight for a while. But the light was so diffuse that finding its center with our optics wasn't practicable. We guessed that the Missile Platform was shooting atomic bombs that were exploded pretty high up, and were told to keep out thoughts to ourselves and our mouths shut.

Some months after we returned to Norfolk, a New York Times article by Hanson Baldwin described our mission as being the high altitude explosion of atomic bombs to measure the electron flow (from fission product decay) around the earth. I asked the XO about our film badges, and he said that they had been lost. A Wikipedia online encyclopedia article states that all the film badges were destroyed or lost. But a related article on the now declassified mission states that one of the oilers had 264 film packets read, with 21 indicating radiation exposures, all negligible. The highest reading was 0.025 roentgens in a control film packet in a radiation-free shipboard space. That equates to 25 millirem (thousandths of a rem, which stands for roentgen equivalent mammal/man), and the highest exposure on an individual's packet was 10 millirem. Our average annual exposure in the U.S. is 310-360 millirem, a daily dose of less than one millirem. So the known highest individual exposure during this operation amounted to about 10-12 days of natural background radiation.

The U.S. Nuclear Regulatory Commission limits dosage to radiation workers to 5000 millirem a year and requires licensees to limit their radiation dosage to the public to 100 millirem a year. And some inhabited areas have natural background radiation levels of up to 3000 millirem a year, with no related harm identified. So our exposures were no big deal.

The unsatisfactory aspect was the loss of the film badges. That no doubt has been construed by some as a cover-up that lends credence to allegations that operation participants have had an above normal incidence of leukemia. To any leukemia victims and their families, I'd expect the badge loss to be a very hot button. To me, it only proves administrative ineptitude.

Our last event on the voyage was a visit to Rio de Janeiro. Before entering port, we lay to, to paint over the sea's ravages, even putting seamen over the side to paint above the waterline. That made our destroyer look so good that a photo of her entry into Rio's harbor made the cover of *Destroyerman* magazine.

Preparations for liberty in Rio included training in Brazil's Latin style of justice, which considered the accused guilty until proven innocent. Also, we were advised that, if we hired a taxi, we were responsible for any accident it had. And, reportedly, any Brazilian driver in an accident, if mobile, went to the nearest phone and reported the car stolen—to avoid being jailed until the trial. Fortunately, we encountered no such problems.

The food in Rio was delightful. Copacabana beach was gorgeous. And several officers, led by the XO, went to the top of Sugarloaf Mountain. We took a long cable car ride to get partway up and another to finish the climb. From the top, we looked down on the tiny city and airport, and watched miniature planes take off and climb in circles until they could fly over the surrounding mountains, getting close enough for us to see that they really were large, four-engined airliners.

We also took advantage of the availability of cheap beef to provide an abundant supply of seared beef strips to the Officer's Mess. I was the Wardroom Mess Treasurer and a few officers complained about the cost, but the Captain had suggested the expenditure and they curbed their displeasure.

Directives

After the South Atlantic cruise, we went through an inspection of our ship's directives. Never having seen any Gunnery Department directives, I asked where they were and was told that I was the

Gunnery Officer and had to have them. After fruitless searching, I started from scratch.

Navy directives came as "Instructions" that didn't expire and as "Notices" that did. At the top were directives issued by the Navy's senior commands. Subordinate commands added on their directives. Individual ships were at the bottom of the cascade. And the models available were insufficient and outdated. So, with a lot of midnight oil, I wrote new Gunnery Department instructions. The inspectors made a lot of comments about improving them, but they passed muster.

Months later, the drawer beneath a previous Gunnery Officer's bunk was taken out. The prior set of Gunnery Department Instructions was on the deck under it, outdated but otherwise better than mine. I kept the two together for the next update. (There wasn't time or support for keeping them current.)

We went through a very trying time trying to get our directives up to speed, and they weren't used to operate the ship. So they made no real contribution to the performance that resulted in our ship being awarded the Battle Efficiency E for being the best destroyer in the squadron.

Admiral Arleigh Burke

Long after my Gunnery Department Instructions fiasco, I read a lengthy Navy Department Notice about the need to reduce paperwork. It was signed by Admiral Arleigh Burke, the Chief of Naval Operations. On the notice was his penned in comment: *This Notice is an excellent example of its own subject.* That raised my high opinion of the man.

Admiral Burke, a living example of derring-do, was known as 31-Knot Burke for the high speed of his destroyers. He was also famous for having mistakenly engaged another squadron of American destroyers at long distance during a Pacific sea battle. The Commander of the other squadron identified the mistake by radio. Arleigh Burke ceased fire and reportedly replied: *Please excuse the next eight salvoes, they're on the way.* He also won the last classic destroyer sea battle by using the classic "Crossing the T" tactic.

Crossing the T is crossing directly ahead or astern of an enemy to keep it abeam. By doing that, warships can bring most of their guns to bear on the enemy while the enemy is limited to using just his forward (or aft) guns. If the enemy ships are steaming in column, Crossing the T has an even greater advantage: naval guns fire very accurately in bearing but less so in range, and Crossing the T increases the chances of hitting an enemy ship.

Reserve Training Cruises

Before the pride over winning the Battle Efficiency E had subsided, our destroyer was assigned to reserve training duty. That meant a substantive cut in crew members and another in funding. Our operations then consisted of taking aboard a group of enlisted and officer Naval Reservists in Norfolk, getting underway on Monday, steaming to the Caribbean for training, spending the weekend there, returning to Norfolk on Friday of the next week, having Saturday and Sunday to prepare, and getting underway with the next group on Monday.

Having fewer permanent crew and less money and less in-port time, the ship's appearance and morale suffered. But the standards didn't change. So, instead of getting the weekend of Caribbean liberty they had looked forward to, most of the enlisted reservists' Caribbean weekend was taken up in sprucing up the ship, along with the ship's crew. Some complained to their congressmen and senators, who sent letters asking what was going on. Our replies were defensive. (I later learned that the best way to answer was to clearly describe our actions and state the related conditions.)

The money shortage became acute. We couldn't afford the paint needed to keep up the ship's appearance. But our Boatswain's Mates didn't accept that. When we moored alongside a fleet destroyer, they saw that she was having her Peak Tanks repainted. Those triangular "tanks" were dry spaces just behind the bow, typically used for storing paint. The adjacent fleet destroyer's paint was on deck, under a tarp, until their Peak Tank repainting was done. And, after we got underway, we had plenty of paint in our own Peak Tanks.

I didn't know where the paint came from, but a betting man might wager that selected members of the other crew had been enticed to look the other way, and had stored discarded empty paint cans in their Peak Tanks so that the loss wouldn't be discovered until it was too late to trace the disappearance.

The Willie D. Porter

Destroyer duty reminded me of the frustrations and difficulties that Morris had humorously described in *Warm Bodies*. But our troubles were as nothing compared to the tribulations of the USS William D. Porter (DD-579), a Fletcher Class destroyer that became infamous. My first awareness of her travails came through a *Destroyerman* magazine article (there now are rafts of similar articles online). The Porter, named for a Civil War Navy Commodore and nicknamed the Willie D, was commissioned in 1943 and home-ported in Norfolk, Virginia.

In November 1943, the Porter was assigned to support/escort a highly classified mission involving the USS Iowa (BB-61), which was taking President Franklin D. Roosevelt to summit meetings with England's Prime Minister Winston Churchill and China's Generalissimo Chiang Kai-shek (in Cairo) and then with Russia's Premier Joseph Stalin (in Tehran). Accompanying the president were Secretary of State Cordell Hull, the Joint Chiefs of Staff, and a slew of aides and VIPs.

Commanding the Iowa's task force was Navy and Atlantic Fleet Commander-in-Chief Fleet Admiral Ernest J. King, who was notorious for ending the career of any subordinate who disagreed with him. He also was described as perhaps the most disliked allied leader in World War II. A former submarine division commander and a naval aviator, he designed the Submarine Warfare Insignia (dolphins) but didn't qualify to wear them. In 1940, he was "rescued" from the General Board (an elephant graveyard for senior officers awaiting retirement) and assigned as the Atlantic Fleet Commander. Then, three days after Congress established the five-star rank of Fleet Admiral in 1941, and two days after Admiral Chester Nimitz, the Pacific Fleet Commander, was promoted to that rank, Admiral

King was so promoted. When he reached mandatory retirement age and informed President Roosevelt of that, the president replied: *So What, Old Top.* So he was secure in his position.

The Porter's first gaffe was while getting underway from Norfolk to join the Iowa. As she backed away from the pier, her secured anchor raked another moored destroyer's side and tore off that ship's railings, life rafts, lifeboat mounts, a small boat, and sundry other items.

The next day, a depth charge from the Porter fell off the ship and exploded because its safety wasn't set. That prompted the task force to take evasive action to avoid a potential submarine attack—until the Porter reported the cause.

Not long after that, a rogue wave took away the topside equipment that wasn't securely lashed down on the Willie D's deck, and washed a man overboard. He wasn't found.

Then a fireroom on the Porter lost ability to steam one of its boilers. The Willie D was now firmly fixed in Admiral King's stern eye, frequently reporting her status to him.

When, to show the president the Iowa's air defense capabilities, weather balloons were launched and shot at, the president and Admiral King watched from the bridge. The Willie D contributed by shooting down missed balloons that drifted toward her. And the Porter then simulated a torpedo launch at the Iowa. The lunacy of that became strikingly clear when the Willie D actually fired a torpedo at the battleship. That the Iowa's thick armor belt and size made one torpedo unlikely to sink her was immaterial. The Porter had fired at a U.S. ship carrying the President of the United States and his august entourage.

After two unsuccessful attempts to visually signal the flagship, the Willie D broke radio silence to report the danger. Reportedly, the unperturbed president asked that his wheelchair be moved so he could better see the incoming torpedo. Iowa took evasive action and trained her guns on the Porter in case this was an assassination attempt. The torpedo exploded in the knuckle put in Iowa's wake when the ship increased speed. (So it would have missed in any case.)

Also, at the reported range of about 6000 yards, the Mark 15 torpedoes carried by World War II U.S. destroyers would have reached that distance in about five minutes. It would have taken quite some time to twice unsuccessfully try to visually signal the Iowa, to then warn her by radio, and for Iowa to then maneuver to evade. So the tale may be embellished, but no one would have dared to dispute the Fleet Admiral. (In addition to the fear the Admiral elicited, he was surrounded by the false, impenetrable aura of Infallibility that accompanies the powerful.)

It's also unrealistic to expect an unguided single torpedo fired at a moving target 6000 yards away to be a hit. For a torpedo fired at the center of the Iowa with a 6000 yard run, a 1.5° inaccuracy in the torpedo's course would be an error of about 470' in the torpedoes' intersection with the target's track. That's over half Iowa's 861' length, and therefore a miss. And, if the torpedo's angle of intersection with the target's track is more or less than 90°, a smaller torpedo course error would cause a miss. (A 45° angle of torpedo intersection with the Iowa's track would have made 0.97° the torpedo course error that would cause a miss.) Also, each one-knot error in calculated target speed across the line of sight produces, for a 6000 yard torpedo run, about a 300' error in the point of intersection. That's why short torpedo runs were sought and torpedo attacks were salvos spaced out along the target's track.

But the uncertainties of torpedo firings lessen Willie D's wrong not one whit. Admiral King placed the Porter and her entire crew under arrest (a first for the U.S. Navy) and sent the Willie D to Bermuda. There, marines maintained the arrest while an inquiry was held. The Chief Torpedoman responsible for the torpedo tube mount eventually admitted to not having removed the primer charge as required, with the firing of that charge causing the torpedo to be launched. And he admitted to throwing the fired primer charge casing overboard to try to conceal his mistake. The Navy sentenced him to 14 years at hard labor. President Roosevelt asked that no punishment be meted out because the firing was an accident.

The Porter's Captain and several officers and enlisted men were transferred to obscure shore assignments. Those officers' naval careers were over. What actually happened to the Chief Torpedoman is unclear, but it seems unlikely that the intent of the president's no-punishment request was fully met.

The Willie D was exiled to the Aleutians. There she fired a 5" shell that landed in the front yard of the Naval Base Commander's home during a party for officers and their wives. That supposedly happened because a drunken sailor returning from leave fired one of the ship's guns before anyone could stop him, with the only damage being to the destroyer's reputation. Even in wartime, however, the hazard of leaving cannon ammunition readily accessible and untended dictates against doing that. If the firing happened as described, the drunken sailor removed a shell and a separate propellant charge from storage, took them to separate hoists beneath a gun mount, energized and operated the hoists, went topside to the gun mount, undogged and opened it, entered, opened the gun's breech, loaded the shell and the propellant charge, closed the breech, and fired the cannon. Even a sailor who knew how to perform each of those evolutions couldn't do them quickly while drunk. Also, that the sailor was returning from leave is suspect. There was no doubt some liberty on the Naval Base, but being able to get wartime leave in, or wasting it on, the cold, barren Aleutians is farfetched. {I've heard sailors derisively describe the Aleutians as having a girl behind every (nonexistent) tree.} So the described sequence may be a cover story. But there's no doubt that this incident increased the Willie D's infamy.

From the Aleutians, the Willie D was shunted to the Pacific Fleet. She was greeted by other ships with the message *Don't Shoot. We're Republicans!* Porter performed well in combat, but shot up the side and superstructure of another Fletcher class destroyer and downed several American fighter planes in addition to the Japanese ones she shot down. Her saga ended during the battle of Okinawa when a Japanese kamikaze (suicide bomber) crashed alongside and continued its forward motion while sinking. The kamikaze's payload exploded under the Willie D's hull, lifting the ship clear of the water. Fatally damaged, the Porter sank three hours later. No crew member was lost. The Captain was the last to leave, damning his failure to bring his wallet along because the pay records went down with the ship and it would take months to get paid again. But her crew kept the Willie D afloat for three hours after the explosion, with each and every one of them coming away alive. So they ended up being more than dangerous stumblebums.

Destroyer Duty Summary

The Porter's troubles show that my destroyer duty was far better than it could have been. It provided me with good times at sea and ashore, acquainted me with good people, and taught me a lot about the benefits and penalties of small warships. Also, exposure to highly intelligent individuals without a college education and ones who had virtually no useful schooling emphasized the realization that: "There but for the Grace of God go I." In addition, reading about the problems of today's frigates (the "Ghetto Navy") showed that my destroyer experience has counterparts today—and no doubt will tomorrow. But the strongest feeling I now have about my first sea duty involves how much my shipmates did to teach me their trade.

II-2 Submarine Training

Prelude

The toy submarine I played with in the bathtub as a small boy was supposed to go ahead, dive, and surface. It did the first two steps well but failed to surface at all. I recalled that when I heard a submariner wisecrack that: *All ships can submerge, but only submarines can surface.*

Submarines didn't really get my attention until 1955, when the first nuclear submarine, the USS Nautilus (SSN-571), sent its widely publicized message: "Underway on Nuclear Power." The Nautilus set underwater speed records and demonstrated for the first time the ability to stay submerged indefinitely.

Along with Nautilus came awareness of Vice Admiral Hyman G. Rickover, the "Father" of the Nuclear Navy. A ruthless workaholic, Admiral Rickover had exceptional engineering competence. He gave total dedication, demanded it from his subordinates, and was infamous for his abrasiveness to and humiliation of others. His promotion to Rear Admiral occurred despite his not being selected by the Navy for that. As the story was told, his professional reputation and ability to ingratiate himself with Congress were so great that the Navy promotion list was rejected until his name was added. That gained him no popularity in the Navy. But even his greatest detractors knew that his efforts produced an incredible advance in warship capability. And his shadow was over the entire submarine force the whole time I was in it.

One of the first submarine duty hurdles was being closely packed with other prospective submariners into a Chamber normally used to decompress divers returned to the surface too quickly. That

EBE CHANDLER MCCABE, JR.

Decompression Chamber was then pressurized to the point at which all speech sounded like Mickey Mouse talk. Such testing occasionally identified some individuals who had claustrophobia and didn't know it.

We also were psychologically screened. That included being shown a landscape of a farmhouse and surrounding scenery. The colors and shapes were out of whack. It looked like a scene from the Disney movie Fantasia to me. Inkblot tests came next. They ended when I described a blob as two hobgoblins creeping up to a building corner and about to peer around it and scare each other to death. The tester laughed.

The Silent Service

One of the first things we were told at Submarine School was that the Submarine Force is the Silent Service. The reason given was that, during WWII, a US Congressman had asked why our submarines were so successful. He was reportedly told that the Japanese set their depth charges at 100' and our submarines were at 400', made that public, and the next week we lost three submarines.

That tale's basis was confirmed in the US Naval Institute book Submarine Victory. It did not name the congressman or confirm the three submarine losses. But a Wikipedia article identifies Historian Clay Blair's attribution of the revelation to Andrew Jackson May, an eight-term Democratic Congressman from Kentucky, after being briefed in Pearl Harbor.

Vice Admiral Charles Lockwood, the WWII Pacific Submarine Force Commander, wrote to Fleet Admiral King's Chief of Staff that he had heard that Congressman May had said that the Japanese depth charges were not set deep enough and would be pleased to know that they are being set deeper now. After the war, Admiral Lockwood wrote: "I consider that indiscretion cost us ten submarines and 800 officers and men."

A 1946 bribery scandal made Congressman May's reelection bid unsuccessful. That scandal involved excessive Garsson Munitions profits and defective mortar shell fuses that resulted in the deaths of 38 U.S. soldiers. In 1947, May was convicted of taking bribes to use his influence (Congressional Chairmanship) to secure munitions contracts. He served nine months in prison in 1950, was granted a full pardon by President Harry S. Truman in 1952, and practiced Law for the rest of his life. His cohort Murray Garsson, who also was convicted and jailed, died in poverty.

Kentucky Governor Bert T. Combs named the 49-room lodge at Jenny Wiley State Resort Park in Prestonberg, KY the May Lodge. It still bears that name. Combs was Governor from 1959-63 and a Justice of the Sixth Circuit Court of Appeals from 1967-70 (appointed by President Lyndon Johnson).

My esteem for Harry S. Truman dropped sharply when I found out about the May pardon. It also surprised me to find out that Kentucky has a memorial to someone involved in the killing of over 800 U.S. servicemen. (I thought that uncharacteristic of the way our States honor their war dead.)

The lesson I took from Congressman May's treatment is that cronyism enables those well enough connected politically to get away with murder.

"Boat" vs. "Ship"

The Submarine School also noted that submarines are called boats, not ships, despite a boat being a vessel that can be carried aboard a ship. (The earliest submarines were in that category.) Boat, in the submarine context, also has been described as a shortened form of pig boat, a term describing the foul smell and living conditions of early submarines.

We also were told that Rear Admiral "Fearless Freddie" Warder, Commander, Submarine Force, Atlantic, had ordered that submarines be called ships. The reason given was that he had been ribbed by other admirals about their commands being of ships while his was of boats.

Admiral Warder had captained the USS Seawolf (SS-197) during World War II. A tale told about that was that, while he was having a cup of coffee in the Wardroom after being depth charged, an excited sailor popped his head out of the battery well (beneath the Wardroom) and yelled "Fire in the Battery Well!" (a serious problem).

Fearless Freddie, unmoved, gruffly responded "Put it Out." But, despite being very highly regarded, and right about submarines being ships, his directive to call them that produced little terminology change (except, no doubt, in his presence).

Buoyant Ascent

One of the hurdles of submarine school was training in the buoyant ascent means of escape from a sunken submarine. The training was conducted in a tall, flooded tower with entry locks (chambers) on the side. The lock 50' below the surface was the one used. We wore life jackets inflated by air cartridges and equipped with valves that let air escape when the jacket pressure was a couple of pounds above water pressure. After we entered the lock, it was flooded to just above the top of the hatch into the tower, pressure was equalized with the tower, the life jackets were inflated, and the hatch to the tower was opened. Each trainee ducked under the water, entered the tower, let go and ascended to the surface exhaling all the way (to prevent chest/lung rupture as the pressure decreased during the ascent). Divers were stationed on the way up to grab anyone who stopped exhaling and stuff him into an air-filled bell-shaped chamber. The ascent left me with a sharp leg cramp, but it kneaded out quickly and I concluded that it had been caused by fear-induced tension.

Submarine operations were very seldom conducted in water shallow enough for buoyant ascent. That may be why the tower was dismantled a few years later.

The School Boat

At Submarine School, we studied the design of the USS Becuna (SS-319). She was a "Fleet Boat" of the kind that had been so successful in World War II (NavPers 16160, available online, contains a fine description of the Fleet Boats). These boats had been modernized after the war based on knowledge gained from captured German submarines. (Germany had the most advanced WWII submarines.) Many years later, when I was in a Philadelphia Naval Reserve

Unit, the decommissioned Becuna was a museum ship moored at Penn's Landing, outboard of another museum ship, the cruiser USS Olympia (C-6). Touring Becuna was enjoyable, but the tour guide wasn't pleased when I corrected his spiel three times before we got out of the Forward Torpedo Room.

Some aspects of submarine school classes were a chore. An example was analyzing air conditioning unit problems such as "short-cycling" on the "high" or "low" side.

Many Submarine School students had mechanical aptitudes and knowledge that far exceeded mine, and I found keeping up with them difficult in classes about machinery.

Approach and Attack Training

The submarine school had trainers with Torpedo Data Computers, and we ran simulated approaches and attacks in them. I enjoyed that training. There also was a captured Japanese periscope set up to view ship images and develop skill in calling target angle on the bow (the angle between the line of sight to the target and the target's course). It was a big help. By the time the six-months at Sub School were over, I had a sound basis for becoming good on the periscope.

Diving Training

Another challenge at Submarine School was the diving trainers. There we simulated dives and putting an out-of-trim submarine in diving trim. That was supplemented by going to sea for training on actual submarine dives.

An in-trim submerged submarine has near neutral buoyancy. Blowing the water out of the ballast tanks with high pressure air provides the buoyancy needed to get to and stay on the surface.

Diving started when the order "Clear the Bridge" was given by the OOD. The Lookouts started below on that command, and the OOD followed after sounding two blasts (A-ooga!, A-ooga!) on the diving klaxon, shutting the Conning Tower Hatch right after he went through it. The klaxon prompted immediate opening of the ballast tank vents, shutdown of the ship's engines, shifting propulsion to the battery, and shutting all hull openings. The first thing the former OOD, now the Diving Officer, looked for in the Control Room was a "Green Board" on the panel above the ballast tank vent operating levers. Rows of red lights just below the green ones showed the open components, but an unlit red light wasn't enough—all the lights had to be green.

The goal was to submerge as fast as possible. WWII submergence had been made faster (less than a minute) by partially flooding the aft ballast tanks to lower the stern in the water. (Sea state and the danger of attack were factors.)

I watched my first dive in a submarine from the Control Room, hoping that my apprehension didn't show. After several dives and surfaces, it was my turn to go to the bridge to be the diving officer trainee. There were four of us on the bridge—the ship's OOD, two Lookouts, and me. I asked the OOD about the Port Lookout, who looked scared. The OOD said that this Lookout had been left on the bridge twice on dives and was very edgy. To demonstrate, he said *Watch This*, raised a foot, and stomped it noisily. In a flash, the Port Lookout went down the hatch into the Conning Tower. Then, the OOD ordered *Clear the Bridge*, sounded the diving alarm, and followed the other Lookout and me below.

Being left on the bridge on a dive was a planned for SNAFU. The bridge watch had to clear it promptly, OOD last, and the watch in the Conning Tower kept a count of the number of personnel topside. If the count didn't add up when the OOD came down, an emergency surface was ordered (three blasts on the diving klaxon), the ballast tanks were blown, the screws were reversed, and the ship surfaced to retrieve the possibly dunked individual(s). Another initiation of this sequence was for an individual left on the bridge to use its MC system to call out "You left me on the bridge; you left me on the bridge!..."

One of the drills conducted at sea was to have another station on the MC system call out "You left me on the Bridge!" to see how the in-training personnel handled that report. Not surfacing was a drill failure because, had the report been valid, time was of the essence in preventing loss of life. But a submarine under attack would continue to submerge—one life vs. 80 and the loss of a warship leaves no choice.

I only heard about one other case of being left on the bridge during a peacetime dive. That occurred on the submarine on which I went to sea to complete my submarine qualification. The submarine had surfaced without shutting the ballast tank vents, and the OOD and Lookouts went to the bridge (getting there promptly to check for nearby shipping is vital). The boat started to submerge as soon as the air blowing the ballast tanks was secured. The victimized officer matter-of-factly told me that the water had gotten deep on the bridge, but that his head hadn't gone under.

A related tale told at submarine school was about a submarine operating near the Panama Canal before WWII. In this case, the Forward Torpedo Room requested permission to disable the torpedo tube interlocks for periodic testing. Because that enabled opening both the inner and outer torpedo tube doors at the same time, the Captain's permission was required. It was given. (The Forward Torpedo Room was the only compartment on a Fleet Boat that the submarine couldn't survive being completely flooded.) A few minutes later, the submarine sank. The only survivors were the Bridge Watch.

Fleet Boats had two groups of main ballast tanks, the forward group and the after group. Initially, they had quick-opening vents at the top and slow-moving Kingston Valves at the bottom. During extended surfaced operation, the Kingston Valves were shut to prevent seawater seepage into the ballast tanks. After several surfaced submarines returning from war patrols were attacked by "friendly" aircraft, the Kingston Valves were removed. That lesson reminded me of a famous World War II report: "Sighted Sub, Sank Same." Apparently, nobody asked: "Who's Sub?" But the wartime reaction to a submarine contact is to attack, with the need for quick response, hatred of submarines, and incompetence fostering failure to identify the nationality of the submarine.

The Fleet Boats had other ballast tanks. One was Bow Buoyancy, a small tank under the top of the bow. It gave the ship an upward angle upon surfacing, and increased the reserve buoyancy while surfaced. There also was a Safety Tank amidships, kept flooded but ready to blow if and only if the Captain ordered it blown. Another ballast tank was Negative Tank, located forward of the center of gravity. It provided an initial negative buoyancy to quicken submergence. Once a good down angle was gained and the surface sea action was overcome, the order was given to Blow Negative. But it was kept ready to flood quickly if, for example, emergency deep was ordered, as sometimes happened when a ship was discovered dangerously close while at or coming up to periscope depth. It was also partially flooded to compensate for the buoyancy added by snorkel piping external to the hull not being flooded while snorkeling. When snorkeling ended, Negative was blown to compensate for the consequent flooding of that piping.

In the Diving Trainers and underway, we were introduced to out of trim conditions and how to correct them. Almost neutral buoyancy is not sufficient for proper trim. Being in longitudinal trim is necessary too. For that, the Fleet Boats had a Forward Trim Tank, an After Trim Tank, and two amidships Auxiliary Trim Tanks inside the hull. A Trim Pump transferred water between the trim tanks to change fore and aft trim or pump water to sea. And the trim tanks could be flooded from sea as well. Trim analysis was complicated by submarine speed and angle. We had to learn to handle problems like, for example, the submarine being light overall but heavy enough forward that the resulting down angle planed the boat below ordered depth.

Fleet Boats had bow and stern planes that served to help gain and maintain ordered depth. The analogy used to describe their function was an arrow in flight. If an arrow's point is tilted, it veers toward the tilt without changing the shaft orientation much—because the tail feathers tend to maintain that orientation. Bow planes work like an arrow's point. Stern planes maintain the longitudinal angle of the boat and are used to change that angle to achieve faster depth changes than the bow planes can—their action is analogous to tilting the feathers on the tail of an arrow.

The bow planes, located far forward, were rigged in (parallel to the ship's sides) when surfaced. (That allowed them to be less sturdily constructed.) The stern planes were aft, adjacent to the rudder. They could not be rigged in.

Mark 14 Torpedoes

The primary weapon of the Fleet Boat was the Mark 14 torpedo. When WWII began, those torpedoes had magnetic exploders designed to detonate the warhead under a target's keel and break it in two. But our boats were returning with reports of their torpedoes impacting or passing beneath their targets without detonating. Those failures were repeatedly considered to be due to failure to prepare, set, or use the torpedoes properly. Finally, the Pacific Submarine Force Commander had an armed warhead hoisted by a crane and dropped nose first onto concrete. It did not explode. Removal of the magnetic exploder and installation of a contact exploder then corrected the failure to detonate. That lesson has stuck with me as a reminder of the need to adequately prove designs and the danger of settling for less.

II-3 Fleet Boat Duty

Getting there

My leave before reporting to a submarine ended early, just like it had before my reporting for duty aboard a destroyer. This time, the rationale my new XO gave was the need to learn on and contribute to upcoming operations, before we deployed to the Western Pacific (WestPac). So I struck out for San Diego in my car, which held all my possessions.

My first day of travel was on the day after a blizzard, and I made only 250 miles. But the roads were clear from then on. Two of the four motels I slept in en route were in Texas. When I started out on one of those mornings, I stopped for breakfast at a diner. It was about 4:30 am and the diner was packed with cowboy-booted, ten-gallon hatted Texans. Their amiability made me think that they felt something in common with people who started their day as early as they did. And it made this stop a nice part of my cross country trip. Also, by and large, the diner's customers were a lot bigger than the farmers were where I grew up. But their demeanor and careworn faces made me conclude that these different sets of people had a lot in common.

The First Task

On the day I reported for duty, I was tasked with resolving an off-ship issue. A crew member whose wife was Mexican had driven to Mexico with her to visit her parents. En route, they had a one-car accident. He was uninjured, but she had a severely damaged arm. The Mexican authorities jailed him for injuring another person and detained her as evidence. She wasn't jailed but wasn't getting medical care.

A member of the Navy's Border Liaison staff and I went to see the sailor in the Tijuana jail. It had a large, concrete-floored center area. Along the walls, on all four sides, were tiers of jail cells—with two bunks on each side of each cell, and with a toilet along the outer wall in the center but no wash basin or towels.

One prisoner had his face pressed against his cell bars and howled loudly the whole time we were there. And a small crew was hosing down the cells and their occupants with a fire hose. We talked briefly with the sailor, and assured him that steps were being taken to bail him out and to get medical treatment for his wife. (He couldn't pay the over $600 bail.)

The Border Liaison said that jail inmates in Mexico had to pay for their keep, and had to stay in jail until their cases came up in court, which could take years. That reinforced the lesson I had had on the Latin system of justice before liberty in Rio.

Arrangements were made for a Mexican doctor who had just returned from the Mayo Clinic to repair the wife's arm. An Electricians Mate on the ship donated the entire bail. When it was paid, the sailor and his wife were allowed to return to the U.S.

When we went to pick up the sailor, we found that he had been transferred to the Tijuana Penitentiary, where we found him clothed only in an undershirt and unbelted trousers. He said that his other clothing had been taken by the other prisoners. We brought him back that way. He had to check in with the Mexican authorities monthly until his trial took place. But ship operations prevented that, and he became a fugitive from justice in Mexico.

This episode doesn't justify the USA's legal system, but it does shed light on why some tout it as the best in the world.

Fleet Boat Crews

Unlike destroyers, Fleet Boats were staffed with their full complement. They even had extra crew members assigned to make a larger number of qualified submariners available to the growing number of nuclear submarines. A side effect was a shortage of bunks. The solution, "hot bunking," split up bunk assignments so that, when watchstanders were on watch, their bunks were available to off-watch crew members. That wasn't appreciated, but it was endured with good-humor

Fleet Boats had three enlisted crew components: war veterans who were nearing retirement, qualified submariners who had entered the submarine service after WWII, and unqualified submariners.

Our younger crew members reflected the Navy's increasing emphasis on individuals with high technical aptitude. The war veterans were tough and especially competent. On liberty they might drink too much, and brawl, and stay ashore after liberty ended. But they had special status because they had been part of the submarine force that comprised less than 2% of the Navy, had 6% of the naval deaths due to enemy action, lost 52 submarines, and accounted for over half the enemy shipping sunk. Their country's view of wartime submarine service was beautifully expressed in the following statements by two high ranking submariners.

To those whose contribution meant the loss of sons, brothers or husbands in this war, I pay my most humble respect and extend my deepest sympathy. As to the 374 officers and 3131 men of the Submarine Force who gave their lives in the winning of this war, I can assure you that they went down fighting and that their brothers who survived them took a grim toll of our savage enemy to avenge their deaths.

MAY GOD REST THEIR GALLANT SOULS.
Vice Admiral Charles A. Lockwood, Jr.,
Commander, Submarine Force, U.S. Pacific Fleet

We, who survived World War II and were privileged to rejoin our loved ones at home, salute those gallant officers and men of our submarines who lost their lives in that long struggle. We shall never forget that it was

our submarines that held the lines against the enemy
while our fleets replaced losses and repaired wounds.

Fleet Admiral Chester W. Nimitz, Commander in Chief,
U.S. Pacific Fleet, and
Commander in Chief, Pacific Ocean Areas

One of our war veterans was a First Class Engineman (EN1) who had been stuck at that level since WWII. I saw him on my post-watch inspections of the boat. (Those were required after being relieved as Officer of the Deck.) No matter what watch I had, he was in *his* Engine Room. He even slept there, on the cushions atop two three foot long bench lockers that he shoved together. We often discussed WWII submarining. He adored the WWII Pacific Submarine Force Commander, Vice Admiral Charles Lockwood, and told me that "Charlie" Lockwood cried every time a submarine didn't return from patrol. He also said that being depth charged was like it was depicted in the movies, with the lights blinking out, etc.

The EN1 asked me to help him advance to Chief Petty Officer. So I tried. The two required training courses were *Engineman One and Chief* and *Petty Officer First Class and Chief.* He had taken them many years (and editions) earlier. When I asked which version of the course books he would use if he were going to prepare the advancement exam, he decided to take the current courses. Then I took a course textbook, opened it at random, and asked him to read a section and tell me the most important points. He did. I disagreed, and showed him that the most important points were in the first and last sentences. He agreed. After the next advancement exam, I asked him how he had done. He said he had memorized the first and last part of every course section and thought that had helped a lot. Evidently it did. He was advanced to Engineman Chief. A few years later, I heard that he had retired and had become a naval shipyard worker.

Despite being in ships designated for replacement by nuclear submarines, morale and performance were high on the diesel boats in San Diego. The only discrepancy I remember occurred when I was the Duty Officer in port and a senior petty officer asked to speak to me in private. He was a very competent submariner. And some of his shipmates had even expressed their esteem for the example he set as a husband and father (contrary to the merciless harassment that submarine sailors usually visited upon shipmates). This man asked for my view on "bastards." He said that he was an illegitimate child and had been discriminated against throughout his life. I said that we are not responsible for the acts of our parents and deserved to be assessed upon our own behavior, and that the respect and admiration his shipmates showed for him was an example. He never brought the subject up to me again, but I doubt that his mistreatment changed much—there are those whose self-esteem is dependent upon condemning others. Hurting people because of conditions they had no part in creating is one of the sadder measures of human character.

When I was a Submarine Communications Officer, one of my radiomen was a former steward who changed his rate when the Navy allowed stewards to convert to other ratings. I got my first take on his character when I entered the radio shack and heard another radioman singing:

"Who is that tall dark stranger there, _____ is his name." I was taken aback—until the singer smilingly pointed behind the radio transmitter—at the broadly grinning subject of his song.

The minority radioman later passed the chief's exam. When we got the authorization to promote him, he expressed dismay at the prospect of the expected ceremony. That meant having his brand new chief's hat tossed into the sea and having to swim out and retrieve it, and he couldn't swim. That wasn't anything new to the crew and, when the boat lay to for the initiation of all the newly promoted sailors, they put a life jacket on him and tossed him overboard. A brand new chief's hat was tossed out about 10 yards further. His awkward splashing brought much laughter, along with the spectacle of his salt water-soaked, brand new chief's khaki uniform ensconced in a bright orange life jacket. But determination assured that he would flail his way out to the hat and return with it. And the crew's laughter accompanied great respect for the man. (Becoming a Chief Petty Officer was an envied accomplishment, but there was no rancor evident about this man's achievement.)

That the conversion of stewards to other ratings wasn't endorsed by everyone became obvious when a senior staff officer came aboard to assess the ship's activities. When he interviewed me, he asked what I had done to foster development of enlisted submariners. He made no comment about the WWII EN1 who had been guided on the way to advance to Chief Petty Officer. But when I identified a Filipino steward who was being groomed to take the advancement exam for Electrician's Mate Third Class, he stated that was improper because decreasing the number of stewards had a bad effect on the wardroom. That was the only time I heard a senior officer openly dispute a Navy program.

Fleet Boat Aging

The Fleet Boats were getting old. Funding constraints added to their problems. An example of the toll was a Fleet Boat that, while still submerged before returning to San Diego, tried to rig the Torpedo Rooms for a planned loading of torpedoes. That required fitting crosswise beams from one side of the hull to the other. But the beams were too long—because the hull had compressed excessively. The boat's allowed depth was decreased, but there was still a strong enough need for her services that she continued to perform routine duties.

The Fleet Boats that I served on were 312' long with an about 27' beam, and displaced about 1600 tons surfaced and 2400 tons submerged. They had been modified after the war to provide greater underwater propulsion (GUPPY conversions).

Initial OOD Training

Getting the ship underway and making landings was a significant aspect of becoming a qualified submarine officer. Getting underway didn't seem difficult until I was told to do so without using the check-off list (a task representative of the philosophy of internalizing the submarine's characteristics and the situation to the point where they became second nature). So I visualized and mentally walked myself through the topside and underwater hull and the ship's systems, and surprised myself by accomplishing every preparatory item on the list. After that, getting underway was a snap.

Making landings was a bigger hurdle. The Captain reputedly allowed few errors, and took over ship control very quickly. Fortunately, my first landing was the relatively simple task of mooring alongside another submarine already moored to a buoy. That aligned the approach with the current. Concerned that getting close or coming in too fast might not be tolerated, I came in at a wide distance and backed down early to come in slowly. The Captain asked if we were going to be close enough to get a heavie (heaving line) over. Knowing that the heavies had (prohibited) lead chunks inside the "monkey fists" at their end (a general practice), I said Yes Sir. The heavies made it easily, the mooring lines were pulled over, and though we had to use the capstan to winch ourselves in, I made the landing without incident. But prolonged at-sea operations and shipyard overhaul combined to limit my chances to make more landings.

Riding the Waves

Going to sea introduced me a ship characteristic new to me. Submarines have relatively little reserve buoyancy, and tend to burrow into the wave following one that they ride over. GUPPY conversions made that worse by making the bow narrower to enhance submerged performance. On the surface, that could produce a rush of seawater along the main deck when the bow knifed into a wave. The bridge, which sat atop the forward part of the Conning Tower, had a transparent plastic bubble (one-quarter of a sphere) that provided some wind protection. But it gave little protection from the sea because, when seawater hit the forward part of the sail, it cascaded up and over the bridge, struck the part of the sail behind the bridge, and cascaded down upon the bridge watchstanders.

A "commandment" for safe ship operation required maintaining an alert and vigilant lookout. So the Officer of the Deck and two Lookouts manned the bridge even when the weather was rough. The hatch to the Conning Tower was kept shut then—except for passage during a break in the seas.

On one rough day, my Lookouts and I were getting thoroughly soaked on the bridge, and I felt that their stations weren't safe enough. Following common practice, I moved them from the edge of the bridge down into the Doghouse, the part of the sail forward of the Conning Tower. There they could look out "windows" in the sail and fulfill (poorly) the requirement to maintain a lookout. Not long afterwards, we went over a big wave and plunged into the next. Seawater filled a good part of the sail. I couldn't see my Lookouts. As the water slowly receded, I saw a head coming out of it. Then shoulders appeared, and then a torso. But I could only see one Lookout—until I saw that he was sitting on his partner's shoulders. Laughing at the spectacle, and realizing that Lookouts were totally useless in this weather, I had the Conning Tower hatch opened, sent the Lookouts below, and notified the Captain what I had done. He had me lay below and I spent the rest of my watch looking through a periscope.

Sail Modification

Our Low Sail configuration was changed, during shipyard overhaul, to a High Sail that raised the top of the bridge to the same height as the rest of the sail. That made for a much more habitable bridge with much better visibility. But the bridge was now much farther from, and higher than, the Conning Tower hatch. To speed the ability to get below, chromed pipes, sized to permit a good grip, were installed on each side of the ladder to the bridge. Upon diving, we descended by gripping the pipes with our hands, straddling them with our feet, and sliding down. That worked nicely unless the pipes were wet, as happened during frequent dives and surfaces. Then the slide down the pipes could be fast. We kept our knees bent to better handle the quick stop, but wet pipes usually meant a three point landing (two feet and one butt) before scrambling over to the Conning Tower hatch and getting below. By the time that happened, the impact was forgotten.

Watchstanding

Until a new officer qualified as a Diving Officer and as an Officer of the Deck, the other watchstanding officers were typically standing port and starboard (alternating with one other individual on a specific watch). That meant standing watch 12 hours a day. When everyone was qualified, the normal watch rotation dropped to one in three. That dropped the time on watch to eight hours a day and 56 hours a week. Incapacity of a watchstander could worsen that, but I never saw an incapacitated officer watchstander during my submarine duty.

Snorkeling

Snorkeling was a big qualification challenge. The Diving Officer had to compensate for a sizable trim change when the snorkel mast was raised, the diesel engines were started, and the snorkel exhaust mast was blown empty. Then the snorkel head (air intake) valve had to be kept far enough out of water to continue snorkeling while keeping it low enough to minimize the size of the radar target it presented. Sensors caused the head valve to shut before it dipped below the surface. And the diesel engines pulled a vacuum in the ship while the head valve was shut. The rougher the seas, the more the head valve cycled. The pressure in the boat and in the crew's eardrums cycled with the head valve. To assist in minimizing the problem, an aircraft altimeter was mounted at the Diving Officer's station, and the ordered depth was sometimes specified in altimeter reading (e.g., 4000 feet) rather than in keel depth. Proficiency in snorkeling was a significant part of the crew's esteem for Diving Officers.

The bow and stern planesmen were critical to the ability to snorkel. On my first submarine, the best Diving Officer aboard was reputedly the Chief of the Boat. A hulking World War II veteran, he was said to have become dissatisfied with the performance of a planesman, picked him up with one hand, cast him aside, and operated those planes himself. But that was ship's lore, and he didn't stand Diving Officer watches while I knew him.

Battery Charges

The battery charge lineup was stringently controlled because of the hydrogen the batteries generated then. We were taught that a 3% concentration will burn and 7% will explode. (My recent research identified higher numbers.) Our limit was 2% hydrogen in the airflow from the battery wells.

The rigor was reinforced by an undetected 1955 hydrogen buildup caused by a mis-wired Forward Battery Well exhaust fan that had run backward on a boat in overhaul. The resulting explosion killed five crew members. (The Hospital Corpsman who scraped the remains of the dead from the bulkheads in the Chief's Quarters wouldn't talk about the event.)

Lining up for a battery charge included checking the battery cells (e.g., no loose caps), ventilation line-up, and cooling water flow. There was no cooling water flow meter, so air bubbles in the plastic tubing carrying cooling water were the yardstick. Once, when I could see no bubbles, I stayed in the battery well for so long that the Captain asked what the Hell I was doing. He then ordered the charge started based upon the cooling water pumps appearing to operate normally. I had no qualms about that, but wasn't about to violate a safety rule established to avoid a repeat of a lethal accident—and the Officer of the Deck wasn't going to start the charge without that OK.

Supply Officer Duty

Diesel-powered submarines didn't have a Supply Corp Officer. That task typically fell to the newest Officer aboard, and was my first job on a submarine. The crew's mess was the biggest challenge. Spending the entire food allotment without exceeding it could be tricky. But it had a lot to do with submarines having the best food in the Navy.

The rest of the Supply Officer's duties involved manual management of the ship's parts and supplies—with many thousands of parts involved and one storekeeper to assist. But the crew knew from experience what parts were essential, and that usually kept the submarine in the parts needed.

While I was the Supply Officer, we visited Vancouver, British Columbia. Stories about how openly that city welcomed submariners abounded. The harbor was deep and scuttlebutt made the rounds about how another submarine had come into the port submerged and surfaced alongside its assigned pier to applause from a large crowd. Our surfaced approach to the pier wasn't so welcomed, but there were a large number of lovely young Canadian women standing on the pier to greet us. And, during visiting hours, those young ladies inundated the ship. They even took over the cooking, and I found numbers of them eating with the crew. If it hadn't been for the limited space on the ship, we'd have suffered a crimp in our ability to feed the crew after the visit. But the Captain and XO had no problem with the young ladies' eating aboard. So I made sure that a proper record of the food use was being kept and went off to enjoy the city with another bachelor officer.

Our first encounter was with a parade that we were invited to join by some pretty girls. So we joined them for a few blocks. But they soon lost interest and we left. The next morning, our Captain showed us the reason for their brief interest. He had a copy of the local newspaper's Ban the (Atomic) Bomb parade coverage, complete with pictures of the two of us parading along in our U.S. Navy Blue Service Uniforms. But the Captain wasn't really very upset. We'd have heard a lot stronger and longer admonition if he had been.

The Vancouver visit was followed by a food service problem. Crew members returning from liberty were allowed to "raid" the food stores if they documented their consumption so that a proper inventory could be maintained. Without that, unaccounted for food usage could put us over budget and produce substantive repercussions. After several tries to correct the lack of documentation failed, I had the food storage locked when the evening meal and movie ended in port. The next day I was called in to speak to the Captain. The result was restoration of normal conditions, but with the food use properly documented.

The cooking situation took a turn for the worse when we got down to just two cooks. At sea, the pair shared duties willingly and cheerfully. In port, they took alternating days of duty, coming in early

84

to cook breakfast and remaining to cook the other two meals. Then, after the evening meal and movie, the duty cook made breakfast pastries and left the ship to enjoy a day off. That worked fine until some of the crew started eating the breakfast pastries after coming in off liberty. Considerably put out by that, one of the cooks retaliated. I found out about that when he greeted me one morning by gleefully stating: *I got those greasy dicks! I got those greasy dicks!* Seeing that he was aboard on his day off, I asked him what was going on. He happily described his action. Instead of preparing breakfast pastries the night before, he had poured melted lard in pie pans, liberally layered the top with cinnamon and sugar, and hid his product in a galley cabinet. As he expected, the returning liberty party found and consumed his revenge, and the guilty parties were afflicted with severe cases of the trots. That affected only miscreants who knew their actions were wrong, and the crew accepted the retribution as just. Besides, these cooks were more than deserving of considerate treatment. Some time before this incident, the lard pastry preparer had come down with a skin infection and been removed from cooking duty. The other cook just said *One submarine, one cook!* and cheerfully fed the ship until his partner returned to duty.

We went to the Mare Island Naval Shipyard for overhaul while I was the Supply Officer. Soon after we arrived, the ship took its turn at running the mess for all the subs in overhaul. I still had shipboard duty and department tasks like, with one storekeeper seaman to help, trying to inventory and upgrade the spare parts list and inventory (a task that, if it were possible to do thoroughly, was beyond my abilities). Oversight of the shipyard-provided mess hall and cooking and supplies for about six submarines presented a few problems for me as well. I once opened a freezer and found Nutty Buddies (chocolate covered vanilla ice cream cones). Turning to my lead cook, I said that we couldn't afford those and hadn't ordered any. He said that those weren't Nutty Buddies but Surplus Dairy Products (e.g., milk) for which we paid little or nothing. So I had another peccadillo to handle unofficially. (Decreasing the quality/ variety of the food and airing out improper handling was a lose-lose situation.)

My biggest shipyard mess problem was with cash sales of meals to personnel on ComRats (Commuted Rations, a monetary payment to individuals living ashore and not obligated to eat in a ship's mess). When ComRats recipients did eat in our mess, they had to pay for the meal. One weekend, our cash box disappeared with over $600 in it. Investigation of the theft by the shipyard was unproductive. And several officers in the shipyard told me that Supply Officers who had funds go missing had to pay the amount out of their own pocket. I fruitlessly pored over the Supply Regulations—until I came up with the idea of surveying the money loss the same way a food loss (e.g., from spoilage) was surveyed and the cost accounted for, and attached the Shipyard's theft investigation report to the survey report. The Captain had never heard of surveying money and asked me for the basis. I said that I had found nothing specific but it was a loss and surveys covered losses. He concluded that the survey was worth a try and signed off on it. It was submitted with the next regular commissary report, which went through without incident. I have no doubt that the mathematics of the report were checked thoroughly, but I'm not sure that the details of the purchase records and surveys were as carefully examined. And I still wonder if the regulations were changed to explicitly cover this situation (and if a kind-hearted reviewer had deliberately overlooked the survey).

WestPac Tours

My Fleet Boat duty included two six-month deployments to the Western Pacific (WestPac).

A preparatory ritual was firing a Mk 14 torpedo at a cliff on a munitions testing island off the coast of California. Its explosion showed that our warshot torpedoes functioned. I was on the bridge with the Captain when one was fired, and thought that the water eruption on the side of the cliff wasn't very impressive. He said it was typical.

Note. The inadequate submarine torpedo testing before WWII does not appear to have been unique. More thorough pre-war testing of U.S. torpedo bomber torpedoes might have made those bombers more than sacrificial lambs that drew enemy fire and enabled more dive bombers to reach their targets during the first part of the war.

The about 5500 mile voyage to WestPac involved a long transit on the surface, typically with one daily dive to assure the ship was kept in diving trim. We only needed one officer on watch the rest of the time. That would have helped a lot with submarine qualification if the wardroom poker game hadn't interfered. But the Captain thoroughly enjoyed the game, and officers who didn't want to play were sent to take the watch for an officer who did.

Qualified submarine officers seemed to enjoy this lifestyle, including the few who didn't play poker. But I and the only other unqualified officer aboard had different approaches to the poker game. He preferred standing extra watches to playing poker. Feeling that standing at least 56 hours of watch a week was enough, I opted to play poker. The relatively low stakes (5¢ ante, table stakes, pot limit) kept the damage low, and I learned enough to come out slightly ahead (but not enough to become a good poker player).

On my first trip to WestPac, an experienced submariner gave us a heads up. He had been the Officer of the Deck on a night watch when a seabird flew into a Lookout leaning out from his station. The Lookout was knocked overboard and wasn't found. We became more alert to the hazards to our Lookouts.

The voyage to Japan from San Diego included a layover in Pearl Harbor, and subsequent ones in Chichi-jima and Okinawa. At Chichi-jima, we saw parts of the incredible tunnel warren in the rock. Had we not bypassed that island during the war, its 25,000 soldiers would have wreaked an awesome toll on us.

Note. I then had no idea that the mission our future 41st President, George H. W. Bush, was shot down on was a raid on Chichi-jima, or that the submarine that rescued him {the USS Finback (SS-230)} had picked him up close to the Chichi-jima shore. Nor was I aware that eight captured crew members of other U.S. planes had been beheaded by the Japanese on Chichi-jima. It was also a revelation to find out that we had convicted and hanged Lieutenant General Yoshio Tachibana and four of his subordinates for those beheadings and the cannibalism of the victims.

My first in-port time in Yokosuka, Japan, included the unofficial task of contracting for faux Zippo cigarette lighters bearing the ship's emblem and the purchaser's name. That involved contracting with a non-English speaking craftsman, establishing a price, collecting the money from the crew, and delivering the lighters. The craftsman was experienced at the process, and the lighters were soon obtained. Our sole unsatisfied customer felt that his nickname was inscribed wrong and wanted the lighter replaced. I felt that the lighter was inscribed as requested, and offered to take it and return his money instead. He kept the lighter.

The poker games continued during WestPac operations. Oddly enough, the Captain often was a loser. The big winner was a Lieutenant who enjoyed playing as much as the Captain did. Once, when he was asleep when the game started, another officer took two poker chips to his stateroom and rubbed them together. The sleeper immediately awoke, said *I'll be right there,* and promptly joined the game.

Another memory of that officer is his frustration when he came off watch while we were snorkeling in heavy seas. He exasperatedly said that *everyone felt safe because the Conning Officer was on the periscope and watching out for them, but the Conning Officer couldn't see a damn thing in this weather!*

That capable and personable submariner decided to leave the Navy. His reason was that diesel submarines were on the way out and he didn't see a future for himself in the service. But I learned something else from him before he left the ship. He was the Conning Officer during a night watch. I was his watch relief. He briefed me on the situation, including a distant helicopter. After a while, I realized that the helicopter had been there for longer than its fuel supply would permit. Careful re-examination revealed that what looked very much like a distant helicopter was a twinkling star. I was chagrined (and now think that my leg might have been pulled).

Before going to sea from Yokosuka, we put our civilian attire in the Naval Base's Submarine Sanctuary, a place where submarine officers could bathe, sleep, and eat. When we returned, the Sanctuary attendants had had those clothes cleaned and pressed.

On extended operations, our aging submarine's ability to distill enough fresh water to keep up with the leakage from the diesel engine cooling water jackets was sorely stressed. That made us unable to shower until the day before entering port. So it was common practice to put a new layer of clothing over the present one when one's smell got too bad. That wasn't frequent because prolonged submergence, battery charging, and diesel fuel impeded one's ability to smell. But it was still a pleasure to smell fresh air on the bridge shortly after surfacing. Laying below after that could be unpleasant until the smells dissipated into the fresh air circulating through the boat. A couple of days later, however, rotting of the now above water growth on the hull made the bridge smell bad.

After taking a shower and donning clean clothes the day before entering port after an extended stay at sea, I tied my smelliest clothes around a weight and heaved them over the side. Then, when we moored, I and the other officers not on duty went to the Submarine Sanctuary, showered and shampooed under abundant hot water, soaked in a neck-deep bath, showered again, and donned clean civvies. Next we went to the base barber shop, got a haircut, a very close shave, and a facial mudpack to clean out the pores.

At that point, some of us went to the Officer's Club. Others went into town for a hot bath and massage at the Grand Palace. That started with a steam cabinet session followed by a masseuse vigorously using a scrub brush to apply a full body cleansing (except for the genital area). Then, after a vigorous massage that included the masseuses walking up and down our backs, we went to celebrate at a local bar. The barmaid looked, leaned forward, sniffed the air, and said: Ah—Sensuikan Sailor. (Sensuikan is the Japanese word for submarine.) That's how strong the diesel submarine smell was.

A permitted, but not endorsed, evolution in WestPac was a ship's party. In Yokosuka, submariners held theirs at the Kanko Hotel. Its bar was on the first floor, and the sailors who could stay overnight rented rooms on the second floor, where there was also a big party room. For our party, I got the duty of being a pseudo shore patrol officer—with the task of keeping things from getting out of hand. The rooms the sailors rented had paper walls, and one of the things they were wont to do was see who could run through the most walls. (The cost was added to the bill.) But our sailors weren't doing that, and I observed what was going on in the upstairs party room.

The first trick played on me was by a war veteran. He called out: *Hey Look at Me, I'm Going to Commit Suicide!* Then he ran across the room and jumped out the Second Story Window. I hurried over, looked out, and saw him crouched on a ledge, grinning gleefully. He was pulled back in and he and another war veteran started talking about their war patrols. They had been on different submarines, in adjacent patrol areas, and one of them described being depth charged. The other replied that he knew that had happened because his submarine had watched it. That produced a roar of outrage because they hadn't fired a pickle (torpedo) at the depth charging destroyer. The disputants were calmed down by their shipmates, and then started singing old war ditties that involved repetitive use of the phrase *The Dirty Little Yellow Bastards*. But that too was put to a halt, and the Japanese in the room took no obvious offence. (Conquered peoples endure worse things than non-violent "Ugly American" behavior.)

In the evening, the party shifted to the big bar on the first floor. A non-crew member whom the crew had invited drank too much. He had several times been put into a room to sleep it off. But he kept returning to the same stool and sliding to the floor. He wasn't hurting himself and had stopped drinking, so no one bothered him as he repeatedly tried to climb up the side of the stool, failed, and slid back to the floor.

The entertainment soon started—a stripper. That was allowed because she was a Class A stripper and didn't remove everything. When this one came out on the dance floor, several crew members in the front row called out to me to come down and sit with them. Unwisely, I did. The stripper promptly came over and jiggled her oversize breasts against my head. When the raucous laughter subsided, she went back to center stage and showed that she was a Class B stripper. At that point, a crew member crawled out on the floor and bit her on a gyrating buttock. The stripping, and the party, soon ended. But the on duty crew hadn't been able to attend, and the party resumed the next day. Since the edge had been taken off, that part of the party went more sedately.

Submarine operations in WestPac kept us at sea a lot, but we did get to see something of Japan. In one case, we took a day tour of the area around Yokosuka. The bus driver's uniform was similar to what we were accustomed to, and the second person conducting the tour was a young Japanese girl immaculately dressed in a similarly colored skirt and jacket. We took her to be about 16 (but that have been due to a youthful appearance that many Japanese retain). When the bus parked for the walking parts of the tour, she proceeded to the parking spot and used a whistle to guide the bus driver in backing in. Her spiels were informative and her personality was captivating. The crew members on the tour were delighted, and asked her to sing for them. She protested, stating that the Japanese didn't have songs like Americans do. But they persisted and she obliged by making up a ditty and singing it. I remember it as:

Sho-Sho, Sho-Sho-Ji,
Sho-Sho-Ji is a raccoon.
He is always hungry,
That is why he thinks of Koi, Koi, Koi

That little girl did more to dispel any remaining World War II animosity against the Japanese on the part of our crew than all the pronouncements about how Japan and the U.S. had become allies. Her demeanor showed that the Japanese, whom we had been taught to hate during the war, and who had been ruthlessly inhuman to those they conquered, had a human side as considerate and caring as our own. The crew responded with considerate behavior and a noteworthy absence of vulgarity.

The WestPac ports we visited included Kaohsiung and Keelung in Taiwan, the island taken over by Chiang Kai-shek and his Nationalist Chinese government after China became a communist country. In Taiwan, we met a Chinese official named Chiang. (Chinese forenames are the family name, so he was a member of the same family as Chiang Kai-shek.) The night club we were in was extremely deferential to him, and when the evening was over, there was no bill for us. Then, along with the official who had made us his guests, we watched the totaling up of the club's take. The money wasn't counted but weighed on a scale like those used in a Chemistry Lab.

Another WestPac experience was visiting Hong Kong. The food there was exquisite, and the shopping amazing. We had good suits tailored and even bought tailor made shoes, all at a surprisingly low price. The sailors found a bar they liked and frequented it heavily. One of the younger unmarried sailors was notably religious and avoided the young Chinese ladies there. (They would have been called B-Girls in the U.S.) Reportedly, the Mama-San overseeing the place asked him if he would like female companionship and he wised off by saying *No, I Like Boys.* In about 15 minutes, she brought in a young boy to meet him. He promptly, and red facedly, returned to the ship—to be ribbed incessantly by his shipmates.

On my second WestPac tour, I was the ship's Navigator, Operations Officer, Communicator, Battle Stations Fire Control Coordinator, and Submarine Qualification Officer for the enlisted crew. We had eight officers aboard, the Captain, the XO, and six watchstanders. One of the six was the Supply Officer. I had the Operations and Navigation Departments, and the other four staffed the Engineering and Gunnery Departments. It was a terrific experience. The only hitch was a calibration that took so many hours on the periscope that I shortly afterwards had blurred vision and a headache so severe that I could only speak very slowly. But a good night's rest ended that.

When I first became the navigator and took star sights to fix the ship's position, I went to the bridge early to get in as many star sights as I could, and had a junior quartermaster write down the time, altitude, and star identification for each of my star sights. My QMC (Chief Quartermaster), a war veteran, usually came up at just about the middle of my stay to shoot his stars. He held his timepiece in one hand, his sextant in the other, and wrote down the information himself. By the time I went below to plot my navigation fix, the QMC's fix was already plotted. It almost always was one of position lines intersecting so tightly that there was no space in the middle at all (a "point" fix). My fix typically portrayed a multi-sided enclosure, with his fix usually inside mine. I trusted his positions.

On this trip, overcast skies necessitated using ship's course and speed, and ocean current estimates, to "dead reckon" our position. The evening before we were to dock in Pearl Harbor and meet with ComSubPac, I quickly shot six stars before the QMC came up to find no stars visible. All six of my star fix lines intersected in the same point, making the only "pinwheel" star fix I ever shot. It showed that we were substantially behind our dead reckoning position. We increased speed to full and the Captain let me know that, if we were late for our meeting with the Admiral, my name would be Mudd. So we didn't slow down until we were close to the Pearl Harbor Entrance Buoy.

For the rest of the trip to Yokosuka, I planned to get as far ahead as practicable. Unfortunately, our scheduled arrival time in Japan was such that it required too high an average speed. So, instead of laying out a course by rhumb line, I laboriously plotted out the shorter great circle route.

Note. Rhumb lines are straight on Navigation charts, which are Mercator projections—analogous to the projection of a point of light at the earth's center onto a circular roll of paper whose diameter is the same as and extends around the earth, touching it at the equator. The higher the latitude, the larger the spacing between minutes of arc of latitude, and the closer the spacing between minutes of arc of longitude. But a nautical mile (6076') is one minute of latitude at any latitude. And the shortest distance between two at sea positions is along the intersection of the ocean's surface with the plane defined by the two end points and the center of the Earth (the Great Circle Route).

My movement report wasn't accepted because, if it was, the Command Center would have to separately compute the great circle route. Having me establish a series of rhumb line positions along the route meant they could just plot those. (No one, aboard ship or in the Command Center, was going to validate my multitude of pages of laborious manual logarithmic calculations defining the positions along the great circle route.) So I revised the movement report to define specific positions along the route, it was accepted, and we made the voyage on schedule. The only problem was the Japanese Current (Kuroshio). It flows northward in the Western Pacific Ocean, and the projected set of the ship was so great that I mistrusted it. But the northward set was even greater than projected. So, upon sighting land, we had to turn southward sharply for about an hour to get back on track. Having been careful to assure that we were well ahead, we easily made the adjustment.

Getting to Yokosuka involved entering Tokyo Bay and turning to port past Kannon-Zaki Light. That was the point at which the crew considered themselves as having arrived in Japan. So I took a look at the lighthouse and the adjacent shoreline. Parked a short distance beyond Kannon-Zaki was a civilian laundry's truck with a canvas sign on the side facing us. That sign, in big letters, welcomed our boat by name. Since our deployment was classified and the ship's hull numbers had been painted out before we left San Diego, that meant that, in the Pacific as well as the Atlantic, the local businesses had knowledge of U.S. ships' classified movements.

Our Captain on this deployment was a remarkable man. On our first at sea experience with him, we were apprehensive about the tremor in his hands. (His coffee cup clinked when he held the saucer.) But, when he quietly and calmly ordered "Make Your Depth 250 feet, Use Negative" right after coming to periscope depth and we heard, through the hull, the loud whoosh, whoosh, whoosh of screws turning overhead as we executed this emergency maneuver, we knew the debility was purely physical. And he soon demonstrated exceptional poker playing ability. But his superior knowledge of submarining was his greatest skill. An example was intelligence messages. Those that he considered faulty were routed to us stamped by his own stamp, which printed "BULLSHIT" in big, bold, black letters. That not only delighted us, it got an appreciative laugh during our post-patrol debrief. Our Captain also was a delight because his mode of operation was to come to the conning tower before an evolution, discuss it, and then lay below and leave the conduct of the evolution to the people on watch.

This Captain also had great distaste for paperwork. He was fond of citing the short operation order for Commodore Dewey's destruction of the Spanish Fleet. My memory of the way he stated it is: *Proceed to the vicinity of Manila Bay, Philippines and protect American interests there. Exercise at gunnery en route.* But I found, online, the following different version of sailing orders issued to Commodore Dewey by Secretary of the Navy John Long on April 26, 1898: *War has commenced between the United States and Spain. Proceed at once to the Philippine Islands, and initiate operations against the Spanish Fleet. You must capture or destroy. Use utmost endeavors.* That's 14 words longer than what I remembered, but it carries the same message about paperwork.

During this WestPac tour, we circumnavigated Honshu, Japan's largest island. That involved a lot of piloting, and I was again on the periscope for prolonged periods. But I enjoyed the experience. At appropriate points en route, the Captain recounted significant aspects of submarine operations. One of these was the sinking of the Japanese aircraft carrier Shinano by the USS Archerfish (SS-311). A little over halfway on Shinano's trip from Yokosuka (9 days after commissioning) to complete fitting out in Kure, Archerfish fired a six torpedo salvo at Shinano. Four torpedoes hit and exploded. Shinano sank 9 hours, 15 minutes later, with 1435 deaths and 1080 survivors. At 68,000 tons displacement, she was the largest warship ever sunk by a submarine and the largest aircraft carrier built until well after the war. (We were told at submarine school that Archerfish sank Shinano right after she was launched.)

An officer who stood the same watch stations that I did was a heavy sleeper who often came up to assume his late night watches late. Befuddled and gurgling down the strong coffee left over from the previous evening, he typically also was slow to get ready to relieve the watch. One morning, he was especially difficult to wake for his 0400-0800 watch. We were snorkeling, and I was in the Conning Tower on the periscope when he struggled sleepily up the ladder from the Control Room. I watched him walk to the ladder to the bridge, start to climb up it, bang his head into the shut Conning Tower hatch, let go his coffee cup, tumble to the deck, get up, glare at me, and angrily ask why I hadn't told him we were submerged. I said something to the effect that I was tired of standing half his watch, and if he wasn't even able to tell when the submarine was submerged, he had no bleeping business taking over responsibility for the safety of the boat. Taken aback, he gathered his wits and retorted: *You can't get to me, you sonuvabitch, I've been had by experts!* Then he went below, cleaned himself up, and came back prepared to relieve the watch. His retort went through the ship like wildfire, and became a standard response to peer harassment. When we reached port, it spread rapidly throughout the other boats.

Being the Navigator put me on the periscope to fix the boat's position when we entered or left port. That gave me the chance to improve my periscope skills. By plotting periscope bearings and radar ranges to other ships, I was able to calculate their courses and check my angle on the bow estimates. The radar ranges also enabled me to check the number of horizontal periscope markings (divisions) between the waterline and the top of the highest mast, determine mast head height, and keep on checking a ship's range by calling off the number of divisions. So I got to the point of being able to estimate angle on the bow to the nearest five degree increment. Range (in divisions) I got down to the nearest half a division, then to the nearest fourth of a division, and then to a tenth of a division. And my speed at making an observation got down to three seconds. (The quickness resulted from the need to place prime emphasis on monitoring the ship's position and track.) Overall, I felt that my periscope obsession was meeting my goal of matching the vaunted periscope skills of those magnificent submarine warriors of World War II.

Japanese Ethnicity

When we were acting as a drill target for the Japanese Maritime Self Defense Force antisubmarine forces, our operational commander sent us a message asking whether the prescribed operations were being conducted. The Captain's reply noted the meticulous nature of the Japanese by stating in part: All events on schedule like Japanese train. So the operation continued and we were treated to port visits in Ominato and Hakodate on the island of Hokkaido. Traditional Japanese politeness and courtesy was evident in Ominato, whose people seemed economically deprived and physically worn more than Yokosuka's populace. Hakodate's harsher climate wasn't pleasant, but there was no apparent cultural difference there either. In Hakodate, we also learned a little about the Ainu people. Those were described as an aboriginal Caucasian tribe who revered the bear. Carved bear figurines abounded in stores, and many of us bought some as souvenirs.

Recent information indicates that the Ainu are an example of the universality of ethnic prejudice. For many years, the Mainland Japanese considered themselves a "pure" race. But DNA analysis labeled them as a mixture of the Yayoi people {closely related to South Koreans and to Chinese indigenous to the central part of China's east coast (Jiangsu Province) and of the Jomon (Japanese hunter-gatherers traceable back to 14000 BC)}. The Ainu were described as heavily bearded, beetle browed Caucasians who have been assimilated into and are now physically indistinguishable from the ethnic Japanese. Ainu DNA was described as indicating descent from the people of Siberia and Mongolia, with similarities to the Ryukans (Okinawans). Overall, the Japanese people were described as being a mixture of the Ainu, the Ryukans, and the Mainland Japanese. Identification of mixing with the Ainu caused a furor that was worsened by assertions that Ainu genes were behind some of the best features of the Mainland Japanese. The Japanese response seemed akin to what many Americans who considered themselves "white" would exhibit upon being told they had American Indian ancestry too and were therefore "breeds." (Embracing that kind of diversity is learned, not natural, behavior.)

Finishing Qualification

Being in the shipyard had kept me from getting in all my practical factors for submarine qualification. A new Captain came aboard during this period. He went over my qualification progress, outlined a plan for completing it, and gave that priority attention. A key step came when we were scheduled to move from a pier-side berth to drydock. The Captain told me to get the ship underway and make the move, and that I would be doing so on one screw while the shipyard was testing the other one. And he had me do so with no other officer on the bridge. Getting underway was easy, and traveling to the drydock was no problem because the screw I had control over and rudder effect enabled me to overcome the other screw's action. But when it came to lining up to enter the drydock, the uncontrolled screw's varying action and the slight current combined to foul up my approach. So I asked the Captain for control of both screws. He came to the bridge, gave me full ship control, and we easily entered the drydock. That pretty much finished off my qualification prerequisites, and my submarine qualification session underway on another submarine was soon scheduled.

That underway qualification was on the USS Rasher (SSR-269). She had sunk 99,901 tons of Japanese shipping, and was the second most successful U.S. submarine in that category. But what mattered to my qualification was the bridge modification made incident to her conversion to a radar picket submarine. The bowed out sail area on both sides of the bridge produced a significant lift when submerged. At periscope depth, that produced an increased tendency to broach (put the top of the sail out of the water). Doing that greatly increases the enemy's ability to identify the submarine's approach, visually and/or by radar, and evade or attack. So broaching is potentially lethal. Rasher's sail won our first confrontation, and I got the standard screamed reproach from the Conn: *YOU BROACHED ME!!!* But not broaching again got me through.

The next challenge was new to me. A bracket in the conning tower held a portable, air-operated foghorn (a backup for the ship's installed foghorn). The conning tower watchstanders dragged it over to the hatch to the control room and sounded it from about four feet over the diving officer's station. The deafening noise caught me unawares but I was having no depth control problems and the green board told me that there was no problem with hull openings. So I just stood there looking at my indicators. After the foghorn blast, the Captain called the Conn to ask how that had gone. He was told that I had passed that test.

My diving officer skills also were tested by ringing up dead slow speed while well below periscope depth. That less than two knots of headway substantially reduced the effect of the bow and stern planes and made neutral buoyancy even more important. An associated trick was to then raise a periscope, changing buoyancy by 100 pounds or less. On those boats, pump and piping size made pumping out or flooding in less than 200 pounds touchy, and judicious periscope raising and lowering could play havoc with depth control at dead slow speed. But I had been caught by this trick before, and was able to anticipate the buoyancy changes enough to maintain depth control.

Through having visited the Rasher in port on the days before getting underway (as my Captain suggested), I had practiced starting their diesel engines (different engines with a different startup process than the diesels I had learned to start up), lighting off the ship's radio transmitter, and numerous other evolutions. So, when I was sent to perform such tasks, the Rasher crew reported that I had already done that and, after a few confirmations, some such reports sufficed and I didn't have a lot of other operations to perform.

An evolution I couldn't practice in port was to "throw the sticks" (operate the levers that changed the power lineup between the various diesel and battery propulsion modes). That was tricky for the inexperienced, especially those tentative in their stick throws. Mistakes also had a potential for severe arcing—sometimes described as having rolling balls of fire in the Maneuvering Room, the compartment where propulsion line-up and speed were controlled. (Fleet Boats had two batteries, each with 126 cells, and each cell weighed about three quarters of a ton. The pure DC current from them could create substantial plasma arcs.)

Submarine electricians' reputed eccentricity didn't add to my comfort level. An example I had been told about was The Rat, a submarine electrician who saw a little Japanese boy staring wide-eyed at a horse harnessed to a peddler's wagon in Yokosuka. The Rat asked the boy if he liked the horse. The kid nodded. So the Rat bought the horse, gave the kid the reins, and watched him lead the animal away.

An experience on my first submarine duty also made me a bit leery of submarine electricians. I was the Duty Officer in Port when we had a fire in the Maneuvering Room. The smoke was so thick that an electrician and I donned OBAs (Oxygen Breathing Apparatus) and crawled into the room to find the source. We used battle lanterns, but they showed only about a foot ahead of us. The fire's source was some smoking rags in the lower level of the room—close to a prohibited electrical contact cleaning solvent canister marked highly inflammable.

I also knew a submarine electrician who talked in a very slow drawl. That had gotten him the nickname BULLLETTT, which was drawn out extensively when his shipmates wanted to point out that his speech was too slow. No performance problems were associated with that, but it added to my perception of submarine electricians as being different.

Despite my apprehensions, the Rasher's electricians were fair and supportive, the maneuvering evolutions I did came out fine, and my underway submarine qualification was successful.

Soon after earning my submarine dolphin insignia, I was ordered to Washington to be interviewed for assignment to the nuclear power program. Admiral Rickover's staff made a big point of my taking over a year to complete submarine qualification. I said that the ship's operations had delayed my qualification. Then, in my interview with the Admiral, he angrily berated me for about a minute before ordering me to get out and never come back. I left intending to pursue a naval career that didn't involve nuclear power.

The Pueblo's Impact

By and large, I saw support of advancement into nuclear power on the part of Fleet Boat submariners. But many of them undoubtedly had hard feelings about not being eligible.

Among the apparent victims of Admiral Rickover's selection process was Pete Bucher, the Executive Officer of the USS Ronquil (SS-396). Ronquil came into the shipyard for overhaul when the boat I was on was there. I first encountered Pete while I was on liberty in San Francisco. He and several other Ronquil officers were walking down the street. Every time they saw a pretty girl, they struck up a cheerful chorus of: *There she is, Miss America!* By the time I saw them, they had accumulated a lovely entourage.

I learned more about Pete at the BOQ (Bachelor Officer's Quarters) bar, where the standard drink was Olympia beer, and from which liberty forays initiated. Pete was always welcome on those because he introduced all the foraying bachelors to pretty girls. But he presented a different picture when I was working late one evening and stopped in at the BOQ bar for a nightcap. Pete had left the partying bachelors in town and was having a nightcap too. Our discussion portrayed him as being devoted to his wife, with the liberty forays being a well-enjoyed indulgence that camouflaged his basic family orientation. But that didn't alter his wild man reputation. One tale told was that he once asked the BOQ bartender for another beer, was told that it was past closing time, walked over to the clock, took off the face, set it back to before closing time, and got his beer. Another tale was about his borrowing an officer's Volkswagen and breaking its wheels/axles by running into a pile of construction rubble.

I don't know how much truth there was in those tales, but I did see another aspect of Pete when he and I went to a hockey game. During the action, a puck sailed into the stands near us. I scooped it up. Pete asked to see it, and I handed it over. Then Pete tapped the shoulder of a boy seated in front of us and, to the lad's delight, gave him the puck as a souvenir. Pete then said that the puck meant nothing to me but a great deal to that boy. I remember that as a minor epiphany—a rare moment when an unseen truth was suddenly thrust upon me. And I wished that I had initiated the giving.

Pete went on to duty on a submarine staff before becoming the Commanding Officer of the USS Pueblo (AGER-2), a former AKL (Auxiliary Cargo Light) vessel converted into an intelligence gathering ship. In 1968, the North Korean Navy captured Pueblo and imprisoned and tortured its crew. The movie portraying that had a scene in which the ship's corpsman was trying to treat Pete's injured foot. The line the actor (Hal Holbrook) portraying Pete spoke was: *The Hell with my foot, it's my ass that hurts!* I saw that as being entirely in character.

When the Navy promulgated information about the Pueblo incident, I was stationed aboard a nuclear submarine. The chronology of events showed the wisdom of departing the area a day earlier. But I didn't see anything about the ship's mission, which seemed to have been at least in part akin to the in-your-face harassment by Russian intelligence gathering trawlers that tried to get in the path of our fleet ballistic missile submarines as those boats were going on patrol.

Shortly after we got the Pueblo chronology, a Navy Captain came aboard to brief us on it. We had also heard things like a statement that our Pacific Fleet Commander had been unable to take action when the Pueblo was attacked because he was en route to Washington at the time. The briefing seemed to me to be the same sort of self-serving claptrap. Believing that our powerful aircraft carriers had the ability to prevent such a capture, I asked about the contingency plans for such an event. The answer was ambiguous. I opined that, if we hadn't had such a plan, we certainly should have had one, and that the Navy had put the Pueblo in harm's way and left her unsupported and vulnerable. The briefing officer packed up his materials and left. That he didn't give me a royal ass-chewing led me to believe that he felt the way I did about the Pueblo incident. In any case, that was the last Navy pronouncement I heard about the Pueblo.

Other information that has since been publicly reported is that the light armament the Pueblo possessed was basically unusable, the ship's material condition was abominable, the inadequate security provisions resulted in the capture of a lot of highly classified information, and the ship's communications capabilities were inadequate. One of the things I recall being reported about the Navy's inquiry was the statement by the Commanding Officer of the shipyard that had fitted out the Pueblo. He reputedly justified the adequacy of the shipyard work by stating that, upon the ship's departure, he had asked the ship's Commanding Officer whether the Pueblo was ready and had received an affirmative reply. That sounded to me like a deliberate evasion.

The Court of Inquiry recommended a court martial for Pete Bucher and for his Executive Officer. Secretary of the Navy Intervention scotched that. I later concluded that the Pueblo incident had been a direct result of the orders and actions of the highest levels of our civilian government.

I never saw Pete Bucher after leaving the shipyard, and he didn't answer the letter of support that I wrote him. But one of his former shipmates told me that Pete had become a quiet person unlike the gregarious, outgoing man I had known.

Enlisted Submariner Qualification

When I became the submarine qualification officer for the enlisted crew, I decided that they would not be delayed in qualification as I had been, and kept after them. The war veterans thought that was good, but some of the rest of the crew thought the unqualified submariners were being worked too hard. It was one of the sailors who wanted the standards for the new to submarines group to be softer who presented a significant performance error on my check of Rig for Dive.

Basically, an operating submarine is either Rigged for Dive or Rigged for Surface. Being Rigged for Dive means that everything is lined up for submerged operation. Rigging for Surface secures systems needed only during submerged operations, and is better suited to maintenance and repair work. Transiting to readiness for diving involves an extensive line-up of the ship's systems. A basic premise in submarine school was that any crew member can misposition a component and sink the boat. Rig for Dive was always checked by an officer, and the penalty described for improperly rigging for dive was submarine disqualification.

The Rig for Dive error I found was in the Forward Torpedo Room. The Petty Officer in charge of the compartment when I found the mispositioned valve admitted that he had based his reporting of being Rigged for Dive upon the valve positioning he thought was the case. So I had the compartment re-rigged, and then rechecked it with no discrepancies found. Then I reported the matter to the XO (Executive Officer), along with my belief that the petty officer involved had become complacent (was "riding the vents"). The result was a personal interview of the individual by the Captain, who concluded that this sailor's past record and revised attitude would result in no recurrence. Nor was there any. This was another lesson in the difference between dogma (in this case, disqualification) and reality (compassion for one's shipmates and case-specific review).

The Thresher's Impact

Overall, we had great confidence in our submarine and our shipmates. An example was a daily dive made during a surface transit. I awakened to find that the boat had enough of a down angle to have tossed me to the head of my bunk. Knowing that the Diving Officer had been standing Conning Officer watches for so long that he had become unused to being a Diving Officer, I put my hands on the bulkhead, thrust my feet back along the bunk, waited for the boat to level out, and went back to sleep. But our confidence decreased when we had been at sea for about 45 days and received a broadcast stating that the USS Thresher (SSN-593), then our most advanced submarine, had sunk with the loss of all hands. That sharp shock was a personal tragedy for our newest officer. Thresher had been his previous duty station. Her sinking involved the loss of essentially the whole crew that he had gone to sea with. Still, the only lasting effect on our submarine was a stronger barrier against complacency. And, though no one became a non-volunteer, a subsequent incident indicated increased concern.

That incident happened when I was in the rear of the Conning Tower plotting the ship's position. A Conning Officer came up to man the Conn for a trim dive. I paid no attention until I heard splashing and saw a vertical sheet of water up by the Conning Tower Hatch. I ran to the hatch, saw water pouring in around it, ordered *All Back Full* and *Shut the Lower Hatch* (the one to the Control Room), and sounded three Blasts on the Diving Alarm. That was an Emergency Surface. When the Conning Tower Hatch was out of the water, I saw that the Diving Officer had bounced it, spun its operating handwheel and inserted the securing dogs between the hatch bottom and its seating surface. I undogged and seated the hatch, and dogged it shut. Other than wetting equipment designed to withstand that, we were OK and made the dive.

The Captain later took me aside to make the point that, if I had undogged and shut the hatch without an Emergency Surface, the dive could have been continued without the scare that the crew had experienced. But, though the Captain's experience made that response feasible for him, he saw that mine didn't. After our discussion, as the Captain suggested, I discussed the event with the crew in each compartment. The crew then had no problem either. {But it was apparent that the Emergency Surfaces practiced on the east coast during Officer Submarine School underway training were (or had become) unusual to enlisted west coast submariners.}

The crew concern about the emergency surface didn't change my assessment of submarine sailors—I had seen them perform professionally too many times. And their temerity remained obvious. An example was a submerged operation during which the boat had not snorkeled or otherwise taken in fresh air for long enough that the oxygen was getting low. I was the Conning Officer. Movement was being minimized, and we were sitting on the deck. Smoking hadn't been prohibited, and the on watch quartermaster had unsuccessfully tried to light a cigarette several times. Then he exclaimed that he had figured it out, opened one of the cabinets in the Conning Tower, stuck his head inside, lit the cigarette, and puffed away until that pocket of fresher air was exhausted.

Wardroom Discussions

As was standard Navy practice, submarine wardroom discussions steered clear of two prohibited subjects—politics and women. But we did have a lot of discussion about how the Pacific submarine fleet was superior to the Atlantic submarine fleet. The perceived reason was the lessons learned from World War II Pacific Fleet submariners, with the credit attributed to greater individual incentive and daring. The Atlantic boats were described as being much more staid, and more closely controlled by higher commands—because of being closer to Washington, DC.

An oft touted example of the Pacific submariners' superiority was UNODIR (Unless Otherwise Directed). That was described as altering an operation by sending a message stating something like UNODIR we will not do_and will do_instead. The most touted use of UNODIR was making an unscheduled liberty port visit. I once analyzed an operation and concluded that such a visit could readily be incorporated. So I suggested that we UNODIR ourselves to a liberty port for a couple of days. The Captain quickly rejected the idea. Subsequent thought led me to conclude that UNODIR may have been used right after World War II, when the battle scarred Navy may have been given more individual license. Later, UNODIR could have turned into a subordinate being perceived as telling his superiors something like: you didn't plan this so well, so we're going to do it this way. But, even if UNODIR was ever real, I never heard of an actual case of it being employed while I was in the Navy.

Integrated Operations

Being on a submarine didn't completely eliminate the problems of Aircraft Carrier operations. On one occasion (it may have been

Navy Day), we were operating with a task force and assigned to make a "show" surface at a high up angle as a display for the surface forces and their guests. Such surfaces put a large portion of the submarine hull out of the water. The key to doing them successfully was to maintain a high speed, use maximum rise on the stern planes to get a big up angle, blow the ballast tanks, and put full dive on the stern planes as soon as the bow broke water—to level out and avoid sliding back and down to an unnecessary deep submergence.

After we surfaced in the middle of the formation, the task force began high speed maneuvers. We had put up the tactical radio circuits in the radio shack but couldn't pipe them to or answer them from the bridge. Moreover, our radiomen were, like all the ship's officers but me, far separated from carrier task force operations, maneuvering boards, ATP-1 (Allied Tactical Publication1), etc. When the formation started making black smoke and white water, I had radio notify the Task Force Commander of our much slower maximum speed. His response was to order us to "Clear the formation." I looked around, saw multiple ships going in different directions at high speed, cleared the bridge, sounded two blasts on the diving alarm, and got the Hell out of there by submerging. That avoided circumstances that I felt were unsafe. But the Captain expected the Task Force Commander to be very irate. When we were clear of nearby contacts and came to periscope depth to communicate, we heard that Admiral's wrath. But the Carrier Task Force got its show, and we got away safely.

We also participated in simulated oppositions of carrier transits. For one of these, I felt that the planner had given the carrier better odds by positioning us too far from her most likely route. I proposed stationing ourselves at the limit of our designated area (or slightly beyond) so as to better hear the carrier. The Captain rejected that and lectured me on the value of carriers and obeying both the intent and letter of orders. But we never heard that carrier and I saw this operation as an example of slanting a performance measure to better the performer's record.

Drill Target Duty

In operations off San Diego, we were often a drill target for ASW (anti-submarine warfare) exercises, mostly with S2F aircraft. Pilots being pilots, the associated Operation Orders seldom made it to us before we got underway for the evolution. But the communication frequency assignments were all we needed, and we made up the exercises as we went along. These were basic training exercises for the pilots, so we made ourselves an easier target most of the time, but practiced evasion tactics a bit when an exercise was nearing its end. The main thing I got from those exercises was that the ocean is so vast that, absent a decent first point of contact, it's extremely difficult to locate a submarine (or anything else that isn't a good visual or radar contact and maintains electronic silence).

One S2F that we were working with abruptly terminated the operation and headed home. When we reached port, we found out that it had suffered engine trouble and jettisoned everything it could in order to better assure getting back. One of the plane's passengers was a submariner who had been assigned as liaison officer to the ASW command involved. He was wide-eyed about the experience.

Experts

There was, at about this time, a relatively high incidence of "experts" reviewing submarine activities. That came to an end in the Pacific when Rear Admiral Roy S. Benson, the Pacific Submarine Force Commander, proclaimed that submariners are the experts in submarines and any other "expert" was *an S.O.B. from out of town with a briefcase*. We hadn't seen any of the now fired experts, but I did get to see a real and very special submarine expert at the submarine approach and attack trainer at Mare Island Naval Shipyard. That Navy Captain's short training course substantially improved my approach and attack skill—it's amazing what a real expert can impart in a short period.

Oral Communication Limits

My third Captain in submarines extended another drill by simulating a total loss of the MC systems, and then a loss of the sound powered telephones. That left us with only word of mouth relay. Then he dispatched a sailor to the After Torpedo Room to tell the watchstander there to report flooding. That meant shouting the flooding report to the Maneuvering Room, then to the After Engine Room, then to the Forward Engine Room, then to the After Battery, then to the Control Room, and then to the Conning Tower. That's six relays. And when the report got back to the Conning Tower, it was "Fire in the After Torpedo Room." Having shown that the more minds a message goes through, the less valid the recounting, the Captain secured the drill.

The Cuban Missile Crisis

Late in 1962, the Cuban Missile crisis, a 13-day U.S.-Russia confrontation, developed because of the placement of Russian missiles in Cuba. President Kennedy decided to blockade Cuba, and told the then CNO (Chief of Naval Operations), Admiral Anderson, that it was now up to the Navy to do the job. The Admiral's response, *Mr. President, the Navy won't let you down,* evoked strong pride in the Navy and an appreciation for the Admiral. When Russia publicly agreed to remove those missiles, and did so, and the U.S. secretly agreed to remove its intermediate range ballistic missiles stationed in Italy and Turkey, in range of Russian targets, war was avoided.

Admiral Anderson also impressed me with a warning message he sent about at-sea casualties, it stated in part: *The Sea merely lies in wait for the innocent; it stalks the careless and unwary.*

The Admiral, who was expected to become the next Chairman of the Joint Chiefs of Staff, clashed with Secretary of Defense Robert S. McNamara. Their issues included the Secretary's intrusion into aircraft choices. The Admiral, a naval aviator, considered a plane the Secretary wanted put on aircraft carriers unsuitable for that service. Congress agreed and the Secretary lost out. But he reportedly considered the CNO mutinous and scuttled his career. After two years as CNO, Admiral Anderson retired. The appreciative president later made him Ambassador to Portugal, and the Admiral was subsequently successful in business.

For his perceptive succinctness, his statement to President Kennedy, and his gutsy stand against a non-expert, my admiration for Admiral Anderson was and is unbounded. (That his first wife died young and he outlived both his sons before passing on at age 85 also attests to a difficult life.)

Secretary McNamara also raised some Navy pilots' hackles when he reputedly endorsed a fighter that was 50 knots slower than its Russian counterpart. He was described as opining that a 50 knot speed differential in a 1000 knot aircraft wasn't worth the cost of building a faster plane. A Naval Aviator I knew contended that the Secretary would have a different view if he had to fly a fighter with the 50 knot faster aircraft on his own tail.

Swim Call

The Pacific Ocean was, at times, remarkably beautiful. The hue of the clouds near sunrise and sunset was especially appealing, despite their tendency to obscure the horizon and make star sights more difficult. And, occasionally, there were especially calm days. During one of those, the Captain acceded to the crew's request and we stopped for a Swim Call in mid-Pacific waters. A group of us were enjoying the ocean on the starboard side of the boat. We were recalled and quickly clambered back aboard as rifle shots began sounding from the bridge. Once aboard, we saw an about 6' long hammerhead shark on our port beam and swimming slowly toward us. Initially, the shooters were using M1 carbines, which fired slower, blunter, less penetrating rounds than the M1 rifles that should have been used. But when M1s replaced the carbines, they seemed to make no impact on the shark's course or speed either. When we got underway, it was still slowly approaching us.

The shark didn't get close enough to present an actual threat, but a reason Swim Call was permitted was the fact that we didn't expect to encounter dangerous fish in mid-ocean. And, while I never had another swim call opportunity in the Navy, the crew didn't alter its practice of indoctrinating newly qualified shipmates by heaving them overboard. Once, while we were moored in a Pacific port, that was done and, within about five minutes of the newly qualified sailors' return aboard, two large sea snakes swam through the spot where they had hit the water. That didn't seem to faze the still wet new submariners.

Rewards

After my second WestPac tour, the crew was savoring the prospect of an operation that included a visit to Eureka, California—which scuttlebutt claimed to be the world's most hospitable liberty port for submariners. That was the reputed reward for our performance in WestPac. I was transferred before the trip and didn't like that timing but left with a letter of commendation from the Captain. It stated that he had been commended by the Pacific Submarine Force Commander for completing a mission of great importance to our nation, and that the accomplishments that had earned that commendation were in large measure due to my performance.

Squadron Evaluation

My second Navigation Leading Petty Officer was a Quartermaster First Class (QM1), not a Chief, but he assured me that our charts and the department records were immaculate. When we were scheduled to be inspected, my pre-check found no discrepancies, and the QM1 assured me that the inspection party wouldn't find any either. He was right.

The inspection critique was presented by a field grade officer who assigned Navigation an excellent grade of 92 (out of 100). I asked what had been found wrong. The reply was that an outstanding grade had to be so good that it would be promulgated to the entire submarine force as an example. So we had been examined, got everything right, had nothing to change, and didn't get a perfect grade. I also believed that, by this time, Fleet Boat navigation procedures and practices had evolved to the point that doing something so unusual and beneficial that it merited promulgation to the entire submarine force was a ridiculous criterion. That made me sure that the rationale was utter B.S.

Also, as part of our ORI (Operational Readiness Inspection), we made approach and attack runs on a destroyer. After all the exercise-configured torpedoes in the forward torpedo room had been fired, we had one run left. The exercise Observer directed that an officer other than the Captain or Executive Officer make the last approach and attack. The Captain picked me. This run was complicated by the need to turn the submarine away from the target in order to bring the stern torpedo tubes to bear (so the torpedo wouldn't have to make a drastic turn). When we reached firing position, I turned to bring the stern tubes to bear and raised the Attack Periscope for a final check. But the target had zigged away. I made the observation, lowered the scope, waited until the new angle on the bow was set, saw that the torpedo run was an undesirable 3000 yards, raised the scope for a final bearing again, and fired. The torpedo intersected the target's track at an ideal angle.

While the torpedo was running, the Observer opined that I had lost control of the approach. But, when we surfaced, the destroyer reported: *Your unit passed under me. My evasive action was ineffective.* We then adjourned to the wardroom, where the target's actual track was superimposed over, and fit very well with, the track determined by my periscope observations. The Observer then described the evolution as a fine example of understanding the situation and reacting to it.

During a check of my service record before one of the periodic inspections, I found that I had been charged with a week of leave. But I had taken none. So I went to the Executive Officer (XO) to get the error corrected. He said that the leave entry was made because someone had to be charged with leave to avoid the ship being downgraded. I was flabbergasted. The XO thought I was making a mountain out of a molehill because I wasn't going to be taking leave and would soon be back at the maximum leave permissible. That was correct. (All accrued leave over the 60 day maximum value was forfeited.) But I made a mental note not to put myself in that position. (Sooner or later, an inspector would collate leave records with the ship's logs and discover that officers had been assigned leave when they were standing duty and signing the logs. That would have had far greater repercussions than a finding that officers weren't getting any leave—which the Division and Squadron Commanders undoubtedly knew already.)

The culmination of the inspections was the Captain coming back from a squadron meeting and telling us that the Battle Efficiency E had been awarded to the USS Salmon (SS-573). He also said that we had the highest overall grade but the award had been based on the Squadron Commander's personal evaluation of Salmon. (I had no awareness of his having evaluated our boat, or even coming aboard.)

At the time, the submarines in San Diego were all World War II Fleet Boats except for Salmon, a post-war diesel-electric design that displaced about 500 more tons on the surface. She also was about 40 feet longer and had 10 more crew. An obvious difference from the modernized Fleet Boats was that her rudder extended above the hull as well as below it. I knew nothing of her crew, and never met her Captain, but he had quite a reputation. An athlete who had played football at another college, he then went to the Naval Academy and was an outstanding player there too. He became an All-American and was elected to the college football Hall of Fame.

While I was an Academy midshipman, this officer had served a short tour there to assist with coaching football. He told one of the team members, a lineman who earned honorable mention in the All-American voting, that, when being charged by an opponent, he should get his forearm under the incoming body and flip the opponent up and over onto his back. The lineman expressed disbelief and the coach flipped him just that way. Since that coach was not in football playing condition, that was a remarkable demonstration.

A submariner who had served with the Salmon Captain when they were both junior submarine officers described being in the wardroom when their ship's Captain asked a question about the boat. The former footballer pulled out his little green memo book, selected a page, and read off the answer. The tale teller said that he had been sitting next to the footballer, looked at the book, and saw that the page was blank. (So the answer was tactfully provided without showing superior memory.)

The Salmon CO's distinguished career was based on far more than being a football player. (He became a Rear Admiral.) But respect for him didn't change the other boats' ire about perceived special treatment for the Salmon. And, reportedly, a sunrise revealed that the part of Salmon's rudder extending above the waterline was a very visible salmon pink. (If that happened, it was no doubt promptly repainted.)

My Seagoing Cap's Demise.

I had a battered (by years of sea duty) officer's cap that I was fond of. One day, our highly respected Chief of the Boat (COB) came to the bridge as we were leaving port, remarked that we were going to be diving soon, and offered to take the cap below so it couldn't get in the way. I let him have it. After diving, I asked the COB where my cap was. He expressed surprise that it was missing, but it was obvious that it wasn't going to show up again. The other officers were amused, but those who had similar caps kept them out of the COB's reach.

Departure from Fleet Boats

My duty on Fleet Boats ended when I was transferred to the Navy's Postgraduate school in Monterey, California for two years of study leading, if I got good enough grades, to a Master's Degree in Operations Analysis (computerized analysis/research).

II-4 Nuclear Power Training

Re-Interviewing

I soon found postgraduate (PG) school demanding, but wanted very much to meet its challenge. After a few weeks, however, I received orders to go to be interviewed for nuclear power training again. My protest put me in the PG school Commanding Officer's office. That Admiral listened to my story about Admiral Rickover angrily telling me to get out and never come back. Then, in a severe tone, he said: *Mr. McCabe, do you know how to obey orders?* After my *Yes, Sir,* he replied: *Go back to Washington and be interviewed by Admiral Rickover!* My requisite Aye, *Aye, Sir* ended the matter.

In the re-interviews, my position was that PG school was a lot harder than I expected, but I was learning a lot, wanted to stay, had been rejected by Admiral Rickover before, and didn't want nuclear power training. I also opined that, though nuclear power requirements were high, they couldn't man a sizable submarine force if they only took officers better than me.

The interview process ended, again, in the Admiral's office. He asked me what would happen if I were ordered into the nuclear power program. My response was that it would probably drive me out of the Navy. I don't recall his subsequent diatribe, but it ended, like my first interview had, with an angry *Get Out!* Concluding that he had sent me packing again, I quickly left the Admiral's office. His secretary promptly said: *Congratulations, Mr. McCabe, you've been accepted for the nuclear power program.*

The Students

My nuclear power school class contained sea experienced officers (including the first non-volunteers) and volunteers who were recent college graduates. One student had a Master's degree in nuclear engineering from Stanford. The student I sat next to had graduated first in his class at the Naval Academy. Of the 60 students, virtually all had graduated in the upper quarter of their college classes, and had engineering or science degrees.

The Pace

The school's schedule was daunting. We took four college or postgraduate level courses at a time, with each set of four courses lasting two weeks. The difficulty of the program was quickly shown in an electrical engineering exam. Out of a possible score of 100, my grade was 40. That was about average for the sea experienced officers.

Few of us could finish the study assignments, but most of us hit the sack each night around 1 a.m. in order to be alert in class the next day. After the first marking period, I found myself in about the middle of the class. But long study hours and the reawakening and improvement of my study habits raised my final standing to 19 of the 57 class graduates. As I recall, the top graduate in his Naval Academy class stood about fifth (I suspect that his non-engineering college course grades were even higher than his engineering grades). The Stanford Nuclear Engineer stood, I think, about seventh.

The Goal

Our training focused a lot on the WHYs behind power plant characteristics. Some of the things we were exposed to, like the ratio of incident radiation to reflected radiation (albedo) became vague memories without operational significance to me. Others became considerations vital to assuring safety of nuclear power plant operation and maintenance. (One of those, radiation safety, is covered is another part of this book.) Overall, the purpose of the training was expressed as providing the understanding needed to take appropriate action if a circumstance that wasn't covered by the procedures developed. That reflected the Navy's assessment of personnel knowledge and capability as the first line of defense against a nuclear power plant mishap, and incorporation of the same philosophic basis as the General Prudential Rule of the Nautical Road. My later experience affirmed the validity of that.

The Prototype

Prototype training followed the classroom phase. My assignment was to the prototype nuclear plant for the USS Nautilus (SSN-571) in Idaho. After a celebratory last evening in California, I headed out about noon the next day. The road was good, the traffic was light, and Nevada had no speed limit. So I made about 350 miles before having a pleasant supper and evening in Winnemucca, Nevada.

The rest of the trip started out as an easy jaunt. Not long after crossing into Idaho, I saw an entrance road angling off toward what looked like a rustic country store. The sign next to that road stated, in big letters, "Free Wocks." Several hundred yards further on, the return road to the highway had a similarly sized sign. It stated: "For Throwing at Wabbits." The smile that brought didn't last very long. Springtime's gigantic potholes (labeled Tank Traps by another trainee) slowed travel considerably.

The arrival at my apartment brought another surprise. My roommate, another trainee, had had an accident along the route he took. He said that he had been stopped at a red light when a woman driver rammed into his trunk, and his car ended up upside down in a field. The bottles of red wine in his trunk had shattered and soaked his clothing, but he was unhurt and managed to get to our new duty station on time.

At the reactor test site, we went on shift work involving study and watch station performance. Studying during the midnight to 8 am shift was extremely difficult. Walking around to shake off the lethargy helped but little. Self-condemnation of sleeping on duty didn't help, nor did bringing to mind the penalty for a Lookout being asleep on watch. Late nighttime studying remained a continual battle to stay awake.

There were Quonset Huts on site that served as bunk rooms for those who stayed overnight when not on watch. Such stays often were necessary. But the huts were so infused with hot, dry heat that most of us made the 40-60 mile bus ride to and from the site whenever practicable. But some stayed onsite for many days at a time. One of those once asked another trainee to stop by his house and bring him the toothbrush he had forgotten. Even after his irate wife adamantly refused, he continued to stay onsite. (His dedication was commendable, his wisdom questionable.)

There was one big benefit to shift work—time off between shifts. One of the trainees, an avid trout fisherman, and I went fishing on our days off. Being experienced at fishing from creek and river banks, he typically managed to bring home a cutthroat trout or two. I used the same kind of rig and caught nothing. Then I bought a 17' outboard-powered boat and my fishing companion, another trainee, and I went to Henry's Lake to fish. The proficient trout fisherman soon caught the first cutthroat trout, and the other trainee then caught our largest fish of the day. They both then compared their fishing skill to mine, ungraciously and at length. But, after easing out my line until it ticked along the bottom, I reeled in a fish, and another, and another. Neither of my companions caught another fish, and the fishing ended when I had caught the rest of our three limits (seven pounds and one fish apiece). Then I revealed my tactic and said that nicer companions would have benefitted from that information much earlier.

My fishing boat also was remarked upon during the bus ride to the site one day. The bus driver commented about having seen a little white boat scooting down the road with no towing vehicle in view. He had sped up to get a better look and saw a little white car pulling the little white boat at 70 MPH. I told him that he had seen my Corvette Sting Ray pulling my boat, and that the boat traveled quite nicely at high speed because the trailer had such large wheels. (In Idaho, the considerable distances between towns made high speed driving commonplace.) But the look on the bus driver's face indicated that he had doubts about my good sense. (His employer reputedly ensured cautious driving by firing any driver who had an accident, regardless of who was at fault.)

The boat brought another memory when the Fourth of July came and I was between shifts. Several of us stayed in a cabin in Yellowstone Park, and awoke on the Fourth of July to find the boat chock full of snow. The waterborne part of the stay was aborted, but the snow melted and the water drained out on the return trip.

Another group of trainees took advantage of a shift break by camping in a remote part of a national park. One of them opened the car's trunk to get a sandwich. A bear came up beside him, stood up, reached into the trunk, and grabbed a sandwich. The offended trainee said something like: Hey, that's our food! He grabbed the sandwich from the bear, put it back, shut the trunk, and somehow came away unscathed.

In Idaho I married a divorcee with a young daughter, and found having a family a great improvement over bachelorhood. Having my wife's support was especially beneficial when a hemorrhoid attack incapacitated me.

My hemorrhoids were lanced in a doctor's office. That didn't solve the problem but did convince me that dying is preferable to torture. The Navy then planned to send me to a Naval Hospital in California for surgery. But my inability to sit resulted in surgery in Idaho. That hospital stay lasted a week (until I stopped taking the painkilling pills). And my qualification was delayed.

When I resumed work, I was soon "caught" by a trick played on one trainee in every class. (After that, the word spread and no one else was caught by it.) My incapacity had made me miss that, so I was subjected to the ruse when I returned. It started with having a non-operator (e.g., a civilian janitor) take an announcing system microphone and shout into it: Trip the plant, Trip the plant! (I've changed the wording for simplicity.) The purpose was to get the trainee officer to do a sudden shutdown. And I did just that. When taken to task, I regurgitated the dogma that this was a shore-based plant where any indication of a safety problem should be very conservatively handled. The instructor said something like: *Just so you had a good reason.*

This was a thought provoking event. The training staff was justifiably accustomed to being founts of wisdom. But the resulting complacency produced a specious drill. If the initiating announcement had first occurred with a well experienced operator controlling the plant, that operator probably would have had enough experience with the plant and its instrumentation to ask WHY before taking the power plant offline. But any operator (or trainee) who took the safer route and shut the plant down would have to be found by competent review to have acted properly. Still, the drill made the training staff's point about the importance of maintaining operating status, while my response affirmed the primacy of safety. And the rest of my delayed by illness qualification was more straightforward.

II-5 Fleet Ballistic Missile Submarines

Background

Late in 1960, the USS George Washington (SSBN-598) began the first Fleet Ballistic Missile (FBM) submarine patrol. The slogan *41 For Freedom* was coined to describe the building program for the first 41 FBMs (Boomers). These boats became the primary deterrent force against a nuclear attack on the United States. They were assigned two crews (Blue and Gold) that made alternating patrols to maximize the ships' time at sea.

The Kennedy Era

John Fitzgerald Kennedy became President of the United States in November 1961, early in the days of the Polaris submarine. He won the election by only 0.1% of the vote. But his performance in the Cuban Missile Crisis endeared him to the country and especially the military. So did his patriotic eloquence (e.g., *Ask not what your country can do for you, Ask what you can do for your country!*). We hoped that he would begin a new government era and correct a lot of mistakes. But Washington's entrenched political hierarchy kept his legislative program from being implemented. When he was assassinated in November 1961, the country, and its military, was deeply shocked, and supportive of what he had tried to do. That enabled his successor, the tough and powerful political insider Lyndon Baines Johnson, to strong-arm JFK's legislative program through Congress.

My Initial Exposure

I reported to duty during an off-crew period. That gave me time to learn some things about the ship before deploying. As the designated DCA (Damage Control Assistant), I was responsible for auxiliary machinery. My first concern was the electrolytic oxygen generators that replaced the oxygen the crew's breathing took out of the air during submergence. The high school chemistry experiment of electrolytic reduction of water to hydrogen and oxygen, the Hindenburg disaster, submarine school, and the Fleet Boat hydrogen explosion had all made me aware of hydrogen's danger. I also knew that an increased oxygen concentration causes fires to burn hotter and stronger, to the point of being virtually inextinguishable. (A U.S. submarine in port had an oxygen-fed fire that wasn't extinguished until she submerged alongside the pier to flood the affected compartment.) So, reading about a prior lethal explosion of a submarine oxygen generator was not surprising. Fortunately, my division knew their oxygen generators well, and proved to be up to the task of keeping these temperamental machines operating. (Today's oxygen generators are no doubt a major improvement.)

Taking over the ship was an initiation into a gigantic workload. Seven day work weeks and well over 12 hour work days were routine. The upkeep intensity kept the ship's officers aboard except for a dinner ashore at about the midpoint—a welcome chance to talk about something besides work.

Also, these ships had first national priority and, if a needed part wasn't readily available, it was taken from other programs and air shipped to the Polaris boat that needed it.

Going on Patrol

Going on patrol was a huge relief for everyone but the Navigator. He constantly monitored the SINS (Ship's Inertial Navigation System) to confirm that it was tracking properly. When he finally concluded that everything was working well, he hit the sack for an extended snooze. A Navigation Electronics Technician took a poke at that by writing a note for the next watch to go to the Navigator's bunk and shake his wrist so that his self-winding watch wouldn't run down. The note-writer wasn't named, but I suspected the ET who, when first briefing me on the navigation system, stated: *This is the SINS. You tell it where it is, and it'll tell you where you are.*

The DCA was the Battle Station and Ship's Diving Officer. So Diving Officer qualification was a high priority. The size of these boats and their Albacore (rounded and streamlined) hulls required surprisingly more trim adjustment near the surface than a Fleet Boat did, but prior experience helped me to finish diving officer qualification early.

It wasn't long afterwards that we had an unannounced weapons system test. As we were preparing to simulate missile launch, we received the report "Flooding in AMR-1" (Auxiliary Machinery Room One). Before anyone else had a chance, I ordered the shutting of a large valve that was open between the sea and a tank used to adjust buoyancy. The flooding stopped and we simulated an alternate launch procedure. Within a few hours, the faulty valve was repaired.

Our only definition of flooding was a submarine school instructor's reply to a question about the difference between a leak and flooding: *If you find it, it's a leak; if it finds you, it's flooding.* But, notwithstanding its imprecise definition, flooding had to be promptly reacted to—to avoid sinking the boat.

After this event, nothing was said to or by me about it. But it was contrary to a practice that I wasn't properly aware of at the time. My experience in the Pacific Submarine Fleet was in attack submarines in which WWII operational considerations persisted. I was now in the Atlantic Fleet and no longer in the small ship Navy. These Boomers (FBMs), though only 3-4 times the tonnage of the Fleet Boats, were Capital Ships. And the atmosphere on this one was unlike that of the Pacific Fleet Boats. Boomers not only weren't aggressive unless and until a valid launch order was received, they had to take highly selected but new to the Navy officers with no prior at sea experience and turn them into accomplished submariners. They did that remarkably well, but there was a corresponding strong emphasis on compensating for their inexperience. Checks and rechecks of activities necessarily became even more important than in Fleet Boats, and checking with one's supervisor(s) before taking an action was practiced more intensively.

One of the items that had surprised me on this Boomer was coming up to periscope depth. On the Fleet Boats, we had internalized that process. But I now had an about 20 page instruction on how to accomplish that evolution—a reflection of the difference in operating philosophy.

My qualification as Conning Officer (Officer of the Deck Submerged) soon came up. The drill held for my practical test simulated a condition requiring the Captain to be contacted. I was expected to call him in his stateroom, then in the wardroom, etc., while he went from place to place to avoid contact—testing my tenacity at informing him. The drill started when sonar made the report: *Torpedoes in the water bearing xxx.* I ordered the boat turned toward the attack source as I grabbed the General Announcing System microphone to order *Man Battle Stations Torpedo.*

The XO promptly came to his Battle Station in the Conn. The Captain didn't. I asked the XO if he would be taking the Conn. He said no. So I made an approach on the reported source. When the Captain finally came up to the Conn, he asked what was going on. I briefed him. He asked why he hadn't been informed. I said (correctly, but not tactfully) that I had done that by manning Battle Stations Torpedo. The Captain and the XO left the conn to discuss the matter, and the XO returned to discuss the drill with me. I showed him the procedure paragraph that stated that option in a dire emergency. The XO left again, and returned to tell me that I was qualified.

I, and other officers ordered into nuclear power training as non-volunteers, were chosen because of the need for more at-sea experience. But I didn't recognize the basis of the difference from my previous experience, or see that I should have responded to the Captain's query by quoting the part of the procedure that I was following. (Had I had the interpersonal skill that the Salmon CO showed in his earlier career by reading the reply to his Captain's question from a blank page in his memo book, I'd have been a better officer.)

Boomer Captains were either experienced Commanders or full Captains in rank, and carried a major responsibility. For example, one of the things we had been told was that each Polaris Missile Submarine carried more firepower than all of mankind had exploded in all of history, including all of World War II. Moreover, when I was finishing off my active duty on the Atlantic Submarine Force Commander's staff, I learned that my first Boomer Captain had distinguished himself to the point of being highly regarded by the Force Commander and his senior staff—individuals whom I held high regard for.

Patrol continued. As the exhilaration of completing the upkeep and resuming a role in the nation's first line of defense settled down, the monotony of operating quietly in order to maximize the likelihood of remaining undetected became boring. A notable morale uptick began when the patrol's midpoint was reached. That was marked by decorating the Crew's Mess and having a Casino Night.

I was put in charge of Casino Night on my first Polaris Patrol, and thought that the dice table odds favored the House (the crew's Welfare and Recreation Fund) too heavily. The Chief of the Boat said that was necessary to account for the crew beating the odds (cheating). But I shaved the odds anyway. We started losing money, restored the old odds, and the Welfare and Recreation Fund came out a few dollars ahead.

On this patrol, the Captain also broke out a case of "champagne" for the wardroom on Casino Night. A few officers acted a bit tipsy until they learned that they were drinking non-alcoholic sparkling grape juice. They then avowed that they hadn't been affected at all.

During this patrol, I was the Conning Officer when a message notifying me of the birth of my son was delivered. It ended with: Mother and son doing fine.

There was a weekly wardroom poker game on this Boomer. One of the more senior officers liked to play Seven Card Stud, High Spade in the Hole Takes Half the Pot. He won that game a lot. But I once had good cards, saw things out, and caught the Ace of Spades on the last card. I sandbagged (bet nothing). He bet big. My raise doubled the pot. I won the whole pot because my spade Ace high full house beat his spade King high one. He asked if I had caught the Ace on the last card, and my yes answer upset him. The money was no big deal—at patrol's end the winnings and losses were prorated so that the big loser lost $50 or less. But I would have been wiser to not press my advantage that hard.

As the patrol neared its end, I was encouraged to complete Engineering Officer of the Watch (EOOW) qualification before we returned to port. But my previous qualifications had involved feeling an intimate knowledge of the jobs involved, and I didn't yet feel that with the engineering plant. Slow and quiet patrol steaming wasn't helping any. So I held back.

When my fitness report came through, I wasn't graded as high as a successful officer would expect. (A classic potshot about fitness reports was that they ranked 90% of the officers in the top 10% of the Navy.) This report's text contained words to the effect that: Mr. McCabe is a highly intelligent officer. To his credit, he completed his Diving Officer, Ship's Diving Officer, Officer of The Deck, and Duty Officer in Port qualifications during his first patrol. But he did not complete his Engineering Officer of the Watch (EOOW) qualification.

Being able to access and concentrate more intensively on the engineering plant before the next patrol enabled me to qualify as EOOW during our next upkeep. Then, when another newly qualified EOOW was lighting off the propulsion plant, we were obviously not going to be ready to get underway on time. He was having each step performed sequentially, and that was taking far too long. So the Engineer had me take the EOOW watch. My more integrated understanding of the plant enabled me to order non-competing steps to be done simultaneously, and we got underway within a few minutes of the scheduled time. The EOOW I relieved had done everything safely, but wasn't confident of his ability to oversee multiple operations. I was far from being a Super Nuke (nuclear plant qualified and also having innate exceptional machinery aptitude), but I now had all the steps and their inter-relationships down pat.

My first XO (Executive Officer) on a Polaris submarine was exceptionally capable. His good sense of humor once surfaced when he routed a batch of the incessant stream of directives and correspondence that we all had to wade through. It included a multi-page document with the typical routing slip attached and the document carefully stapled shut all around. Each officer who had seen it before me had initialed the routing slip, with no indication of any attempt to remove the staples. I passed it on the same way.

This XO was replaced by another exceptionally capable individual. He once came to the off-crew office covered with poison ivy blisters. The cause was his having removed the poison ivy vines from his property because his children were as allergic to them as he was. (Association with especially dedicated people is an advantage of submarine duty.)

Drills on my first Polaris submarine began differently from what I had come to expect. Before each power plant drill, the Captain would walk through, and the Engineer would be standing just outside the EOOW's station. After the Engineer told the Captain that everything was ready, the Captain would head forward. So we knew a drill was coming, and were as ready as we could get.

That changed when the next Captain (a Super Nuke) arrived. The first drill he pulled on me came while we were submerged and I was writing up my EOOW log in preparation for being relieved. Without warning, the plant tripped and we had to recover it. That went smoothly because, although the initiation was startling, the recovery steps didn't change. More such drills raised the crew's confidence and alertness.

NESEP

The Navy Enlisted Scientific Education Program (NESEP) took some capable enlisted sailors, sent them to college, and commissioned them as officers when they graduated. Aboard my first Polaris submarine, the selection of the ship's NESEP nominee was a hot topic. When I was the Main Propulsion Assistant, I had a very capable first class petty officer in my Division. He was married, stable, reliable, smart, and a hard worker. I proffered him as a NESEP candidate. His competition was a young, smart, single sailor who wasn't in the Engineering Department.

The non-engineer was selected by the ship. I asked why and was informally told that it was time that somebody who wasn't nuclear trained had a chance. That's a theme compatible with not choosing the best qualified individual. (Another example would be: *It's time we had an Eskimo become the Governor of Alaska*, with that sentiment ignoring who is the best qualified candidate.)

Many years later, when I went to the Submarine Base for my annual active duty as a Reserve Officer, I saw my former NESEP candidate at dinner in the Officer's Mess. He had been promoted to Warrant Officer. I asked about the sailor who had been sent to

NESEP. He said that he had written his former shipmates often about how great the college parties were, but had flunked out and been returned to sea duty to finish out his enlistment. I considered that a typical outcome when one chooses less than the best qualified candidate for a job—in this case selection of a capable individual who didn't have the maturity to take advantage of the opportunity given to him.

The Vent Condenser

One of the first things that happened to me when I became the Main Propulsion Assistant was an out of the blue delivery of an unordered infrared temperature sensing "gun." I thought it might enable me to confirm my hypothesis about our vent condenser problem.

Like other pressurized water power plants, ours had two parts, the nuclear power generation part that generated heat, and the secondary system that boiled water for steam turbine operation. Apart from the steam generators, the secondary system was a lot like ordinary steam power sources. Water had to be added to replace losses, and that water was de-aerated in a tank that was heated by a steam coil. A minute amount of steam issued from the tank and went up a pipe. A section of that pipe went through a vent condenser, which consisted of a small jacket containing a light flow of cooling water that served to condense the steam in the vent pipe, resulting in the condensed steam dropping back into the tank. This rudimentary condenser was shaped much like a quart oil can with a hole in the center of each flat end and the vent pipe running through the holes.

The seams between the vent pipe and condenser were welded connections. Those welds repeatedly cracked, and the condenser leaked and was secured. After each re-welding, the weaker weld seam cracked again. Usually, air cooling of the vent pipe condensed the minute amount of steam. So the condenser leakage was just a minor nuisance. But I thought I might be able to define the cause with the infrared gun.

In a submerged submarine, minute compressed air leaks increase the internal pressure over time. That, and atmospheric pressure changes, can be significant when the boat surfaces. These effects are compensated for by equalizing interior and exterior pressures before opening the hatch to the bridge upon surfacing. That's necessary because the hatch has 600 or more square inches of area, and a boat with its internal pressure a half an inch of pressure per square inch higher than atmospheric has a total upward thrust on the hatch in the 300 pounds force range. (Hatches between compartments, being bigger, can produce injury-causing forces at smaller pressure differentials. When compartments are isolated for any reason, equalizing pressure is necessary before breaking the isolation.)

Feeling that a sudden small drop in boat pressure might be a factor in the condenser weld failures, I stationed myself at the vent condenser before we surfaced and measured the temperatures of the condenser exterior and the vent pipe going through it. When the ship's pressure was equalized, a cloud of water vapor issued from the vent pipe, and the vent pipe temperature soared. The small pressure decrease had lowered the de-aerating tank water's boiling point temperature slightly. That produced a slug of steam that heated up and lengthened the vent pipe. The condenser around it was much less affected, showing that the differential increase in vent pipe and condenser length was the cause of cracking the welds connecting them.

I reported the cause of the nuisance as the lack of an expansion joint in the vent condenser. After repeating my test and graphing the temperature transient, the ship submitted a report on it without identifying the root cause (because it was considered improper to suggest the solution). If there was any feedback to the ship, I wasn't aware of it.

When I met my former NESEP candidate in the Officer's Mess at the Submarine Base, I also asked him about the Vent Condenser. He said that the fix that had come out in about two years replaced the condenser with one made out of heavier metal without changing its dimensions otherwise, and the fix had promptly experienced the same failure as the original design. That *if it doesn't work, get a bigger hammer* approach was, I speculate, because the problem was so minor that it was given to someone too inexperienced to deduce the root cause and correct it—a consequence fostered by not identifying the differential expansion consideration in the ship's report.

Engineer Officer Qualification

My primary focus during this time was studying for qualification as Engineer Officer of Naval Nuclear Power Plants. I was advised to study some things that I had little awareness of, like reactors that had a homogenous nuclear fuel and coolant mixture that remained subcritical in the piping to and from the reactor vessel and became a critical, power-generating mass when inside the large diameter reactor vessel. This sounded pretty far-fetched and impracticable to me, but I learned something about it and otherwise tried to bolster my nuclear engineering knowledge. Then, when I went back to the Office of Naval Reactors, I found that the examination was solely about my ship's power plant, and realized that my study should have focused on its Power Plant Manual, a set of volumes that almost filled a tall shelf on a good-sized bookcase.

I did poorly on this examination, and was summarily booted out by Admiral Rickover again. And I returned to the ship to report my failure to the new Captain—who had recently taken command. He agreed that I needed to intensely study the ship's Power Plant Manual. Moreover, he was a Super Nuke and his encouragement and support were invaluable. When he sent me back for re-examination, I was ready. On the written exam (a three-four hour ordeal), I felt I had a firm grasp of every question asked but one. For that question, I stated my rudimentary knowledge and why I hadn't been able to get more.

Next came the oral exam. The Examiner asked me how I thought I had done on the written exam. I said that I thought I hadn't disgraced myself this time. He asked me what the difference was, and I explained the change in my study focus. Things seemed to be going smoothly on his other questions, and he changed the focus by stating: *Let's look at some history of your ship and see how familiar you are with that.*

Expecting to be asked about something I had little knowledge of, I was delighted when the obscure item he pounced upon was the ship's report on the Vent Condenser. Mindful of the "Answer the Question Asked" (and then shut up) dogma, I answered his questions carefully. After a thorough interrogation, he asked how I had obtained my detailed knowledge of the matter. I explained the out-of-the-blue arrival of the infrared temperature sensing gun and how I used it to confirm my hypothesis. He then commented that my name wasn't mentioned in the report. I said that my identification of the problem had prompted a more detailed retest, and the oral exam ended without my being asked anything about the root cause of the vent condenser problem.

My next step was the interview with the Admiral. He vigorously and briefly castigated me again. This may have been the time he said that I had improperly supported one of the sailors in my Division for participation in NESEP (the Navy Enlisted Scientific Education Program) leading to a college degree and an officer's commission. I responded that the sailor I had supported was the best man, and the Admiral summarily dismissed me (again). But I left qualified as an Engineer Officer of Naval Nuclear Power Plants.

Another memorable event on nuclear submarines was the ONR (Office of Naval Reactors) assessment of the crew's ability to operate the power plant. Ships that failed that evaluation weren't allowed to go to sea. Their nuclear trained personnel drilled and studied incessantly until they passed re-examination. Their ships were outcasts, moored and silent, with other ships' personnel crossing over them quietly and quickly.

Before the only ONR assessment on a ship I was on, we heard that a current favorite test was plant startup from cold shutdown with no outside power source available, and with the least experienced EOOW aboard in charge of the evolution. So we practiced it, and failed our own drill the first time. But when ONR gave us that test, we did it easily. And we passed all the other aspects of the examination as well.

Ship Turnovers

The friendly ribbing during turnovers for my seven Polaris patrols revealed a lot about the officers on both crews. One Engineer

Officer was a Super Nuke who could regurgitate the name, number, location, and function of every valve in the nuclear power plant. (He eventually advanced to flag rank.) Having five very active sons and no daughters colored his reputation. One of the tales about his family was that his wife said that three kids are more than you can handle, so it doesn't make any difference how many more you have.

One officer was continually ribbed about his experiences before he qualified as an "Engineer Officer of Naval Nuclear Power Plants." A statement that was repeatedly mentioned was his exasperated reaction to a cross-threaded bolt in the ship's air conditioner. He reputedly had asked the petty officer involved: *Did you cross-thread that bolt when you were putting it in or when you took it out?* And, during this upkeep, he increased the ribbing onslaught when he used a toilet in the officer's head, forgot that the tank to which the toilet drained was pressurized, opened the flushing valve, and treated himself to what an instructor at submarine school once described as the old submarine disease—freckles.

Another officer was noted for his behavior the night before his Crew left for the States and the two wardrooms went out to celebrate. The oncoming crew had essentially taken over responsibility for the ship and was very restrained. But the offgoing crew had just shed a tremendous responsibility and was more inclined to celebrate. During one of those celebrations, an officer on the oncoming crew won a bet that his counterpart on the other crew would fall off his bar stool, with his drink still in hand and unspilled. By the end of the evening though, the faller seemed bright-eyed and bushy tailed, and fully ready for the next day's flight home. (I later heard that wasn't the first time that same bet had been made and won, but never heard whether the bet was a set-up.)

Return to the United States after turnover was a cause for concern that some individuals might rush back into activities ashore. But I only recall two potentially related incidents. One was a sailor who started out too hot on his motorcycle, spun out, and got skinned up. The other was an officer who had his own airplane. He made too hard a landing and broke some of the plane's parts. But he met the Navy's definition of a successful landing: one that you walk away from. And there were no personnel time loss events ashore during my seven ballistic missile patrols and one shipyard overhaul.

Reassignment and Moving

There was no turnover after my last patrol on this submarine because it ended in the United States so that the boat could begin shipyard overhaul. Shortly after the return, I was ordered to Ship's Inertial Navigation System (SINS) training for subsequent assignment as a Fleet Ballistic Missile Submarine Navigator. That meant moving again.

Moving from Idaho to my first Polaris submarine's home port had been complicated. We had to rent a house in New London for a year before being able to move into Navy Housing. Then we lost submarine base Navy Housing eligibility when I was ordered to SINS training in Virginia, and I moved my family there with me to minimize the family separation. Another move became necessary when, shortly after moving to Virginia, I received orders to become the Executive Officer of one crew of a Polaris submarine in overhaul at the Portsmouth, New Hampshire shipyard. The first step was going to Prospective Commanding Officer (PCO) School at the submarine base, so we rented a nearby beach house before moving to Portsmouth for the duration of the overhaul. When we did move to Portsmouth, the house we rented there turned out to be unsuitable after a few months, so we moved to a better one. Then, when the overhaul was over, we moved back to the submarine base area. That was seven moves in about three and a half years.

The moves helped a bit with my wife's unhappiness about a husband being at sea and unreachable half the time and leaving early and returning late the other half. But the brunt of the moving fell on her and that had a big negative impact.

Prospective Commanding Officer School

When I was ordered to duty as the Executive Officer of a Polaris Submarine, I was told by the Bureau of Naval Personnel that I was the first officer in my year group to be chosen for such duty. (At least one other classmate was told that when he was assigned to an FBM submarine XO billet.)

PCO school began with classroom study of the latest submarine tactics, followed by torpedo firing exercises on a Fleet Boat. The acoustic torpedo firing exercises were like the ones I had participated in during operations out of San Diego. On the one I had the conn for, when my gut confirmed our firing solution, which had just tracked the target as coming within firing range, I told the PCO school instructor that. He asked why I wasn't firing, and I said that I didn't feel that comfortable in water I had little experience in. Later, I fired on a correct solution. Afterwards, the instructor said that his pre-knowledge of target initial position and course and speed held the target as being just within range when I stated that it should be.

The next approaches were World War II Mark 14 torpedo firing exercises. On my first one, I saw a large merchantman (an oil tanker) coming into the exercise area. The instructor asked what my plan was, and I said I'd go deep, speed up, go under the merchantman, come up on the other side, and resume the attack. He said that was an unnecessary danger, and I should go behind the interference. I said that would abort the attack, but did as specified. We ended up behind the target and unable to catch up.

My next approach went nicely. When the torpedo was fired, sonar reported that it was running "hot, straight, and normal." But I saw a trail of bubbles through the periscope and reported the torpedo malfunction. We surfaced and followed the trail. It ended where a steady stream of bubbles was breaking the surface. That location was plotted and reported, but the Navy decided not to try to retrieve the torpedo.

After this event, the instructor told me that the other students were all going to Commanding Officer tours and needed the practice more. So I became the Fire Control Coordinator for the rest of the exercises, and have never fired another torpedo.

When the firing exercises ended each day, the submarine typically acted as a sonar target for the destroyer we had been making approaches on. Destroyers now had improved active sonars. Roundtable discussion of that increase in destroyer capability held that Fleet Boats could no longer evade destroyer sonar. So I asked to try and was given permission.

The Conning Officer on watch was a Naval Academy classmate of mine. (We had compared experiences and skills earlier. His 20-10 eyesight enabled him to see ship features like hull numbers through the periscope better than I could. But I was better at calling angle on the bow.) He was enthusiastic about my plan for breaking contact. We got permission to use evasion devices and were allowed to put the batteries in series to increase our speed capability. Then, at the standard time for watch relief, we cranked up flank speed, got behind the destroyer, released two kinds of evasion devices, blew air bubbles to further confuse the situation, and quietly retreated from the location we had noisily established. After we were well clear, my classmate reported losing contact with the destroyer. His Captain chewed him out.

When I dropped down to the Control Room, the sailors on watch were grinning from ear to ear at their restored sense of superiority. But the PCO School Instructor and the Captain evinced no pleasure.

I left PCO School giving more credence to tales about World War II British and American submarines becoming more effective after their Commanding Officers were replaced with younger and more daring ones.

The Overhaul

When I reported to my second Polaris submarine, the Captain told me that he had personally selected me to be his XO. That was especially flattering because his knowledge of submarines was awesome.

One of the first bits of wisdom my new Captain imparted was that our goal was to minimize our time in the shipyard. His sound rationale was that shipyard overhaul was like any complex construction activity: it cost the same each day, and the longer it took, the more it cost.

This Captain demanded that we be on top of all shipyard activity related to our ship. His own impressive knowledge was accompanied by a fiery response to any indication of lack of awareness. But his sometimes volcanic style didn't alienate the crew or the shipyard. He was a classic example of the man who, when he said Jump, was only asked How High? I felt that his crew would trustingly go to Hell with him, or for him.

A standard ordeal for ships completing overhaul was proving the operability of systems to the Bureau of Inspection and Survey (InSurv) during an at sea operational period especially for that purpose. InSurv Examiners typically ran a ship's crew to near exhaustion. But that didn't happen with us. We grouped together all the tests that could be performed simultaneously. And, instead of the InSurv Examiners waiting for the ship to get ready, we had several tests ready to be done together. The word most frequently announced on the 1MC was: Will the InSurv Inspector for _____ please report to _____ to observe the test. We finished the testing successfully in less than the allotted time and saw off an exhausted InSurv staff.

The post-shipyard trials to prove operational proficiency were demanding. The Captain took the Command Duty of overseeing operations during the day and early evening. I had the Command Duty at night and slept a few hours or minutes during daytime periods when things were running smoothly. When anything displeased the Captain, however, he had me awakened and called to the Conn, where he chewed me out for not having trained the crew better, and sent me to correct the problem.

After the USS Thresher (SSN-593) sank with the loss of all hands during its post-overhaul trials, the Navy developed an upgrading program (SubSafe) for nuclear submarine seawater systems. The SubSafe program had been performed on our ship during this overhaul. Nonetheless, the touchiest of the post-shipyard tests was diving to test depth. We approached that depth cautiously and, when there, the Engine Room reported sea water in-leakage around the propulsion shaft. The Captain dispatched me to assess the situation. I saw that the leakage was copious and wondered how the Hell I could safely say that things were under control. But the leakage wasn't increasing, and the compartment watchstanders indicated that to have been the case before I arrived. So I reported that the leakage was not getting worse. We then ended the test depth dive. But I was never more acutely aware of my lack of innate understanding of machinery, or of how one mistake could result in the loss of a submarine.

Post-Overhaul Shakedown

The overhaul was followed by an extended shakedown period that tested the ship and crew thoroughly, and provided a lot of shiphandling opportunities.

Although this Captain was a very skilled shiphandler, he was typically very testy while we were entering port. That was the only aspect of submarine operations that seemed to elicit any concern on his part. (These boats sacrificed surface maneuverability for submerged performance, and were unpredictable with sternway on.) Once, when we were entering New London Harbor to moor alongside a submarine tender, a Navy tug, commanded by a Chief Petty Officer, was coming alongside to assist. The tug bumped us hard, and the Captain, from an about 20 yards eye to eye distance from the Tug's Captain, told him: *Get the Hell away from my ship!* The Captain then kept the Conn for the landing, which was expertly made without that tug's assistance.

Later on during shakedown, when we were getting ready to enter port, I went to the Captain's stateroom to report our readiness and found him ill. He expressed doubt about being able to go to the bridge. I said that he had trained us well and he could safely stay in bed. But shortly before we entered port, he came up to the bridge, wan but in complete control, and oversaw the landing.

One of this Captain's firm beliefs was that: *If you haven't done it, you can't do it.* So he drilled and trained us incessantly and realistically. One of the results was that he made me a superior shiphandler, perhaps even better at some aspects than he was. The other officers benefitted too.

Post-overhaul operations provided another out-of-the ordinary experience when one of our sailors became ill. We didn't have a doctor aboard, but our First Class Hospital Corpsman diagnosed appendicitis and recommended immediate transfer to a hospital. We radioed for a helicopter, made the rendezvous, strapped the patient to a Stokes Litter (a rigid, steel mesh stretcher), and watched the helicopter smoothly take him away. He had a successful emergency appendectomy within two hours of arrival at the hospital. We were quite proud of getting him the care he needed, and especially of our Corpsman.

Unclassified post-overhaul operations provided yet another lesson in submarining and this Captain's exceptionalism. We were submerged at night. I was at the Conning Station to take the Command Duty from the Captain. The OOD reported sighting the light of a probable fishing boat through the periscope, and the Captain proposed that we each estimate the range to it. I voiced the standard knowledge that the periscope provided monocular vision and it takes binocular vision to tell distance. The Captain said that experience compensated for that. So I looked through the periscope and watched the boat's single white light bobbing, guessed the range at between 3000 and 3500 yards, and gave my estimate at 3250 yards. The Captain's estimate was about 1000 yards higher; the OOD's estimate was about 750 yards lower. Then the Captain ordered the periscope radar turned on. I again demurred, stating the dogma that periscope radar was not to be used because it provided a detectable signal. The Captain said that we were on an unclassified operation and this use was justified. And the range to the boat turned out to be less than 100 yards over my estimate. The Captain was pleased with the results and with proving his point, and I had a new affirmation of how experience and practice could enhance capabilities beyond normal limits.

This Captain remained as demanding as he was intelligent. On post-overhaul shakedown, I went without sleep for so long at a stretch that I developed tunnel vision, having to turn my head from side to side to compensate for the loss of peripheral vision. A couple of hours of sleep remedied that, but I had no time for anything but ship's evolutions. So, when the crew decided to take the door to my stateroom and hide it as a prank, I ignored that. (The door reappeared in a few days, at the Captain's order.)

Not long afterwards, I was developing nervousness and sought out our hospital corpsman. He asked me how much coffee I was drinking. I couldn't count that high. He suggested that I go off that stimulant. I did. My sense of well-being returned. My caffeine tolerance never has.

One of our next evolutions was submerged sound trials involving closely passing by underwater sensors. The Captain and the Engineer collaborated on these during the day. Each evolution was discussed so thoroughly that they were several evolutions behind when I took over for the 12-hour night stint. Unimpeded by consulting, and discovering a flair for the maneuvering, I usually managed to get ahead of schedule by the time they relieved me. That perplexed me. The Engineer was a Super Nuke, the Captain the sharpest submariner I had known, and together they were doing less than I was. That gave my ego a boost, but the probable cause was the difference between day and night staffing at the sound range—with too many cooks spoiling the broth during the day.

One of the post-overhaul evolutions was an actual missile firing. That was preceded by training at Cape Canaveral. By this time the Captain was beginning to relax and spend an occasional evening ashore. One morning, as we were getting ready to get underway, he hadn't returned to the ship. The full Navy Captain who oversaw our progress was aboard and on the bridge. When our Captain came aboard, at just about the time we were scheduled to get underway, I reported that we were ready. He ordered that we get underway and went below. We were proceeding down the center of the channel when the Overseer commented that we would be better off on the starboard side. I looked askance at him, because we could damn well take our ship in and out of port, but had the OOD move the ship over to the Starboard side of the channel. (Being in the center of the otherwise empty channel was safer, but the right-hand side of the channel was safe too.)

Although I was apprehensive, our Overseer's behavior was entirely proper, and he was worthy of respect. For example, the first time he came to the bridge, he took one look at the gyrocompass repeater and said: *That gyro is gimbaled wrong.* He was right, and no one on the ship had noticed it. (He became a Rear Admiral and commanded the Submarine Base.)

The firing date arrived and the Captain ordered me to complete the countdown with no holds. That meant controlling things we couldn't control, like an aircraft coming too near the airspace the missile would traverse. But I knew the Captain well enough to respond *Aye, Aye, Sir* and hope that nothing requiring a hold would come up. Nothing did. When we reached the firing point, the Captain gave me the firing key and ordered me to fire the missile. It went off on time and fell on target.

138

As we were nearing the end of shakedown, the Captain said that we could finish two weeks early, tie up the ship, send him and half the crew on leave for the first week, and send me and the other half of the crew on leave for the second week. I said that would push the crew to its limit. He replied that, if I sold them on the idea, they would do it willingly. So I made the proposal to everyone (in small groups), and found that the Captain was right.

We finished shakedown two weeks early but never found out if the Captain's plan would work. (I had doubts about the second week.) Another Polaris submarine ran aground while submerged, had its hull penetrated in the Torpedo Room, bounced to the surface, pressurized the compartment, and remained afloat. The officer who jumped into its flooding Torpedo Room and supervised the damage control had been a trainee at the nuclear prototype with me. I remember him most for his reply to another trainee's comment about things finally getting better after we finished prototype training. He said that we had been expressing such hopes for a long time, and he was tired of wishing his life away. I never saw him after prototype training, but heard that he became the Captain of a submarine tender.

Post-Overhaul Patrol

Going back in the line of battle early didn't alter our trip to Annapolis to show off the ship before going on patrol. En route, when I was overseeing the piloting, we made a wrong turn. Within a couple of minutes, the Captain was in the Conn correcting the situation. Later, he called the OOD and me to his stateroom to say: I *thought I had made every mistake in the book during my career, but you two S.O.B.s just showed me a brand new one.* (After I resigned from active naval duty, and that OOD had as well, I was told that our Captain had expressed great regret about both resignations.)

At Annapolis, the Captain promptly went ashore to make the expected formal calls, and to embroil himself in the local and Washington social scene. While he was gone, we toured a raft of midshipmen and senior naval officers through the boat. We also were making missiles ready and preparing for departure on patrol. I spent most of the days supervising that and briefing Admirals, and most of the nights preparing the myriad of reports due before we departed. The Captain returned to the ship when we were ready to get underway. Before going below, he signed all the outgoing reports. They were stuck in envelopes and taken ashore for mailing by the boat that brought him to the ship. We weighed anchor as soon as that boat departed.

During the first days of our trans-Atlantic voyage, a steady stream of messages arrived from flag officers who had toured the ship. They expressed thanks for our hospitality and most of them commended me by name for my briefings. The Captain chewed me out because they had named me but not him. I said that I had no control over Admirals and got away with that, perhaps because we had just received good grades for post-overhaul training and shakedown. Both crews received a grade of 92$^+$, with our Crew getting a grade a few tenths of a point higher than the other crew. The other crew's Executive Officer had been the Captain's XO before the overhaul, was with the Captain throughout the overhaul, was highly respected, and the Captain said I had done well to beat the other crew's grade.

The transatlantic crossing was a high speed one. And we had a challenging depth excursion. To facilitate understanding, the following public data on a Polaris submarine is relevant: over 20 knots maximum submerged speed and 1300 feet test depth. Test (maximum permissible) depth is the depth at which the water pressure compresses the hull to the point at which it will return to its original shape when the pressure is removed. Beyond that elastic limit, the hull is permanently misshapen. (Submarines that descend below test depth can survive if crush depth isn't reached and the hull penetrations remain intact.)

A 20 knot speed is slightly more than 2000 feet per minute. At 20 knots, a submarine with a 30° down angle descends at about 1000 feet per minute. At a 45° down angle, the descent is about 1400 feet per minute. So, at high speed and big angles, the action needed to keep the ship safe must be taken promptly.

Our depth excursion occurred while the Captain and I were inspecting the ship. We were in the Missile Compartment when the boat suddenly nosed over, and we ran for the Control Room and Conning Station. I walked up the sides of the steps of the ladder

140

(which was more like a 45° staircase that was now level) to the Conning Area, pulled myself up hand over hand to the railing around the Conn, and looked at the situation. The Captain had climbed up behind me and pulled himself up to the Conning Station. The Conning Officer had reversed the screw thrust and blown the ballast tanks. We ascended rapidly, and surfaced.

The depth excursion was initiated by a hydraulic leak. A watchstander had shut an upstream valve to secure it. That took the pressure off one side of the stern planes' operating mechanism, and the pressure on the other side put the stern planes on full dive. Prompt corrective action had stopped our depth excursion at less than 200 feet. We repaired the leak, recharged the air banks, submerged, and went on our way undetected (as far as we knew).

The crew knew how well the transient had been handled and had no concern. But the sailor who had secured the leak had to be evaluated. The Engineer Officer did that and reported that the man had violated a cardinal rule by securing the hydraulic supply without first reporting the leak. Also, this sailor had previously taken inappropriate actions that had caused lesser problems.

My pro forma assessment was that we couldn't rely on this sailor and should disqualify him in submarines. The Captain angrily asserted that the sailor was career Navy, that the sailor's father was career Navy, that we were going to change his rate to one he wanted, and that he would be assigned to surface ship duty without removal of his submarine qualification.

The sailor selected a rating that he couldn't be transferred to. When I told the Captain that, he said: *Damn it, I know that, do it anyhow!* On my second try, I produced a justification that the Captain accepted. That rating change was accomplished and the still submarine qualified sailor was assigned to non-submarine duty. (Compassion had trumped dogma again.)

Later during this transit, I was the Command Duty Officer when the fathometer started showing a significantly decreasing water depth. The navigation chart showed no water depth decrease. So I told the Conning Officer to slow down while we evaluated the situation. In about a minute, the supposedly sleeping Captain was in the Conn with us. He checked the charts and the fathometer, ordered that we resume speed, and went back to bed. We did as ordered and water depth soon returned to conformance with the chart. I still don't know how the Captain concluded that that uncharted peak wouldn't endanger his submarine.

During this Captain's tour, a rumor circulated that the Republican Party in his home state had offered him their nomination as Governor. We certainly considered him capable of high position. And his lovely and intelligent wife would have graced a Governor's mansion. (An accomplished hostess, she once served the wardroom a whole young pig, scraped clean and gutted, with its head on and an apple in its mouth.) It seemed unusual that a man that young, with a career that had kept him out of his home State for so long, would be sought out as a candidate for State Governor. He put the rumor to rest by remarking that no Republican had ever been Governor of his State, and he wasn't going to try to change that.

Operating out of Holy Loch, Scotland involved dead stick (i.e., with the nuclear power plant shut down) moves that shuffled the submarines from one side of the submarine tender to the other— because of activities like offloading or onloading a missile. We used tugs to move the ship, and the Captain had me do that the first time. I soon overdid the tug thrust and had to reverse it strongly, learned from that, and made the rest of the move smoothly. After several more moves I felt that I had gotten very good at it—the Captain never interjected any direction or advice. Then, when we moved and I saw a sizeable group of submarine officers on one of the tender's upper decks, I wondered aloud about that. The Captain said that the other boats' officers were up there to watch us move to learn from it. He also said that our moves were known among the other Captains as the ___ and Ebe show.

My belief in my shiphandling was taken down a peg when we entered a Floating Drydock. I slowed the ship to enter the drydock gently, and the current started to swing the stern. The Captain increased speed, put the rudder over to counter the swing, and backed down sharply when the bow was well inside the drydock. Then he calmly explained the importance of getting these big boats in and out of drydock quickly.

During sea trials, the Captain scheduled some approach and attack training, and made a fine illustrative run on a Submarine Rescue Vessel. Then he had me make an approach. When we plotted the target's actual track for my run, it superimposed closely on the track established by my periscope observations, with my called angles on the bow plotting very closely to the target's course. The Captain made no comment, and I kept quiet about doing better than the cream of the crop.

The Captain was very focused on seeing that his crew was rewarded for their hard work. He was unhappy about their relatively low advancement rate, chewed me out for allowing that to happen, and ordered me to correct it. In addition to their heavy workload, the crew was hampered by advancement exams that covered equipment unfamiliar to them. For example, we had two types of Electronics Technicians (ETs), Navigation ETs who worked on the inertial navigation system and ETs who worked on nuclear power plant instrumentation, and they didn't touch each other's' equipment. And neither group had any familiarity with the surface ship radars that their exams covered. Also, submarine Sonarmen were tested on the active sonars on surface ships, etc. So I made the crew aware of the need for taking the relevant, current courses, showed them the most important parts of their course material, and insisted that they get fully prepared. On the next exam we had a 75% pass rate. On the following exam it was 85%. And the Captain attached a letter of commendation to my fitness report noting the striking improvement in and immense benefit to morale.

What we did doesn't seem to have become a lasting lesson learned. There have been media reports of scandals involving officer-assisted cheating on submariners' advancement exams. That's dishonest compensation for a correctable problem. But that also indicates that examining personnel on systems they don't use may still be an unfair part of Navy advancement practices.

The Captain allowed no one but himself and me to touch his huge service record—gigantic because it was so full of commendations. His reputation for being "star-crossed" seemed to be confirmed by his next duty assignment, Assistant to the Undersecretary of the Navy. Additional confirmation was indicated by his following assignment, which was as the Head of the Guantanamo Bay Naval Station (Gitmo). That post was once held by War Hero PT Boat Buckley, who had cut off the Cuban water supply to Gitmo to show independence from Cuban support.

Note: Many years later, a former shipmate told me that our Captain's career progress ended when he took some black sailors to Captain's Mast at Gitmo and was accused of racial prejudice. Neither of us thought that the man would unfairly discriminate. But, whatever scuttled his career, his failure to gain an Admiral's stars supports the assertion that *One Aw Shit Wipes Out a Thousand Atta Boys*. And finding out that he had died at the age of 84 when he fell and hit his head on a tennis court significantly saddened me.

The New Captain

My first patrol with the next Captain started well. He was new to ballistic missile submarines, but the crew was superbly trained and he was professionally competent. We got through the transition to patrol operations nicely. Then, about midnight one night, I relieved him as Command Duty Officer. After the offgoing OOD reported the ship's status to me in my stateroom (adjacent to the Captain's), we decided to have a movie in the wardroom. About 15 minutes into it, with the offgoing EOOW and the Offgoing Diving Officer watching with us, the Captain strode in, ordered the movie secured, and stalked out. Then he stopped speaking to me (except for Command Duty tasks). The other officers avoided the wardroom except for meals. After three days, the Captain asked: *XO, would you like to know why I haven't been speaking to you?* I said *yes*. He stated that it was because I hadn't invited him to the movie. I said that it was his ship, he would have been welcome, and I would have asked him if I had known that he hadn't turned in for the night. That ended the non-talking. But our relationship remained distant. (Things might have gone a lot better if I had been able to make him feel more welcome as the new Captain.)

When we reached port and turned in the patrol report, the Captain and the off-watch crew went ashore. The Division Commander made a prolonged ship walk-through with me and made a point of the ship's bilges not being spotless. I saw that as caviling. (The bilges were clean, and ready for the upkeep, but not for a white glove inspection.)

Then I learned that the cause was Admiral Rickover having raised Holy Hell because another submarine's bilges weren't spotless.

We returned to the USA on a Friday. I took the rest of that day off. On Saturday, I went to the off-crew office to attack the huge mound of paperwork and went home after about 12 hours, put out yet again by what I considered its lack of value.

On Sunday, I stayed home and reviewed my situation. Reams of minutiae that had nothing to do with our Cold War mission weren't the only burr under my saddle. My trust in the government's management and support of the Navy had taken a big hit when the Pueblo's crew was left hanging out to dry.

The Navy's plan for me also was giving me heartburn. A Detailing Officer from the Bureau of Naval Personnel told me that, since I had become an Executive Officer so soon, I was scheduled for another nuclear submarine Executive Officer tour. I asked when I could expect shore duty. He said that my nuclear power training had been shore duty. I considered that intensive nuclear training a far cry from the respite from sea duty that shore duty reputedly was. Besides, another XO tour, presumably followed by two CO tours, would make me just about eligible for retirement without ever having had real shore duty.

Another concern was that my absences and work schedule were taking a toll on my marriage and family. There was no indication that that would change in the Navy.

I concluded that I sorely needed to enjoy my life more and that wasn't going to happen in the Navy. So I wrote out my resignation.

On Monday morning, I went to the office. The Captain was already there. He said something very much like: *Good morning, XO. I didn't see you in the office yesterday. What were you doing?* I said something like: *I was working on my resignation, Captain. Here it is.* He looked it over, said that he had thought something like that was in the wind, and forwarded it on.

At the time, there was a one-year delay between resignation of a nuclear trained officer and his discharge. The Captain wanted to keep his junior officers from being exposed to the example of a resigning Executive Officer, so my relief was ordered aboard. After our turnover, I was transferred to a staff job at ComSubLant (Commander, Submarine Force Atlantic) headquarters in Norfolk.

I never saw this Captain again, but did see his obituary. It described prestigious accomplishments that included two commendations for performance of missions of great value to the United States.

Note. http:www.chonday.com/Videos/pen1nav1 is a good place to start checking on more modern submarines. It describes the ~18,000 ton Ohio class submarine. And the book *Blind Man's Bluff* describes nuclear attack submarine operations. Those are far different from my ballistic missile submarine experience, but I thought that the book realistically depicted submariners.

II-6 SubLant Headquarters

The Welcome

I was cordially welcomed at the Atlantic Submarine Force Commander's headquarters, and was assigned as the Public Affairs Officer (a job usually filled by a former Fleet Boat Captain.) My staff was two journalists and a graphic artist who planned to take a job with Disney when his enlistment was up.

The Force Commander

ComSubLant, Vice Admiral Arnold F. Schade, was deeply admired and respected. He had been a World War II Executive Officer on the USS Growler (SS-215). The Growler's Captain was Commander Howard Walter Gilmore, the first World War II submariner to be awarded the Congressional Medal of Honor. On February 2, 1943, during her fourth war patrol, Growler made a night surface attack on a Japanese convoy. A 900 ton Japanese provision ship, the IJN Hayasaki, tried to ram her. Gilmore maneuvered and rammed Hayasaki amidships at 17 knots. Hayasaki raked Growler with machine gun fire, killing the Junior Officer of the Deck and a Lookout, and wounding Gilmore, whose injuries immobilized him. Recognizing the danger to his ship, he ordered his XO to "Take her down." LCDR Schade submerged Growler, waited until the seas were clear, and started looking for Gilmore. He wasn't found. His Medal of Honor was issued posthumously.

LCDR Schade captained the Growler back to port for repairs. He commanded her on her next patrol and sank a Japanese troop transport. Growler was later sunk on her 11th patrol. Hayasaki survived subsequent air attack and later hitting a (probably submarine laid) mine, and was taken over by Russia after the war.

Take her down became a legendary phrase. But, at SubLant headquarters, the Growler story was a prohibited subject.

Staff Reaction

A Commander who was probably the staffer closest to my age told me that it cost the Navy $500,000 to bring an officer to the point of being assigned as a nuclear submarine Executive Officer. But no one pressed me about my reasons for resigning. The only clue I got about that came when I was on the War Plans staff and a senior staff officer commented that he had heard about my differences with my last Captain. He saw my anger and changed the subject. There could have been several sources for his knowledge. My differences with my Captain were well known to the officers and crew of the boat. Whatever the source(s), the SubLant staff knew a lot about their submarines.

Duties

The Public Affairs Officer prepared the Admiral's presentations, attended functions with him, and operated the slide projector. Very professional-looking slides were whipped up by the artist. Journalist familiarity with the Admiral's style made the speech writing easy.

Another part of the job was responding to letters from the public. One of those was from the widow of the Captain of the USS Scorpion (SSN 589), a submarine lost at sea about a year earlier. Shortly before Scorpion was scheduled to return to Norfolk, the crew's families were notified. But, when Scorpion didn't report in when she should have, nothing was said to the families, who had assembled on the pier to greet the crew. Hours after the ship was scheduled to return, they were told to return home and await further information.

Because the families the Captain's widow represented deserved special treatment, we carefully crafted a response. I signed it, and put it in the outgoing mail. It was intercepted by the senior staffer who reviewed outgoing correspondence. He thoroughly reamed me out, and said that Admiral Schade personally responded to the Scorpion crew's families. Later, I was given a copy of Admiral Schade's response. It came with the oral comment that there had been "nothing wrong" with my reply. But the Admiral's warmer and more knowledgeable letter showed how deeply he felt the loss of Scorpion's crew and a basic reason why he was so respected.

The security clearance I held made me eligible to stand overnight watches at CinCLant (Commander in Chief Atlantic) Headquarters. That didn't involve processing any situation that could lead to retaliation to enemy attack. But I still remember the stream of incoming cars I saw after being relieved in the morning. Each one ferried an Admiral or General to work. On the shelf in front of each car's rear window, just behind each flag officer, was a red phone. I felt a deep respect for those officers, but was glad that I didn't have a red phone next to me 24 hours of every day.

Occasional at sea time with the Admiral or a senior staff member was part of the job. One of those was for a short submarine indoctrination period for the media. There were no big name broadcasters, just a bunch of eager beavers who avidly took in everything they were told. I had previously had a good experience, while stationed on a destroyer, with a newspaper reporter who went to sea with us for a week or so. This experience was producing even more enthusiasm. The SubLant staff looked at such initiatives as a well worthwhile enhancement of the Navy's image. I thought they were right.

After about six months, a permanent Public Affairs Officer reported for duty and I was assigned to the War Plans Staff. Having a fresh eye produced some thoughts on better ways to do things. Those were listened to, but my time on the staff ended before I found out whether they would be implemented.

My Lai

SubLant duty made me more aware of the impact of the My Lai massacre. Before the Vietnam War, we typically heard only about

EBE CHANDLER MCCABE, JR.

the atrocities committed by our enemies, and even those were often hushed up. That may be why America was so thoroughly shocked when the March 1968 massacre of 347-504 Vietnamese "civilians" at the My Lai massacre was made public in November 1969. Our soldiers were then publicly condemned for killing unarmed women and children.

My contact with Marine Officers at the Bachelor Officers Quarters showed me a different perspective. Their view was that, amidst the Vietnamese people, there was a substantial cadre of war-hardened fighters who were a threat to our soldiers. They also said that even young children and old ladies had hurled grenades at, and killed, U.S. soldiers. That's quite different from, and I think more correct than, the slaughter of unarmed innocent women and children that America reacted to. But it doesn't justify wanton killing in retribution.

Second Lieutenant William Calley, Jr. and 26 soldiers were charged with the killings. The soldiers weren't tried. Calley was court-martialed, convicted, and sentenced to Life in Prison. After 3.5 years of house arrest and no prison time, he was pardoned by President Nixon. His civilian career was as the manager of his father-in-law's jewelry store.

Calley's Company Commander, Captain Medina, also was court-martialed. He was found Not Guilty. But his Army career was over, and he resigned and went to work in a helicopter factory owned by his famous defense attorney (F. Lee Bailey).

Tales indicate that Captain Medina disparaged Lieutenant Calley in front of their troops, and that the Lieutenant wasn't respected. That's a recipe for disciplinary breakdown. And that can foster irresponsibility and the accomplishment of illegal acts.

Calley and Medina have suffered from public stigma. They, and the untried soldiers who participated in the massacre, also have their own personal evaluation of the acts they committed to consider. Denial's ability to shunt their responsibility aside either has stopped or will stop protecting some or all of them. For the moral ones, facing up to their deeds has been or will be traumatic. Whether that accountability is appropriate to their crimes is a matter for a judgment more capable than mine.

Insofar as My Lai was mob behavior by undisciplined armed youths and not a planned execution, there's justification for Calley's pardon. (I've been told that there's no one crueler than a 19 year old soldier away from home for the first time and armed with an automatic weapon.) Further, we should all be aware that moral people who succumb to mob mentality in any situation put themselves in a position similar to the one of the killers at My Lai.

Calley's and Medina's other subordinates, colleagues, and supervisors who considered the Vietnamese less than human "gooks" also fostered the My Lai massacre. So did the rest of the culture that regarded this enemy as subhuman.

The closest I came to seeing the nature of our soldiery in Vietnam was during training we participated in with a group of marines in WestPac. We approached a "hostile" shore submerged, surfaced the submarine, debarked the marines in rafts, submerged and departed. During a preparatory walk-through, when the heavily laden marines climbed up to the deck to launch their rafts, a burly one slipped on the ladder and smashed his nose on a rung. He continued topside, blood dripping. His sergeant ordered "Give me 50." And, with his heavy pack on his back, the marine did 50 pushups. That seemed to be an example of the kind of discipline that prevents deviation from mission requirements and rules of conduct.

A substantive example of American values was displayed in the Vietnam War by Lieutenant Colonel Hal Moore's Seventh (airborne) Cavalry. The examples of valor, courage, and discipline they set were in the highest traditions of soldiery. But the Seventh Cavalry's performance, and the rigorous discipline that I considered typical among our marines, are not the picture displayed to the world about Vietnam. We not only have the My Lai massacre to our discredit, Hollywood provided *Platoon*, a hugely acclaimed movie that rubbed salt in the open wound.

Platoon portrayed, except for college dropout and volunteer Taylor, draftees with little discipline and less moral character. Their platoon took dope and displayed their crudity in a bunker. Its gargoyle-faced Sergeant Barnes murdered an unarmed woman because her son denied his village's collaboration with the Vietnamese army. He then threatened to kill the man's daughter, and held a pistol to the child's head until Sergeant Elias intervened and the sergeants fought. The murder was reported to the platoon's Lieutenant, who did nothing.

The platoon burned the village, and Taylor prevented the rape of two village girls. Later, during a retreat, Barnes shot Elias twice in the chest, left him in the path of the enemy, and said that the Vietnamese had killed him. When the platoon was overrun, Taylor and Barnes were among the few survivors. Taylor joined his platoon mates as a dreg of society by killing the wounded Barnes with a discarded Vietnamese rifle. Still later, as Taylor was being airlifted from the area, he saw the twice chest shot Elias' (unrealistic) prolonged run from a group of North Vietnamese soldiers, who shot him several more times before he died in anguish. *Platoon* won the academy award for best picture in 1986. Its writer/director, Oliver Stone, was a combat experienced, decorated Vietnamese War Veteran. He was given the best director award.

I personally rejected *Platoon* because it labeled the worst of mankind as characteristic of America, and displayed that to the world. That was made worse in my mind by the failure to provide the world a realistic picture of the beatings and torture the Vietnamese practiced, especially at the Hanoi Hilton. (What we've heard about Jane Fonda's visit to Vietnam and the resultant increase in the brutal beatings of American prisoners there has induced some Americans, including me, to no longer watch movies in which she has or had a role. The apparent lack of other accountability for her alleged behavior has been disappointing.)

Checking Out

Just before I left SubLant to return to the Submarine Base for discharge, I was called in to see the Chief of Staff, a reputed hard nose. He said that resigning officers usually aren't worth much, but I seemed to be an exception who had worked hard. Then he gave me a genuine Zippo lighter with ComSubLant's emblem on it and sent me on my way. My only other sendoff was a phone call from a Chief Petty Officer who told me that, if I ever needed his right arm, it was there for me. I left the active duty Navy with those things in mind, a commission in the Naval Reserve, and a five year prohibition against going to a Soviet Bloc country.

II-7 The Naval Reserve

Initial Affiliation

After my active naval duty, I did nothing in the Navy Reserve until I was promoted to Commander. Then I started attending Naval Reserve meetings. That, and correspondence courses, enabled me to get the "points" I needed to be eligible for continued affiliation.

One of the Reserve Unit's officers was a Professor of Management Science. I asked him about managers whose main focus was on their employees' performance as compared with those whose primary attention was on pleasing their bosses. He responded that those who focused more on their subordinates were likely to get the most personal satisfaction. I've never had occasion to disagree with that.

When I went to work for the Atomic Energy Commission, the Reserve Unit gave me a going away party. The highlight was a gift of a "monkey wrench" to "reward" my ability to throw obstacles into progress. The actual wrench was a small Stillson Wrench. I happily used it for years.

Submarine Unit Affiliation

After another non-pay billet, I affiliated with a Submarine Support Unit as its Executive Officer. After the Commanding Officer's tour ended, I succeeded him. One of the Unit's activities while I was its Captain was removing a crane from a Submarine Rescue Vessel. The ship didn't have the money to make that authorized modification. So our qualified people did it. Doing such productive work helped unit morale considerably.

Low advancement was a Unit problem. I and my senior petty officers came up with a plan much like the ones that I had found successful before. When the next exam's results came through, four unit members were advanced in rate. That gave our unit two-thirds of the total of six advancements achieved in the about 50 Reserve Units in the area.

This unit did its annual active duty at the Submarine Base. There the crew was assigned to productive work and enjoyed the duty.

A previous unit Commanding Officer was then a Rear Admiral in the Naval Reserve. Our unit's highly respected Master Chief Yeoman also had been in the unit when that Admiral was its Commanding Officer. And, in preparing fitness reports for his unit Commanding Officers, the Admiral had solicited that Master Chief's comments. The Master Chief and several other crew members later told me that and said that they told the Admiral that I was the best Commanding Officer the unit had ever had. When I got my fitness report, I believed them and concluded that was entirely due to their pride in doing constructive work and in having the area's best advancement rate.

My next duty was as the Commanding Officer of a unit that supported a submarine tender. For that we traveled to active duty in Norfolk. This tender supported nuclear submarines. Several of my unit's members worked at commercial nuclear power plants, had previous nuclear Navy experience, and could have been a valuable resource. But the Submarine Force didn't want reserve personnel to do any work aboard nuclear submarines, so this unit's ability to take pride in supporting the active duty Navy was diminished.

Additional Training Duty

By taking annual leave from my job, I was able to do two, two-week active duties a year. The second two weeks were done as a participant in the Inter-American War Games at the Naval War College in Newport, Rhode Island. Many of the other reservists at those games did their active duty there every year. Two whom I remember were former Navy pilots. One of those had owned a small shipyard. He said that that had been unprofitable until he sold it, now supported himself by repairing sailboats, and had sailing around the world single-handed as a goal.

(I don't know if he ever tried.) The other pilot had stayed in the Navy until a year or two before having enough time in to retire, and resigned because the civilian airline he now worked for was going to stop hiring pilots. When he took the civilian job they offered him, he flew the same multi-engined aircraft that he flew in the Navy. He said that he now flew for the airline and had plenty of time and the opportunity to fly for the Navy as a reservist whenever he wanted to. His other interest was the farm he owned and on which he raised beefalo. Another reservist at the games was a doctor who also was a PhD microbiologist whose reserve commission was as a line officer. His was (and I hope still is) an outstanding mind.

Another active duty training session was a Senior Reserve Officer training course at Fort Leslie J. McNair in Washington, D.C. The attendees were a diverse group and we enjoyed the participative aspects of the training. One of the attendees was a grizzled, grey haired, crew cut marine Colonel who was a specialist on China. When the course was over and we shook hands and wished each other well, he told me that he didn't have much use for Naval Officers but had to admit that *you* (i.e., me) *have all your shit in one sock.* (I still grin when I recall his saying that.)

Reserve Staff Meetings

Our reserve Rear Admiral asked his unit Commanding Officers to sit in on his staff meetings. He ran them with consummate professionalism. All voices got heard. Comments were solicited. That he was a lawyer, a professional adversary, and had so much leadership skill astounded me at first. But he was a born salesman as well as an accomplished technocrat. (After his extended tour as a Navy Admiral, he became the Director of one of our U.S. Mints.) I still feel that his competence put him on the same level as the best managers I've encountered.

Pentagon Unit Affiliation

My final reserve unit affiliation was a two year assignment to the Pentagon unit supporting the Deputy Chief of Naval Operations for Submarine warfare. An active duty I served there was as a replacement for the on leave project officer for the submarine-launched cruise missile (nice title, but I had no involvement with the actual work on the weapon, and couldn't have had much in two weeks). Duty with this unit also gave me two nice memories. The first involved getting up to hit the road by 4 a.m. on Saturday for an 8 a.m. drill start. My teenage daughter voluntarily got herself up and fixed me an egg-in-a-hat for breakfast. (I called them UFOs, Unidentified Frying Objects, but they were tasty and a nice sendoff.) The second nice memory was the kindness and friendship of another Pentagon unit member. He was a Naval Academy classmate who also had become one of the first Polaris submarine Executive Officers from our class. We didn't discuss the story I had heard about his having told his last active duty Commanding Officer to Go to Hell, and his personality and character didn't confirm proneness to such behavior. On drill weekends, he welcomed me into his home and I spent Saturday nights with him and his family. (It was a sharp disappointment to return to my job after a vacation many years later and hear that he was being buried that morning, too soon for me to get there.)

Naval Windup

I left Naval Duty without having convinced anyone to pronounce submariner as submarine-er rather than sub-mariner. (The common pronunciation connotes subordination—a British Sub-Leftenant is subordinate to a Leftenant.)

My last naval duty was as a member of the Senior Reserve Officer Advisory Staff in my area. It was a "graveyard" assignment and I retired about one year before I had to.

If spending eternity in Davy Jones' Locker with my Active Duty and/or Reserve shipmates had become my lot, I would be in good company.

Part III

Civilian Life

III-1 Diamond Power

Transition

I had no job when I got out of the Navy. My parents took my family of four in. It only took a short time to thoroughly appreciate what my father had gone through when he was out of work and had a family to feed. But, in about a month, I was hired by the Diamond Power Specialty Company in Lancaster, Ohio.

The Company

Diamond Power was a subsidiary of Babcock and Wilcox (B&W), a long-time supplier of power plant boilers. B&W also was a designer of commercial nuclear power plants, competing with Westinghouse, General Electric, and Combustion Engineering.

Diamond Power's part of the B&W nuclear power plant was the control rods and their power supplies and operating controls. (The control rods, when withdrawn, permit the reactor to be taken to power operation and, when inserted, shut down the reactor.)

Psychological Interview

Not long after I started work, the Executive Vice President told me that company procedures had been violated by the hire because the required psychological interview and clearance hadn't been accomplished. So a special session was set up for the interview. A psychologist gave me paperwork tasks to complete, set time limits, and then didn't end the tasks when the time was up. Then an oral interview was held. The psychologist seemed rigidly dogmatic, and I felt that I had demonstrated virtually nothing. But my pleased bosses shared with me the conclusions that I had shown the ability to do outstanding work if given enough time and that I was capable of original thought. (That probably meant independent thought.)

Invalid Prejudices

This being my first experience in a civilian management position, I had some prejudgments to reassess. Among those was the notion that civilian industry may profit unfairly, and even dishonestly, from business dealings. A hypothetical military example is, if one unravels 1000 foot coils of line (which landlubbers call rope), one would find that all the coils would be a few feet longer than the 980 feet that the purchase specification's 2% error permitted. Such tales were dwarfed by ones of cost overruns and allegations of fraud. (I think it was Humorist Max Shulman's writing that first exposed me to the derogatory term feather merchant for military suppliers who provided inferior equipment.) But working at Diamond Power soon confirmed that I was with honorable and conscientious people.

The Staff

My new boss was Diamond Power's Controls Engineering Section Manager. He was a long-time employee who was highly experienced in designing Control Systems for the soot blowers used to clean the boilers in conventional commercial power plants. Those control systems were one-cabinet affairs. The control rod power and control system had over 20 cabinets containing DC power supplies (six phase, half wave rectified AC), a relay logic system, and a solid state control rod position indicating system.

My staff included a very competent senior controls engineer (our primary designer) and a PhD electrical engineer who was reputedly the only not yet retired member of the team that had developed the stators for the Navy's nuclear power plant control rods. We had several other engineers and technicians, and draftsmen were assigned to prepare our engineering drawings.

It wasn't long before my new boss asked me why a West Virginian's dead dog had to be buried three times. He responded to my lack of knowledge with a grin and a statement that the first two graves were too shallow. So I knew that the huge body of derogatory jokes that applies to Poles, Englishmen, Italians, and newbies covers West Virginians too.

I also soon saw that civilian leaders try to humanize themselves to their subordinates. Diamond Power's President was known for, at annual company picnics, playing the gutbucket (washtub bass, a folk music instrument using an inverted washtub as a resonator for the sound created by plucking a taut string attached to it). When this personable individual moved on, his Executive Vice President replaced him. Employees knew their new president as much for having offered to resolve a difference with a customer by flipping a coin as for being a past American Society of Mechanical Engineers president.

When the new Company President was still the Executive Vice President, he came to my desk one Sunday morning, asked what I was doing, and told me to break things down into smaller parts by saying: *The world is hard by the yard but, by the inch, it's a cinch.*

He further impressed me when, as the new Company president, he dispositioned an anomaly that was found in the control rod motor tubes. The tubes met code requirements but he doubted their suitability for the service, ordered them replaced, and accepted the additional schedule setback. At year's end, he also had to personally explain the associated 25% drop in company profit to B&W's President. That only raised the esteem he was held in by Diamond Power's staff.

The new Company President's high standards also became evident to me when a considerable effort was required to correct a glitch in our nuclear controls drawings. My boss took me aside to relay the president's comment that, when he graduated from college, he spent several years making engineering drawings before being allowed to do actual engineering work, and knew very well that such a glitch shouldn't have happened. I said that, if we had draftsmen with our president's capabilities, we wouldn't have had the problem.

My boss (wisely) told me to not say that again, but that was the last I heard about the matter.

It also soon became evident that some civilian bureaucrats could rival anything the Navy had to offer. The eraser on the mechanical pencil I was using wore down. I had to go to the person in charge of consumables to replace it, and was reluctantly given one eraser. The associated time loss cost considerably more than the whole box. When I pointed that out to my boss, he agreed but stated that this situation had come about because consumables had been misused to the point where the expense had become unacceptable. Later, my order for an Electrical Engineering text was rejected because experience had shown that such books disappear. But pointing out that one valid use more than paid for a book's cost ended that restriction.

Diamond Power had a soot blower controls design engineer whose work showed that he was capable of much more. He said that he was doing just what he wanted to do and was satisfied with his pay. That was an ideal situation for him and for his boss.

My biggest problem with my staff came from a deviation from the engineering drawings in the control system being built. My manufacturing counterpart said that my liaison engineer had changed the system. We restored the as-designed configuration. My liaison engineer reluctantly accepted not being able to make changes without lead designer engineer approval and resigned a few weeks later. Several months later, Personnel told me that he had asked to return. But we no longer needed his services.

Cost Disputes

We had continual disputes with B&W Lynchburg about our product costs. The system specification had a huge raft of reference requirements, plus a general clause incorporating any other references that turned out to be pertinent (another General Prudential Rule). That made agreeing on system characteristics and costs difficult. I once pointed out to my boss that we had just spent, in travel and interaction time for the group involved in a meeting, more money than we were contesting—and had then given up when we were right. But, months later, I found out that our Vice President of Finance had adjusted the sale price to cover all our expenses.

One cost dispute triggered a great lesson for me. An electric utility insisted that a feature be added to their nuclear plant's control rod control system at no cost. I, and my bosses, disagreed. But when our customer took umbrage at my tactless statement that they were asking for something for nothing, Diamond Power's president made sure that I knew that such treatment of a customer could end my employment. I didn't have to be told that twice. That experience also soon had a tangible benefit when a General Electric salesman told me that we shouldn't expect to get early deliveries from them because we were competitors. But after our president's discussion with a GE vice president, our components were promptly delivered.

Attacking the Problem

When I began my Diamond Power employment, our nuclear control system was two years behind schedule. In my first month of trying to correct that, I spent more than my entire year's budget. That raised eyebrows but produced no recriminations.

Early in my stint at Diamond Power, the Executive Vice President asked me about ways to speed up the work. I pointed out that I had a PhD electrical engineer who had to stand in a long line to get the drawings he needed. The next morning I was told to hire another technician. And another drawing issue room window was installed and staffed within three days. My Navy experience hadn't made me expect such responsiveness.

My staff grew by up to 25% in 90 days without a net ill effect. That our open work area let me talk directly with five members of my staff, with the others nearby, helped a lot with that.

After some months, Nuclear Controls Engineering became a separate section. The Nuclear Engineering Manager became my new boss and said that I now rated an office of my own. But I wanted to stay where I was, and he let me do that for a while.

The Big Picture

We began catching up on our contracts while there was still hope for a burgeoning nuclear power industry. My boss sent me to a conference on "Nuclear Power for Tomorrow." I already knew about B&W's CNSG (Containerized Nuclear Steam Generator) design for a compact, relatively small power output design that could be built at a factory and shipped intact to a locale in need of power. And I was interested in Gulf General Atomic's HTGR (High Temperature Gas-Cooled Reactor) design that scaled up their prototype to about 1000 megawatts of electricity output.

Another concept was floating nuclear power plants, proposed to be located off the coast of New Jersey. Shipboard nuclear power plants were obviously practicable. But the design lifetime of commercial nuclear power plants was 40 years, and electric utilities had conventional electrical generating stations that lasted a lot longer. That nuclear reactor plants in vessels afloat in salt water would last a lot longer than 40 years wasn't proven. I also saw some of the conference's statements as unduly optimistic. An example was terming floating nuclear power plants "unsinkable," the first usage of that word I knew of since it was applied to the Titanic. Diamond Power's Sales Manager gleefully pounced on that. But that potential problem had little to do with the offshore concept not being implemented. Commercial Nuclear Power foundered because of concern about nuclear radiation.

The Culmination

By the time that I caught up with my work, B&W wasn't selling any more nuclear plants. My boss and I discussed that. He said that he was an engineer and would go on unemployment before taking a different job—my view was that even pumping gas was preferable to unemployment. I don't know what became of him after B&W's nuclear plant deliveries ended, but his considerable expertise should have kept him gainfully employed.

When our nuclear sales ceased, I was assigned tasks in Diamond Power's New Products Task Force. But I didn't know enough to identify suitable new products. And, when I was able to do my day's work in six hours, I found a job with the Atomic Energy Commission. The travel that involved made completing a Master's Degree in Industrial Engineering impractical. (I had completed about 80% of the requirements for earning one at Ohio University, but short-term financial considerations ruled the day.)

The Value

Diamond Power was a tremendous experience. I even redesigned part of our relay logic system because my staff was overloaded. And overseeing the technical writer for the system manual led me to develop a special ("Functional") engineering drawing to depict system interconnections.

Several years later, I ran into a member of my Diamond Power staff at Three Mile Island. He said that something I had done had been patented, but he didn't know what. I suspect that it was the "Functional" logic drawing.

At Diamond Power, I was held accountable for my actions and encouraged to grow. The working relationships I had there and the even-tempered management style are a fond memory.

III-2 The Kent State Tragedy

The Setting

When I left the Navy, the country was in turmoil over the Vietnam War. Tales about anti-war protestors spitting on military personnel in uniform circulated. Dissent intensified when the war expanded into Cambodia.

The Sequence

Late on Friday, May 1, 1970, protests by about 500 Kent State University students, bikers, and transients turned violent. The dissenters became a mob of about 1000 people who yelled obscenities and threw beer bottles at police.

The Friday night rioting reportedly started with spray painting *Fuck the Pigs* on the exterior of a bar that the students frequented. There weren't enough police (Kent had 21 policemen, the university 25). The mob grew. Kent's mayor declared a state of emergency and had the bars closed.

Rioting continued the next day. The mob grew to about 2000 people. Kent's mayor asked the Governor for help. When the Ohio National Guard arrived five hours later, the ROTC Building was afire. Several firemen and policemen had been struck by rocks. The fire hose was slashed. A later statement by the Guard's Adjutant General was that a sniper had fired at the Guardsmen. No Guardsmen or police were shot, and no one died from the fire, but the Guard and Police had to be concerned about potential lethal consequences.

Ohio's Governor made a desk-pounding diatribe at the Kent firehouse about the event being the product of the strongest revolutionary militia in America being bent on destroying higher education in Ohio. But the riot trigger was a national war that he couldn't address authoritatively. And his diatribe did nothing to lessen the mob's unlawful behavior.

The Governor called in the National Guard because there was no realistic alternative. Tragedy resulted when the Guard shot and killed four students and injured nine (one was permanently paralyzed from the chest down). Two of the dead were rioters; the other two were going to class. (That half the dead were bystanders isn't surprising. That the college was still open is.)

Mob fervor escalated. Attacking the Guard was envisioned. But impassioned pleading by a few faculty members dispersed the mob and prevented a much larger tragedy.

Analysis

James Michener, a Pulitzer Prize winning novelist noted for meticulous research, wrote a non-fiction book on Kent State. He assessed the rioting as a college spring frolic involving a core of radical activists abetted by a few real revolutionaries.

Michener also concluded that alcohol and drugs played no role in the Kent State rioting. But beer bottles were thrown at the police and National Guard. And it's unrealistic to conclude that alcohol played no role in rioting that started outside the cluster of bars frequented by college students—or that alcohol consumption didn't add fuel to the throwing of beer bottles at the Police and the National Guard—or that the thrown bottles (and rocks) played no role in the response of the Guardsmen.

Some students reportedly were told that, if the Guard's guns were loaded, it was with blank ammunition. If that was said, it was a dangerously irresponsible statement. Still, for youths to throw rocks and beer bottles at armed men little or no more adult than themselves doesn't make sense.

A mob is dangerous. Typical mob members see themselves as anonymous and unaccountable, and commit acts they wouldn't individually condone. Mob violence can be prevented by removing or intimidating the ringleaders, but an inadequate initial response had enabled this riot's ringleaders to incite the rioting and get away scot free.

Years earlier, while I was a National Guardsman, I had minimal training in mob control, far less than what the 1970 Ohio National Guard had gained by dealing with rioting strikers. But I had been a Guardsman of the approximate maturity of the ones in Ohio. And, as a civilian university freshman, I also was part of a group of college youths newly removed from parental supervision. To me, the Kent State riots pitted a youthful mob against substantially outnumbered Guardsmen. (Reportedly, only 77 Guardsmen were in the group that fired on the 1000-2000 person mob.)

Michener also asserted that a lot of arrests and a lot of small fines would have been far better than a few arrests with substantial jail time for each offender. That's consistent with psychology courses I took at Ohio University, during which the professor (a B.F. Skinner disciple with a BS in electrical engineering and a PhD in psychology) repeatedly asserted that the assurance of punishment is far more effective than its severity.

Much was made of the killing of "unarmed students" and of "our children." But a mob of 1000-2000 18-22 year olds is not the defenseless group that such characterizations portray.

It's nonetheless tragic to snuff out young lives, and to cause parents (who often struggle to give their children a better chance in life) to have to bury those children and endure lifelong heartache. (At whatever age it happens, the hardest death to endure is the death of one's child.)

The military draft set the stage for the Kent State rioting. Expansion of the Vietnam War into Cambodia was viewed by the students as an increased likelihood of their having to fight a war. The rationale that it was better to fight communism overseas rather than in our own country didn't appeal to them. Still, some 80%-90% of Kent State's students didn't join the mob.

Many people were and are justifiably disturbed over this preventable tragedy. But I'm not aware of a reasonable rationale (other than Michener's) being advanced about how law and order should have been restored.

There were post-event assertions that loaded guns must not be allowed in such situations and better ways of handling them must be developed. But a mob of 1000-2000 rioters is a lethal force, and heavily outnumbered, unarmed law enforcers are likely to be its victims, especially when the mob has a *Kill the Pigs* mentality.

Reports that the Guard fired in unison indicate that they may have been ordered to fire, assertions that they spontaneously fired when they were in fear of their lives notwithstanding. The closest individual shot was over 70 feet away from the Guard, and most of those who were shot were over 100 yards away. And no warning shots were fired. (At least one Guard Officer stated that firing into the air could be dangerous and could incite the mob. But carefully aimed warning shots could have showed that the guns were loaded and that restoring law and order was being undertaken seriously.)

The faulty Guard performance was widely recognized and denigrated. But the rioters' misbehavior was disregarded. A simple example of the associated misrepresentation was terming the four killings a massacre (which has a connotation of the brutal slaughter of a large number of helpless or unresisting people). But a mob's very nature is not one of unresisting helplessness, and four deaths are more akin to those in a serious car accident than to a massacre. And this mob's *Kill the Pigs* mentality, combined with hurling rocks and bottles at the National Guard, made the danger of retaliation greater. (Armed men threatened with bodily harm and with threats of death tend to have itchy trigger fingers.)

A criminal case was prepared against the firing Guardsmen. It was dismissed by a federal judge as being too weak to prosecute. Also, the riot instigators suffered no apparent consequences for their role in getting four people killed and nine injured.

To settle a successful civil suit that had been reversed on appeal and remanded, the State of Ohio paid $675,000 (the reputed estimated cost of defending the suit again).

The failure of the campus police to seek out and arrest the instigators was a major contributing factor to the deaths. But that doesn't lessen anyone else's responsibility. The University wasn't prepared for rioting. Neither was the town of Kent or the State of Ohio. Moreover, where college students live under regimes tolerant of their misbehavior, those regimes bear a responsibility for consequent violence. And the people with influence (including some Kent State instructors) who encouraged, directly or indirectly, illegal behavior by students also have a moral responsibility for contributing to the deaths.

If the rioters had limited themselves to the "peaceful assembly" that our Constitution authorizes, four dead students would have lived through the protest, and the paralyzed fifth student would have been able to walk. So every rioter also shares a moral responsibility for the deaths and injuries.

The attempt to control so many Kent State rioters with so few Guardsmen strongly indicates that Ohio's riot control training was inadequate. That also indicates that a primary fault was with the management practices that necessitated reliance on an inadequately staffed and trained law enforcement response to the violence that college students are prone to being enticed into.

Kent State's students did have valid concerns besides the war. An example Michener documented was a professor who was regularly 40 minutes late for his 50 minute classes. He reportedly told his Department Head that he had tenure and nothing could be done about it. And huge class sizes, with the students identified by number, not name, were a sore point. But Universities began in 859 AD with the University of al-Karaouine, in Fes, Morocco. Italy's University of Bologna became Europe's first in 1088, and the Universities of Oxford and Paris date back to about 1096. Harvard became America's first university in 1636. Our educational institutions have evolved for well over 1000 years. Believing that violent university students could do away with them and establish a better system is a colossal vanity. Even with the strong support of a broad cross section of our populace, that would substantially lower the quality of education.

Students do contribute substantially to educational institutions and society. But their educations are incomplete and few of them have been responsible for supporting themselves or others. And violent student behavior besides rioting is an ongoing hazard. An example is the sexual assaults that resulted in President Obama's "It's On Us" campaign to protect women on campus. And instances of student deaths from "initiations" recur. Students are just not mature and experienced enough to redesign a country. Giving them control over their schools or their government is like letting the inmates run the asylums.

Unnecessary deaths were the primary result of the Kent State rioting. Capitalism is still functioning (even in China). And Kent State University now has eight campuses and about 23,000 students. U.S. News & World Report ranks it as the USA's 194th National University. Also, the year after its tragedy, Kent State established its Center for Peaceful Change, and the university offers degree programs in Peace and Conflict Resolution. Memorials to the dead students have been erected at the sites of their four deaths. So the school's students (and faculty) should be well aware of the potential consequences of violence.

Some believe that it's naive to expect mature and sensible behavior from college students. And, to the extent that they are children, students must be protected and controlled. But, to the extent that they are responsible adults, they are accountable for the consequences of their actions. The transition to adulthood is infamously difficult, but granting privileges plus immunity from accountability to anyone is very dangerous.

Hitler's minions killed about six million Jews and about five million non-Jews—almost 14% of the German population. Denial is the way intelligent Germans (and intelligence is a German strength) avoided facing that. Their rationale seemed to be the same *We just didn't know* humbug that people still use as an excuse for activities that produce unacceptable results. That people are still in Denial about the Kent State rioting deaths shows that we're as susceptible as the German people were to being turned into cohorts in murder.

Another cause of the Kent State horror was our Pollyannaish culture that falsely ascribed goodness to our supposedly civilized populace. (That's still a serious fault.)

History recurs because we don't learn from it. A key unlearned lesson from Kent State is that those who do not comply with the directions of those whose duty it is to maintain law and order foster serious and perhaps lethal consequences. A lot more than four lives are at risk because of that. And we have seen more rioting and should expect to see more, and perhaps more lethal, mob-related violence.

III-3 Federal Regulatory Service

Dixy Lee Ray

When I joined the Atomic Energy Commission (AEC), Dixie Lee Ray was its Chairman. A brilliant scientist with a PhD in Biology, she was pro-nuclear, eccentric, and lived in a 28 foot motor home on a rural Virginia lot with her two dogs. She had imposed tougher requirements (e.g., Quality Assurance criteria) on nuclear power plants authorized before those requirements were established. And she separated the nuclear advocacy and nuclear regulatory roles of the AEC. That culminated in 1974 in the inspection and enforcement arm that hired me being made into a separate agency, the Nuclear Regulatory Commission (NRC). She followed her AEC chairmanship with a stint as Undersecretary of State, resigning in six months because of lack of input into State Department affairs, asserting as she was leaving that *anything the private sector can do, the government can do worse.* Then she successfully ran for and became a controversial (and the first woman) Governor of the State of Washington, where her unpopular evacuations of the area around Mt. St. Helens was credited with saving some 5000-30,000 lives when it erupted.

My entry into the AEC occurred soon after the new safety requirements were imposed. Tales of industry disregard for AEC field inspection became stories of yesteryear. One of those was about an AEC inspector stating that a concrete pour could not be made, standing in the way, and being told to get out of there or be deluged by concrete. That such tales described past conditions reflected the knowledge that Dixie Lee Ray greatly increased the role of federal inspection of commercial nuclear power.

Qualification

My first regulatory job was as an Inspector of Commercial Nuclear Power Plants under construction. The Regional Director, whose high intelligence and exceptional knowledge reminded me of the first Polaris Submarine Captain whom I served as Executive Officer, soon ordered the establishment of the first NRC Field Inspector qualification program, with me as the guinea pig. Finishing it gave me a much better overview of nuclear power plant construction, and the realization that the construction specialists' knowledge was so much deeper than mine that their examination of me could be very difficult. But they delved into what I needed to know as a project inspector and didn't try to display their superior knowledge with "gotchas." I answered their questions satisfactorily for some time. Then they stumped me completely, terminated the examination, took a short break, recalled me, and stated that I was now a qualified inspector. (Later, my boss said that they had expected to stump me sooner.) Inspector qualification then became a requirement.

The continuation of the onerous, seemingly unending qualifications and examinations I had undergone in the Navy, and particularly those on nuclear submarines, put a bad taste in my mouth. But, in any field of endeavor, qualification is so necessary that individuals who do not have a qualification program need to establish their own.

Inspecting

My first inspection was on an about eight man team that went to an under construction nuclear power plant. The plant's Quality Assurance Manager was on loan from another company and this nuclear utility had a long way to go to meet the new standards.

Our inspection identified about 25 violations of Title 10, Part 50 of the Code of Federal Regulations (10CFR50). As the newbie, I was tasked with citing them all. Then I became the Project Inspector for that plant and one other one. Typically, that meant an inspection week followed by a week in the Regional Office to write the inspection report. With travel to the site and an Entrance Interview on Monday, and an Exit Interview and return travel on Friday afternoon, that produced about 3.5-4 days of inspection every other week, which came to one 3.5-4 day inspection of each of my sites every four weeks.

Sometimes I was accompanied by a specialist inspector—an Electrical Engineer to review electrical equipment and wiring, or a Civil Engineer to check out structures, or a Mechanical Engineer to review pressure vessels, etc.

After a few months of this, I read an assertion that we inspected about 10% of the construction activity. Knowing there were over 500 workers on construction sites and a lot more at the architect-engineer's home office, I asked my boss how what we were doing could be construed as inspecting as much as 1%. His response showed that our selective checks of both onsite practices and test results covered a lot more than a numeric time tabulation indicated.

Inspection Frictions

The QA Manager for the plant that was further behind in upgrading its quality assurance soon complained that the cost was adding $7 million a year to their expenses. Neither I nor my management sympathized with that.

The other plant I was assigned also had heartburn over the new standards. Their company had been an electricity supplier very early and their practices were well set. Our first dispute was over the diesel engines that provided emergency power to restart the plant in case of a blackout. Those diesels were well-proven engines of the same type as the ones on many U.S. diesel-electric submarines, and were classified and controlled as safety-related. But their fuel was normal commercial supply, with no additional checks. The pedigree oriented licensee stated that classifying the fuel as safety-related wasn't practicable because the suppliers couldn't provide the requisite documentation. They also argued that air was needed to operate the diesels and wasn't safety-related, so diesel fuel didn't have to be.

My position was that air to the diesels was safety-related and was continually proven suitable by the operability of the vehicles driven to and from the power plant. The licensee then pointed out that there were hydrogen tanks on site and a major leak might pollute the air supply to the emergency diesels. I responded that, if that was so, the tanks had to be relocated, but that plant design had to have taken that into account, and the hydrogen added to diesel-electric submarine diesel engine air intakes during battery charging increased their power output for a given fuel use rate. Then, after confirming that the diesel engine technical manual included fuel quality specifications, I cited the licensee for not treating diesel fuel as safety-related.

The licensee appealed my citation to the AEC's/NRC's Licensing Office, which ruled that all consumables required for the operation of safety-related equipment are safety-related. Licensee checks of delivered and stored diesel fuel's conformance to the diesel manufacturer's fuel specifications were then instituted.

The licensee employee who was so insistent about the diesel fuel had a cohort who could be expected to make the same point repeatedly: power plants had to be cost competitive and nuclear power was too expensive. But, when asked why they were undertaking the cost of nuclear power generation, a more senior licensee manager stated that the country's need for power required utilizing every potential power source. (Both licensee employees who often opposed federal regulatory requirements retired within a few years.)

Many years later, I saw another case of a paper-oriented focus on quality assurance raise its ugly head. In this case, a Security Supervisor was concerned about being able to obtain certification that his site's security camera coverage was sufficient. The way to provide the needed assurance became clear when it was pointed out that assurance of continuity of surveillance camera coverage can and should consider not only Mean Time Between Failure ratings of cameras but camera coverage overlap, availability of spares, power source reliability, and time required to replace faulty cameras.

Regulatory Management

My first regulatory boss was even-tempered and made his points clearly and positively, without rancor or derogation. That contrasted with the "ass-chewing" orientation I had occasionally encountered. Overall, he was the best boss I ever had.

Government employment also reintroduced me to a superficial management style. Discussions of problem areas with our headquarters seemed to always include one person who immediately blamed someone (else) for the problem. That input usually was temporarily held in abeyance. (Putting a fire out typically takes precedence over arsonist identification.)

After about a year, I became a section chief who supervised inspectors of power reactors that were preparing to operate. Later, I became a section chief for inspectors of operating nuclear power plants. Initially, my inspectors operated out of the regional office, traveling to their plants on a schedule much like the one I had followed.

Resident Inspection

The inspection process was modified when resident inspectors were assigned to each nuclear power plant site in 1978. Their inspection provided more inspection coverage and better overview of site activities, and enabled better tailoring of inspection to the more safety-significant activities at each site.

Transition to Computers

Inspection reports were reviewed and signed by managers in the Regional Office. So having resident inspectors meant back and forth report mailing time between the regional and resident offices. I advocated using personal computers to prepare and review the reports. That was resisted. (An NRC Regional Administrator once told me that one had to know when change can be made or exigencies would doom it. He also said that better men than he and me put together had gone under trying to fix the things we were talking about.) Eventually, however, my Division Director stated that this was my idea and my job to prove it would work, and asked me where I wanted the trial resident office computer. That one of my resident inspectors had a computer savvy secretary made that choice simple.

Some months later, the Division Director chewed me out for not having enough information on a problem at the computerized site. He said that I needed to get the resident inspector away from the computer and out in the plant. But this was a communication problem. The inspector, aided by being freed up by the computer and part-time secretary, was on top of the situation.

We soon equipped all resident offices with computers, and began issuing reports within a few days of inspection completion. The impact of that on the Regional Office was soon evident. In the large room the typing pool had occupied, there were now about three typists at work and a large number of empty typing stations. That drove home the point that beneficial change can require reconfiguring the work force.

A Responsibility Lesson

When the Regional Office emergency preparedness staff reported to me, we requested a computer that could handle related assessment functions. It wasn't delivered for a long time, reportedly because of budgeting constraints. When it finally arrived, the inspector who unpacked it found an invoice that listed the price. It was higher than the cost of the same machine in a computer magazine ad that identified the government's contract number. The ad price was for one computer and the NRC should have been able to get a group discount. In addition, the computer we had gotten at a higher price came without the monitor included with the advertised one. My inspector was outraged that we had to wait because of money constraints while the agency was paying well over market value. He said that the matter should be reported to the Inspector General. I said that was his right and tried to find out more.

The first feedback was that the invoice shouldn't have been included with the computer. But hiding the cost hid the problem. Follow-up by our Administrative Department Head then identified the purchase as part of the required use of minority contractors by our headquarters. Stating that purchases should be competitive and not a grant of money was followed by competitive, Regional Office purchase of its own computers. I then forgot about the matter until a 2011 college scandal highlighted a related issue.

That scandal hit the headlines when reported sexual abuse by a Penn State assistant football coach went unaddressed. The school's head football coach, Joe Paterno, had relayed a report of sexual misbehavior by his assistant coach to Penn State's Athletic Director, who informed Penn State's President. Nothing was done. When that came out during the Commonwealth of Pennsylvania's investigation of alleged long-term child molestation by the Assistant Coach, the School President resigned and the Athletic Director's and Coach Paterno's contracts were terminated. Reverberations were felt in universities across the nation. The assistant coach was convicted and sentenced to 30 years in jail.

Many people thought that Coach Paterno shouldn't have been fired. But Paterno said he should have done more, and the scandal tainted his legacy. His situation was different from mine, but we both reported wrongdoing. And the lack of follow-up made the impact of the Penn State problem huge.

The lesson here is that simply reporting wrongdoing isn't enough. Those who do nothing more can be held accountable for that, and the more serious the problem, the greater their punishment.

Staff Cuts

Years after its buildup, the NRC experienced staffing cuts. Those applied equally to every government agency, reputedly to avoid unacceptable infighting. (To anyone who tries to change that under our political system, I offer a mocking phrase I first heard in Japan: *Rotsa Ruck, Boy-san.*)

Our field office cuts were compounded by transfers to headquarters. The more we shrunk, the bigger it seemed our headquarters needed to be. The mantra was: *We've got to do more with less.* But, with fewer resources, less gets done.

Entrapment in Trivia

One day, the loudness of a dispute in the office next to mine made me privy to the discussion. No safety issues were mentioned. At issue was the address on an inspection report cover page. The section chief insisted that it be written in possessive form in accordance with the rules of grammar. The inspector insisted that it be in plural form in accordance with the name of the community. (Their dispute was analogous to whether a title was Johns Cove or John's Cove). Anger compounded the vehemence until the exasperated inspector took leave for the rest of the day and stalked out of the office. This inane argument was a lesson in not letting trivia replace substance and in how being right can be insignificant compared to the value of moving on.

Bureaucratese

Each word requires a finite time to read, so the more concise a message, the better. But we suffered from having a lot of long, hard to read memos. So, when the Regional Administrator assigned me to draft a reply to a headquarters memo about a prospective change to our inspection program, my draft just stated that the change would not work for three reasons, each of which was stated in one or two lines. The Regional Administrator had his Technical Assistant put that in "agency format." I had a hard time finding my three points in the three page memo that went out (and raised no hackles).

Our inspection reports also suffered from obfuscating verbiage until a better focus on safety eliminated unnecessary boilerplate. My part in that was recognized when my boss said that he couldn't understand how I, who had taught the whole agency how to write reports, could have produced such a bad licensee assessment.

Networking

The NRC strongly emphasized networking. Knowledgeable inputs and evaluations are essential, but politic inputs and concurrences usually delay accomplishment and diffuse accountability. That can be more harmful in government offices where profitability's Sword of Damocles plays no role.

My diesel fuel issue, if it hadn't been so clear cut, might have been networked within the regulatory staff, with an internal conclusion reached before enforcement action was taken. But the only internal Commission discussion needed in this case was the phone call to me by a headquarters quality assurance specialist to let me know about the licensee's appeal and agree that the citation was valid.

In a different, much later case, I had an inspector use the Student T Distribution to assess a small number of data points. Headquarters referred that to an agency statistician, who said we should have used the Normal Distribution and recalculated the data. His 1% different result changed no conclusion but (I thought) protected his rice bowl.

I didn't always agree with networked outcomes in the NRC. But I never experienced any NRC situation in which I thought the safety concern(s) got less than appropriate consideration.

Work Hours

Power Plant event responses could become over 100 hour work weeks for participants. For example, early on during the Three Mile Island accident (addressed in the part of this book about The Nuclear Boogeyman), for those of us on the site even our meals involved work discussion and the only breaks we took were for sleeping. But my ordinary NRC work week was 50-60 hours, less than the time my bosses typically put in. (Some of their time may have involved the politic practice of not leaving the office while their boss was still there.)

There can be a down side to hard work. We had a Regional Administrator who accomplished much by working about 14 hours a day, including weekends. But he ignored a low grade fever for a prolonged period, and the cancer that caused it was by then lethal. So his priorities were a major contributor to his death.

Dedication

There's usually more than enough work to be done, and work quality and volume determine each employee's value. Those who work harder and longer are favored in pay raises, promotions, and advancements. (Forty hour work weeks are a myth except for those paid by the hour but, when time spent takes precedence over productivity, it's time to consider other employment.)

Some people, if they get to work early, sit in their cars until the designated start time. They're also likely to be among the first ones out the door at the designated end of the work day. Usually, they're advanced only when there's no other choice.

Pick the Best

When recruiting was my collateral duty, a colleague told me that it wasn't in our own best interest to hire individuals as capable as the ones I was bringing in. But top-notch people pay off long term—like a high rate of compound interest. And even if mandates or political correctness require hiring based on official or unofficial quotas, searching far and wide can minimize or prevent lowering the level of competence.

Regulatory Burden

A Small Business Administration Study reportedly found that government regulations cost over $10,000 per employee. That's huge. But a danger like an E coli outbreak morphs the cry for cutbacks in "unnecessary" regulation into excoriation of the failure to protect the public. And we all benefit from the mandatory safety advances forced on the auto industry by the government. Unfortunately, the key factor of the benefit achieved by regulation is too often overlooked.

The QA Manager who told me that the requirements we were imposing cost his utility $7 million a year may have exaggerated, but the rules that the NRC enforces under the Atomic Energy Act are enormously expensive. On the other hand, Russia's Chernobyl nuclear power plant was built and operated under much less stringent rules than the ones imposed on Three Mile Island Unit 2. The Chernobyl accident cost hundreds of billions of dollars and about 50 lives; the accident at Three Mile Island (TMI) cost a billion dollars and no lives. Did we over-regulate TMI?

Such considerations remind me of the discontinued OpNav 34P1, U.S. Navy Safety Precautions. I still associate it with the phrase *Safety Precautions are written in blood*.

Leaving Federal Service.

When yet another NRC reorganization and staff cut began, I recalled that, about ten years after he retired at age 75, my father said that I should retire as soon as I could—so I wouldn't be too old to enjoy it. I also had known an NRC inspector who died two months after retiring after a long career. And I saw no safety benefit in the coming changes. Besides, younger employees were better able to adapt to the new setup. So I retired. I've since been told many times that I did that too soon. But retiring (almost) made me my own boss. And that's Liberty.

Part IV

The Nuclear Boogeyman

(A Personal Assessment of Nuclear
Weapons and Nuclear Power)

IV-1 Nuclear Weapons

Background

Forces that aren't understood are feared. And the fear that the atomic bomb has evoked is a clear example of how emotion trumps objective reason in human affairs. But nuclear energy needs to be logically placed in a valid overall perspective.

My assessment of nuclear weapons (and nuclear power) is based on: skepticism; Navy education and training; duty aboard U.S. Navy nuclear powered and nuclear armed submarines; Nuclear Regulatory Commission (NRC) training in accident review; NRC inspection and enforcement experience with commercial nuclear power plants, including accident stricken Three Mile Island; and publicly available information.

I'm retired with no personal or financial link to nuclear energy or its opposition. That and (I believe) my Navy experience and the safety assurance aspect of my previous regulatory role minimize my bias about nuclear weapons and nuclear power generation. Further, I believe that age has enabled me to seek and, like Statesman and Philosopher and Essayist Michel de Montaigne, speak the truth more than I could earlier.

The Atomic Bomb

General awareness of nuclear energy began with the use of atomic bombs on Japan in World War II. Their horrendous devastation produced great opposition to nuclear weapons. But that opposition has too often been expressed out of context, I suspect mainly by members of later generations that weren't substantially impacted, as my generation was, by WWII (including seeing the Gold Star Service Flags displayed by families who lost a member to it).

Hatred of Japan erupted in America when the December 7, 1941 Japanese "sneak" attack on Pearl Harbor killed 2400 Americans and devastated our Pacific Fleet. It escalated when Japan conquered the Philippines and over 6000 American and Filipino war prisoners died on the 80 mile Bataan Death March. The first Death March atrocity was summary execution of 350-400 Filipino fighters who had surrendered. No medical care or supplies were provided to the marchers, who got no food for the first three days and got their only water from buffalo wallows beside the road. Some fell and were bayoneted. Others were beheaded by mounted officers using samurai swords. The "justification" was that honorable warriors kill themselves before surrendering—the others are subhuman.

Our perception of the Japanese was based on news, movies and propaganda. (An image I retain is a movie scene depicting Caucasians forced to dig a trench-like community grave, lined up along its edge, and machine-gunned into it.)

Japan forced the men on Pacific islands (e.g., Indonesia, Malaya, Singapore) into brutal slave labor and tortured them (having surrendered, they too were subhuman and without honor). Tales have since been related about captive females on a starvation diet being forced to stand in tropical heat and humidity for 24 hours without food, water, or respite. Children, the aged, and the ill died on their feet.

The hatred was mutual. Japan's view that we were barbaric, inhumanly cruel monsters was fostered by its military.

The Japanese preference for death over surrender was shown by mass civilian suicides on Saipan and Okinawa. There were even reports that the Japanese military killed Okinawan civilians unwilling to commit suicide, and used others to draw allied fire to better enable ambushing the attackers. There also are ardent assertions that the suicides were all voluntary. In any case, fear of anticipated atrocious treatment and the code that honored suicide and reviled surrender played major roles.

Aspects of Japan's culture that had to be considered in assessing the consequences of invasion included atrocities that weren't made public at the time. Those included cannibalizing executed prisoners, and even cutting flesh from prisoners who were still alive. (Check Japanese Cannibalism on the Internet.)

Another factor was the insistence on unconditional surrender. It had been imposed on Germany and the Allies were determined to exact it from Japan. (Germany's return to a path of conquest after the armistice that ended WWI was an underlying reason.)

That Japan was destined to lose WWII was indicated about a year into the war. In June 1942, Japan tried to establish an airfield on Guadalcanal, a 2500 square mile island along the American supply route to Australia and New Zealand. Our August 1942 response was a U.S. Marine landing force supplemented by Army troops. By the end of the vicious jungle fighting in February 1943, the U.S. had lost 2000 of its cadre of 60,000 warriors. Japan lost about two-thirds of its 31,400 soldiers, evacuated the rest, and the irreplaceable loss of elite Japanese pilots in the air battles marked the end of Japan's control of the air. But Japan remained determined to wage war.

Saipan was a later marker. In a 24 day assault beginning on June 15, 1944, we captured that island and put our B-29 bombers in range of the Japanese mainland. The Japanese lost three aircraft carriers, 300 planes, and 97% (29,000 of 30,000) of their troops in the battle. There also were a lot of civilian suicides. The Japanese government termed those heroic and encouraged all Japanese to follow that lead when the time came. (Japan was prepared to pay a huge price to prolong the war it was losing.)

Our return to the Philippines was a huge disaster for Japan. In the October 23-26, 1944 Battle of Leyte Gulf, the largest naval battle ever fought, Japan lost 300,000 tons of warships (four aircraft carriers, three battleships, six heavy cruisers, four light cruisers, and eleven destroyers). We lost 37,000 tons (one light carrier, two escort carriers, two destroyers, and one destroyer escort). When our forces moved on to Luzon, they killed about 205,500 of its 287,000 defenders (72%). Our dead numbered about 10,400. Overall, Japan lost about 400,000 lives in the Philippines before we recaptured them early in August 1945. That's about as many lives as we lost in all of World War II.

Japanese dedication also was shown in the five week (February-March 1945) battle for Iwo Jima, a volcanic island eight square miles in area. There were no civilians on Iwo Jima. It was defended by 22,000 soldiers in heavily fortified bunkers, hidden artillery positions, and 11 miles of underground tunnels. We attacked with 70,000 U.S. Marines and control of the sea and of the air. Victory cost us 6821 dead (9.7%) and 19,217 wounded. Japan had 18,844 deaths (85.6%). 216 Japanese were taken prisoner. 3000 went into hiding. (Some Japanese were captured because they were incapacitated.) Projecting that dedication on the entire Japanese Army indicates that five million of its over six million soldiers would have died if we invaded Japan. But that doesn't consider civilian deaths among Japan's 72 million people.

The 82-day (April-June 1945) Okinawa invasion was another indicator. It cost 149,000 civilian lives, 77,000 Japanese military deaths, and 14,000 Allied deaths. The about 225,000 deaths among the 400,000 Japanese on Okinawa were more deaths than the atomic bombings caused. And the 14,000 Allied deaths were 2.8% of the population conquered. A direct correlation to Japan's WWII population of 72 million people is 32 million Japanese deaths and over 2 million allied deaths. But, because Okinawa is about 350 miles south of Japan and not part of the Japanese homeland, that could be a substantial underestimate.

Our Okinawa assault forces numbered about 500,000 and included the U.S. 5th Fleet's 300 warships and 1139 other ships. (Four UK aircraft carriers and 21 supporting vessels, a formidable force, were a minuscule addition in comparison.) A wiser Japan would have capitulated when it saw our ever-increasing onslaught by an ever-increasing force of ever-increasing power.

Most of Japan's air might was destroyed before we attacked Okinawa. Still, kamikaze attacks from Japanese territory (e.g., Kyushu) sank 36 allied ships and damaged 368. But over 1400 more Japanese pilots died, and no allied transport carrying assault forces and no warship larger than a destroyer was sunk.

Japan also committed a national symbol of her Imperial might to Okinawa. In Operation Ten-Go, the 70,000 ton battleship Yamato, whose main armament was nine 18.1" guns, was ordered to proceed to Okinawa, beach herself, and fight until she was destroyed. Her task force included the light Cruiser Yahagi and eight destroyers.

Yamato had a full ammunition load, but only enough fuel for a one-way trip was authorized. (She had more fuel, but not enough for a round trip.)

Two U.S. submarines spotted and reported Yamato. Our carrier-based dive and torpedo bombers attacked. Yahagi sank after being hit by about 12 bombs and 7 torpedoes. Yamato, hit by at least 11 torpedoes and six bombs, capsized and sank about 184 miles south of Kyushu. Over 3000 of her crew of 3332 died. The four remaining destroyers rescued survivors and went home.

Ten-Go was commanded by Vice Admiral Seiichi Itō. He had opposed it until he was told that Emperor Hirohito expected the Navy to attack. But he chose to go down with Yamato.

Near the end of the assault, U.S. Army Lieutenant General Simon Bolivar Buckner was inspecting his troops on the battlefield when a Japanese artillery attack made him the highest ranking allied death in the war. (Hopefully, that curtailed such inspections.)

Lieutenant General Mitsuru Ushijima, the highest ranking Japanese to die in WWII, also died on Okinawa. He reported that he and his troops had done all they could, apologized to the emperor for the failure, and pledged a final attack. When it failed, the General (and his staff) committed ritual suicide.

Note. A Peace Memorial erected on Okinawa in 1995 lists over 240,000 names of allied and Japanese military and civilian deaths associated with the battle.

Invaded countries suffer especially great losses. Of the 60-85 million Word War II deaths, Germany lost almost 6 million people and Russia about 25 million, while the uninvaded United States lost about 400,000 and Great Britain lost about 450,000.

Our projected 400,000-800,000 U.S. military deaths during the invasion of Japan would have doubled or tripled our WWII death total. We projected that 5-10 million Japanese would die during the invasion, and the estimate of Vice Admiral Ōnishi of the Imperial Japanese Navy General Staff was up to 20 million. The actual WWII Japanese death toll was about 3 million.

Those death projections may have been tailored to the estimators' agendas. And the conditions on which loss estimates are based typically change radically when the firing starts. But the Allies were determined to exact unconditional surrender, the Japanese were determined to fight to the death, and the invasion death toll would have been horrendous.

A noteworthy example of Japan's fanaticism was its most famous war holdout, Army Second Lieutenant Hiroo Onoda, an intelligence officer on Lubang Island in the Western Philippines. He lived on scavenged and stolen food and conducted guerilla warfare there for 29 years after the war—until his former Commanding Officer came to Lubang in December 1974 and relieved him of his duties. Onoda returned to Japan as a hero. But he never endorsed its American-style democracy: his post-war book stated: *Life is not fair and people are not equal. Some people eat better than others.*

Japan's determination also was described in a December 1946 article in *The Atlantic* by Dr. Karl T. Compton, a renowned physicist and the president of the Massachusetts Institute of Technology. During a two month stint with General Macarthur and his staff, he participated in the interrogation of a knowledgeable and intelligent Japanese Army officer. That officer said that, if WWII hadn't ended, the allies probably would have invaded Kyushu about November 1, 1945. (That was the since published plan, and the Japanese buildup would have reduced the 3:1 allied manpower advantage on the Pacific islands to about 1:1.) He also stated that he thought that Japan couldn't have stopped the invasion, but: *We would have kept on fighting until all Japanese were killed, but we would not have been defeated* (disgraced by surrender). Compton also noted MacArthur's statement, a month after we occupied Japan, that loss of Japanese government control and its former soldiers taking to guerilla warfare in the mountains could take a million troops ten years to overcome.

Compton (and MacArthur's staff) believed that Japan's defense would have been more fanatic than Iwo Jima's and Okinawa's. He also noted that *"All war is inhuman"* and that the two incendiary bombings of Tokyo killed about 225,000 people and destroyed 85 square miles of the densest part of the city—more damage than the atomic bombs had done.

Additional hundreds of thousands of Japanese were burned alive by napalm bombings of 67 Japanese cities. General Curtis Lemay, the architect of those bombings, reportedly told his cohort, then Lt.Col. Robert S. McNamara, that "If we'd lost the war, we'd all have been prosecuted as war criminals." (Movie *The Fog of War*, as cited on ditext.com)

An alternative to invading Japan came with the successful July 16, 1945 Trinity test of an implosion atomic bomb at the White Sands Proving Ground in New Mexico Ten days later, U.S. President Harry S. Truman, UK Prime Minister Winston Churchill, and Nationalist China's Chairman Chiang Kai-shek issued the Potsdam Declaration. Its provisions included:

We call upon the government of Japan to proclaim now the unconditional surrender of all Japanese armed forces, and to provide proper and adequate assurances of their good faith in such action. The alternative for Japan is prompt and utter destruction...We will not deviate (from those terms). There are no alternatives. We shall brook no delay.

Declaration broadcasts were aimed at Japan in English and in Japanese. Leaflets containing it were dropped on Japan. And President Truman, in a speech picked up by Japanese news agencies, stated that, if Japan didn't accept the Declaration, it could *expect a rain of ruin from the air, the like of which has never been seen on this earth.* Japan's Prime Minister Suzuki then affirmed, to the Japanese press, Japan's commitment to fight on.

Twelve days later, on August 6, 1945, an atomic bomb (*Little Boy*) was dropped on Hiroshima. It was basically a gun that fired one subcritical Uranium mass onto another, creating a highly supercritical mass equivalent to about 15,000 tons of TNT. That explosion devastated Hiroshima. But Japan did not surrender.

Two days later, on August 8, Russia declared war on Japan and invaded Japanese-occupied Manchuria with a million troops. That attack went very well. And the next day, our second atomic bomb targeted Nagasaki. This bomb, *Fat Man*, contained Plutonium surrounded by explosives that, when detonated, compressed the

Plutonium into a highly supercritical mass that exploded with a force equivalent to about 20,000 tons of TNT.

Note. A subcritical mass cannot sustain a nuclear chain reaction. A critical mass does. Nuclear reactors are made minutely supercritical (or subcritical) to raise (or lower) power and return to criticality at the new power level. Only a highly supercritical mass (not achievable in a power reactor) can produce a nuclear bomb.

The atomic bombs killed about 100,000 Japanese. (That total would double in four months.) But the Japanese people were so isolated that the atomic bombings, incendiary bombings, and the failure to hold any Pacific island hadn't changed their conviction that they were winning the war.

Alec Davis (See Gyokusai and Ketsu Go on www.indiana.edu) documented Japan's plan to avoid unconditional surrender by Ketsu Go (massive opposition to the invasion) and by Gyokusai (individual suicide attacks by the general populace). A member of the Japanese General staff reportedly asserted that *20 million Gyokusai and victory will be ours.*

No foreign country had ever occupied the Japanese home islands, and tradition held that no organized group of Japanese soldiers had ever surrendered. Plans were made to mobilize all men from age 14 to age 60 and all women from age 16 to age 40. 5000 kamikaze aircraft were to oppose the landing. Suicide boats were to be used against the landing craft. Soldiers were trained to throw themselves under tanks and detonate explosives strapped to their backs. Elementary school students were taught that anyone unwilling to die for the emperor was a coward. And the night before the recording of the surrender statement was to be broadcast, there was an attempted coup d'état involving occupation of the Emperor's Palace to capture the recording. A Lieutenant General opposing the coup was shot and hacked to death, but the coup failed and its two leaders committed suicide. The next day, August 14, the recording became Emperor Hirohito's first radio broadcast to the Japanese people. It stated:

...We have ordered our government to communicate to the governments of the United States, Great Britain, China and the Soviet Union that our empire accepts the provisions of their joint declaration....the enemy has begun to employ a new and most cruel bomb, the power of which to do damage is, indeed, incalculable, taking the toll of many innocent lives. Should we continue to fight, it would not only result in an ultimate collapse and obliteration of the Japanese nation, but also it would lead to the total extinction of human civilization.

Among the Japanese who recognized the futility of continuing the war was Kido Koishi, Lord Keeper of the Emperor's Personal Seal. He termed the atomic bombings *a gift from Heaven* that allowed Japan to surrender.

Note. We didn't have another atomic bomb. Seven more were expected to be ready by November 1, 1945.

The atomic bombs killed about 52% of the 385,000 people in Hiroshima and Nagasaki. Those two cities now have about 1.5 million people and average background radiation levels.

An August 7, 2014 Zachery Keck article in *The Diplomat* stated:

...It's impossible to know how many people would have perished if allied forces invaded Japan....Hiroshima and Nagasaki were unspeakable tragedies (as was much of WWII). But whether one believes the decision to use atomic weapons was correct or not, and whatever one believes the motives of the U.S. leaders were, that decision ended up saving millions of lives.

Basically, two atomic bombs ended a 3.5 year war in four days. That saved half a million (maybe several million) allied lives and five million (maybe 25 million) Japanese lives at a cost of 200,000 Japanese lives. That's from 25-100 lives saved for each life lost.

The condemners of the atomic bomb did not face the prospect of invading Japan and being responsible for and having to justify the major increase in U.S. deaths in order to avoid killing the hated Japanese who started this war while deceptively conducting peace talks—and waged it with the barbaric cruelty that the Bataan Death March characterized.

A group whose condemnation of the atomic bombings would have had considerable merit was the Gold Star Service Flag families and the military personnel who were vulnerable to being killed if the U.S. Government had used less than the powers at its disposal to win the war—or in any way sacrificed American lives to avoid killing those who started the war.

Japan now renounces war and the use of force to settle international disputes. Strong support by the Japanese people has kept that mandate intact. That's a huge change for a tiny nation that warred against China, against Russia, against the Mongols, and against Korea—and had internal warfare between its competing tribes since about 10,000 BC. (Lack of trust in America's commitment to protect Japan and concern about other Asian nations' intentions could change Japan's rejection of war.)

Eight other nations reputedly have nuclear weapons: Russia, the United Kingdom, France, China, India, Pakistan, North Korea, and Israel. (Iran seems to be on the way to becoming the ninth.) Are any of them fanatic enough to use them on us?

IV-2 Radiation

Basics

Radioactivity is the emission of electromagnetic waves or subatomic particles from atomic nuclei. The word was coined by Marie (Sklodowska) Curie (11/7/1867-7/4/1934). She won Nobel prizes in Physics and in Chemistry and was the first female Nobel Prize winner, the first female professor at the Sorbonne, and the only winner of Nobel prizes in two different sciences. Her scientific discoveries included Polonium (named for her native Poland) and Radium (named for its high radioactivity). Her death at age 66 from aplastic anemia (inability to replace blood cells) was attributed to long-term exposure to radioactivity.

Radiation is the waves or subatomic particles emitted by radioactive materials. It has ionizing properties that damage body tissue by breaking both strands of the DNA helix. The body does have repair mechanisms (Nonhomologous End Joining and Homologous Recombination) for that, but they aren't as effective as its healing mechanisms for single strand DNA breaks.

Acute radiation doses (high doses received over a short period of time) are potentially lethal. Low doses are a different consideration. For example, according to the National Institute of Health's National Cancer Institute website, the radiation that normal tissue can safely receive is known for all parts of the body and doctors take potential damage to normal cells into account during cancer radiotherapy. (That enables oncologists to kill cancer tumors with focused high radiation doses without killing enough normal cells to kill their patients.)

Solar Radiation

There's a long-standing assumption that **all** radiation is harmful. But moderate exposure to sunshine is beneficial, and the sun is a nuclear (fusion) reactor. Its ultraviolet (UV) radiation causes our skins to produce Vitamin D, which protects against weak, brittle bones and osteoporosis. UV radiation also increases melanin production, providing greater protection from solar radiation's ionizing effect. And sunshine and photosynthesis enable, every Spring, the Earth to blossom and its animals to reproduce. In temperate zones, if water and fertile soils are abundant and people are sensible, sunshine is highly beneficial. Then, when Summer and Fall end and sunshine wanes, we come to the season in which "Winter Kills."

The effect of a lack of solar radiation was very evident in extreme Northern Hemisphere cooling in 535-536 AD. (Eruption of El Salvador's Ilopango Caldera caused the cooling, according to a February 25, 2015 *Earth Magazine* article.) The results included snow in summer, widespread crop failure, famine, and flooding. (See ScienceHeathen.com and Knowledgenuts.com)

Concerns about blocking out solar radiation have included fear of a "Nuclear Winter" being caused by nuclear war. That has a sound basis in global cooling events. But sunshine's benefits (and oncology's successes) show that not **all** radiation is harmful.

Radiation Hormesis

Radiation Hormesis is the hypothesis that radiation doses at or near the natural background radiation level cause the body to develop resistance to radiation.

France credits Radiation Hormesis. International authorities reportedly reject it because there's no supporting evidence. But that's true for all low radiation dose effects on the body, and the alleged benefit of Radiation Hormesis is like some effects that we know. Sunshine is one example. Exercise that increases the ability to endure physical stress is another. A third is vaccines that stimulate the body to produce antibodies to disease

Also, tiny doses of some poisons have therapeutic medical uses, and overdoses of substances that the body needs can be seriously toxic. Potassium chloride is an example. It's an over-the-counter table salt substitute. Doctors prescribe it in higher doses to correct potassium deficiency. And its cardiac arrest properties in much higher doses made it a part of a lethal injection used to impose the death penalty.

A reputed instance of Radiation Hormesis was a major decrease in cancers, in Taiwan, among apartment dwellers exposed to radioactive Cobalt-60. (That's further described later.) There are also tales of a lack of related adverse health effects in occupants of stone buildings with above background radiation. And, except for preventable thyroid cancers near Chernobyl, no low level radiation harm has been found near nuclear and coal-fired power plants (that's also discussed later).

On the other hand, blows with a blunt object may increase one's vulnerability to them. And the sunshine that enables life as we know it to exist can be dangerous. One of my high school classmates spent his childhood summers outside wearing only short pants and has since had several melanomas removed. Another basked in the "healthy" sun and turned her fair, freckled skin a dark tan every year. She subsequently has had several squamous cell carcinomas removed. They've survived their cancerous growths, but their experience is consistent with the WebMD generalization that being in the sun (or a tanning booth) increases the risk of developing skin cancer. And Radiation Hormesis, if it exists, has an upper limit.

Radiation Safety Indoctrination

Navy radiation safety training taught about Madam Curie's death and the radiation-induced deaths of workers who painted luminescent radioactive coatings on clock dials (using their mouths and tongues to put a fine point on their brushes). We also heard about dentists losing their thumbs from radiation received by holding x-ray plates in place while taking tooth x-rays. That fostered a lasting aversion to exposure to radiation.

EBE CHANDLER MCCABE, JR.

We were also taught that the allowed 5 rem annual radiation dose was based on that dosage being received for 50 years (actually 47 years) and causing no harm. That's reasonable: life on earth has always been exposed to background radiation, so an ability to withstand and heal its ill effects has developed. (Rem means roentgen equivalent man/mammal, a measure of the ionizing energy imparted to human or other mammalian tissue.)

LD-50

The atomic bombs killed 50% of the Hiroshima and Nagasaki victims who received a radiation dose of 450 rem. That dose was termed LD-50 (Lethal Dose - 50%).

LD-50 has a range of about 340-550 rem (without medical intervention) and about 480-990 rem (with medical intervention). And it may be identified as LD-50/60 to show a 60 day time frame for receipt of that dose. But the 450 rem LD-50 is based on a composite of a huge number of acute, high, whole body radiation dose victims, making it representative for doses without medical intervention—despite the fact that age, health, physical condition, life style, etc. affect each individual's ability to withstand radiation.

The Linear No Threshold Model

The Linear No Threshold (LNT) model has long been used to predict radiation lethality: It has two underlying assumptions: (1) **all** radiation is harmful; and (2) radiation damage is directly proportional to the dose received. That LNT model graphs as a straight line between zero rem, zero deaths and 450 rem, 50% deaths (LD-50). It provides a Lethal Dose Percentage (LD%), for "average" humans, of the rem dose received (R) divided by 9.

$$(LD\%)_{LNT} = R/9$$

Massachusetts Institute of Technology (MIT) Tech Talk, Vol. 38, No. 18 and newsoffice.mit.edu affirm the 450 rem LD-50 and adds that 600 rem killed everyone who received it. (Another source put the 100% lethality dose at 599 rem.) Proportionality (linearity) therefore requires that radiation lethality graph as a straight line between 300 rem, zero deaths and 600 rem, 100% deaths. So, either radiation doses below 300 rem aren't lethal to the average human or radiation's lethal consequences aren't directly proportional to the dose received (linear).

It's also invalid to extend the predicted consequences of radiation doses beyond the range of the data. From 450 to 600 rem, proportionality should closely approximate the actual death rate. But the lack of establishment of radiation-induced death percentages well below 450 rem means that the predicted death rate becomes increasingly unreliable as the dose rate decreases below 450 rem. And the absence of known actual low radiation dose fatalities affirms the invalidity of the LNT model for low doses.

A Nonlinear No Threshold Model

The MIT-cited LD-50 (450 rem) and LD-100 (600 rem) values combine with the zero dose, zero death assumption to define a nonlinear ENT (Exponential No Threshold) upward curving line. An equation for such a curve is:

$$(LD\%)_{ENT} = 9.537\{[9^{(R/540)}] -1\}$$

That model fits the known high dose data. But it too assumes that there's no threshold beneath which radiation doesn't cause a lethal effect on the average human being—and cannot be confirmed by actual low radiation dose mortality (because low radiation doses don't have a measurable death rate).

A Nonlinear Threshold Model

In the U.S. the annual radiation dose limit has been 5 rem for U.S. radiation workers over age 18 since 1958, with no adverse effects shown. And the International Atomic Energy Agency (IAEA) permits an emergency, one-time, up to 500 millisieverts (50 rem) radiation dose for lifesaving (or to prevent catastrophe or a large collective dose). {The corresponding U.S. Nuclear Regulatory Commission (NRC) value is 25 rem (250 millisieverts).}

Rescuers need to know their lethal risk. The emergency dose authorizations don't state any, so there's no known associated lethal potential. Assuming that IAEA's best judgment is that a 50 rem one-time dose has no lethal consequences (or they wouldn't have authorized it), that provides a best judgment assessment of the minimum threshold of radiation lethality of 50 rem

A nonlinear ET (Exponential Threshold) LD% equation based on a 50 rem radiation dose lethality threshold, 50% fatalities at 450 rem dose, and 100% fatalities at 600 rem dose is:

$$\mathbf{(LD\%)_{ET} = 13.52\{[9^{(R-50)/568}] -1\}}$$

That predicts lower, and seemingly more realistic, mortality rates than the preceding no threshold models. But it assumes (seemingly conservatively) an "average" radiation lethality threshold that isn't justified (or refuted) by low radiation dose mortality data.

Assumption's Consequences

The models of low radiation dose lethality are assumptions, not facts. And assumptions are scientifically invalid. They're even disparaged by statements like: *To "assume" makes an "ass" out of "u" and "me."* But we're not going to expose people to radiation doses high enough to kill enough (or any) of them to identify the threshold of radiation lethality. So we're stuck with the assumptions. They need to be kept conservative, but the predictions of radiation-induced deaths from low radiation doses need to be based on the best estimate of radiation lethality instead of by assuming that the Linear No Threshold model is accurate—because LNT projections result in unwarranted fear with, as discussed later, lethal consequences.

An Additional Conservatism?

50% of an atomic bomb's energy is generated as blast, 35% as fireball, and 15% as radiation. If there was conservatism in separating atomic bomb blast and fireball effects from effects due to radiation alone, radiation dose effect models exaggerate radiation fatalities.

The Life Span Study

A sophisticated (regression analysis) assessment of the long term effect of the atomic bombings was made by the Life Span Study (LSS), a U.S. and Japanese consortium's 1950-1997 assessment. The LSS studied a "cohort" of 93,000 people who were in Hiroshima and Nagasaki during the atomic bombings. (It eliminated those who did not survive for five years.)

Initially, the Life Span Study included 27,000 people who weren't in Hiroshima or Nagasaki during the bombings but were there five years later. But "inconsistencies" in mortality data for that group resulted in their data being discounted.

Cancer deaths were the focus of the Life Span Study. At its end, the surviving cohort was 47 years older than when it started, and cancer incidence increases with age. Also, according to cancerresearchuk.org, it's the leading cause of human death except for 15-24 year males, for whom transport events rank first.

The Life Span Study describes atom bomb dose effects as uncertain for doses substantially different from the estimated doses (i.e., for extrapolation). It also noted uncertainties in estimated atomic bomb doses due to shielding and location.

The LSS lost its unirradiated control group, has inaccuracies in radiation dose estimates, and extrapolates (extends the range of interest beyond the range that the data justifies). And 70 years after the atomic bombings and 19 years after the Life Span Study ended, that Study hasn't provided scientifically credible quantification of low radiation dose effects.

Known Radiation Effects

Some atomic bomb victims died immediately. Others soon died from severe body damage. More died later from infection. (High radiation doses drop infection fighting white blood cell counts—down to zero in severe cases—for about three weeks before the body starts ramping them back up.) The LNT model is our best source of prediction of the deaths caused by high radiation doses. But the NRC has found no correlation of within limit radiation doses to adverse health consequences.

People exposed to above normal radiation levels include pilots who regularly fly at high altitude, people who live and work in above normal radiation fields, etc. Along with people who live near power plants, these represent a populace among which adverse radiation dose effects should be evident. That so many people live (or work) in above normal radiation fields without any known adverse health effect supports a conclusion that the doses people receive incident to a considerable variation in Earth's natural radiation are not a health hazard. An example is Ramsar, Iran. Its 1000 highest exposed individuals get a background dose of 600 millirem/year. That's close to twice the sea level dose in the United States. Studies reportedly indicate a resulting protective and/or adaptive effect that's not strong enough to justify relaxing dose limits. But that indicates that low radiation doses do cause the body to better protect itself against radiation. And the studies of nuclear accidents (discussed later) even show that unwarranted fear of low level radiation has caused more known deaths than the accidents did.

IV-3 Nuclear Power

Initiation

On December 8, 1953, President Dwight Eisenhower's "Atoms for Peace" address to the United Nations General Assembly fostered development of nuclear power plants. The first such plant was the 60 megawatt electric Shippingport Atomic Power Station in Pennsylvania. It achieved criticality on December 2, 1957 and operated for over 30 years. Nuclear power plants came to provide 20% of our nation's energy demand. And no known radiation-induced deaths have resulted from the operation of or accidents at U.S. designed commercial nuclear power plants.

Public Perception

A March 6, 2012 Wall Street Journal Opinion Page article by William Tucker stated that, since the Japanese nuclear accident at Fukushima, much of the world is turning away from nuclear energy, with Japan taking all of its reactors offline and Germany planning to shut down all of its reactors by 2022. In Japan, the power shortages and increase in oil and gas imports changed 20 years of trade surpluses into a record $18 billion deficit.

Tucker also noted increasing pressure in the USA to shut down aging reactors. His examples were Indian Point in Buchanan, NY, and Vermont Yankee in Vernon, VT. (Vermont Yankee was shut down permanently in December 2014, reportedly for economic reasons.) The Nuclear Regulatory Commission did, however, issue the first new license permit in 30 years, for two nuclear power plants near Waynesboro, Georgia. To Tucker, that connoted far less than the carry through of the "nuclear renaissance" projected before the Fukushima accident.

Tucker also described an accidental mixture of radioactive cobalt-60 into steel reinforcing bars (rebar). That rebar was used in the early 1980s to build 1700 apartments in Taiwan. When the error was revealed 15 years later, the apartment residents had been subjected to radiation up to 30 times normal background radiation, ~180% of the allowed dose for radiation workers, and ~90 times (9000%) of the dose that NRC-licensed activities are permitted to expose the public to. So the apartment dwellers' cancer incidence was expected to greatly exceed the normal (160 cancer) incidence. But researchers found only five cancers among the 10,000 residents, 97% fewer than expected. Also, birth defects among the residents' offspring were 94% below the expected rate. That was reported in the Journal of American Physicians and Surgeons. (Volume 9, Number 1, Spring 2004, *Is Chronic Radiation an Effective Prophylaxis Against Cancer?*)

The reported drop in cancer incidence correlates to a cancer death drop from about 0.6% cancer deaths per year at a normal background dose of 0.31 rem per year to about 0.02% cancer deaths per year in a radiation field of 9.3 rem per year. But, while that's consistent with the Radiation Hormesis hypothesis, it provides no indication of the threshold dose at which the harm done by radiation meets (and subsequently exceeds) the body's ability to surmount radiation damage.

Tucker saw the Taiwan experience as showing the enormous gap "between radiation science and the popular perception of nuclear power." (Without corroborating evidence, however, the Taiwan case is an unexplained anomaly.)

The Taiwan data was disparaged for not considering the relative youth of the apartment dwellers. A counter-assertion was that the radiation doses were significantly low even when that was considered.

Tucker also noted that 100 U.S. coal plants have been shut down because of mercury and carbon emissions, while the alternative sources of solar power and wind energy "that are supposed to take their place are proving to be much more intractable and land-consuming than previously imagined." That bolstered his argument about the need for power, which is the same view expressed to me many years ago by an electric utility executive who said that we need every available power source.

Tucker did not consider that radioactive material naturally existing in coal goes up the smokestacks of coal-fired power plants. The per person radiation dose from a coal-fired power plants that generates the same amount of power as a nuclear power plant is over 100 times the dose from the nuclear power plant (Alex Gabbard, ORNL Review Vol. 26, No. 3&4, 1993; NCRP Reports 92&95). So people living near coal-fired plants should have over 100 times the radiation effects from nuclear plants generating the same power. But no adverse radiation health effect on the public is evident from either power source.

The absence of radiation ill effects near power plants is only part of the picture. Nuclear power plant accidents have had a major impact on the public's perception of nuclear power. A not so brief summary of my take on that follows.

Three Mile Island

When the Three Mile Island Unit 2 (TMI-2) accident occurred in March 1979 and the Nuclear Regulatory Commission (NRC) Section Chief who supervised the TMI resident inspector's office went to the site, I took his place in the NRC regional Incident Response Center, was later relieved to get a few hours rest, and returned to man the Center overnight.

The lowering of plant pressure that had occurred raised concern that a primary credo—Keep The (Reactor) Core Covered—was getting short shrift.

The plant pressurizer was a particular problem indicator. Such pressurizers are big metal cylinders with a steam bubble in their upper parts and water in their lower parts. Their bottoms are connected to the reactor coolant system. Heaters In the pressurizer water volume maintain system pressure by boiling the water. That water, when it turns to steam, increases in volume by a factor of about seven. So increasing the heat supplied to the water in the pressurizer increases the pressurizer steam volume and system pressure. Conversely, decreasing the power to the pressurizer heaters allows some steam to condense and reduces system pressure. In normal operation, small changes in pressurizer heating maintain operating pressure.

The pressurizer is also a surge tank. If, for example, an increased demand for secondary plant steam occurs, the steam drawdown lowers steam generator pressure and temperature. That increases the difference in temperature between the secondary (steam) plant and the primary plant. More heat is thereby drawn from the primary plant, decreasing its temperature, pressure, and volume. As the lowered pressure lowers the boiling point and converts more pressurizer water to steam, water leaves the pressurizer and keeps the primary system full of water.

Charging (adding) water to the primary system normally causes a pressurizer water level increase. That compresses the pressurizer steam bubble and increases system pressure. Removing (letting down) water from the primary system has the opposite effect. It was baffling that, when water was charged into the TMI primary system, the pressurizer water level decreased instead of increasing. And, when water was removed from the primary system, pressurizer water level increased. It took until about 3 a.m. for me to conclude that such an opposite response would occur if a second pressurizer on the system was large enough that the amount of steam change in it caused by system pressure changes was large enough to reverse the effect on the installed pressurizer. That condition was later called the reactor vessel bubble (caused by boiling part of the water in the reactor vessel).

When morning came, I was relieved of Incident Response Center Duty, and briefed the Regional Staff on TMI status. To questions about the problem cause, I said that the exact cause hadn't been determined, but my view was that there had been a loss of reactor coolant accident. Then I caught some sleep, drove to the site, relieved the exhausted cognizant Section Chief, and remained in charge of the onsite TMI resident inspection office for about two months. In a few days, NRC Licensing staffed their (more senior) office onsite as well. A few weeks after that, a senior NRC Licensing representative told me that he had known it was a loss of coolant accident early in the event sequence.

Early in my time at TMI after the accident, I went to the control room. When I asked why the radiation monitor in the top of the Containment Building was pegged high, an operator said that it seemed to be a false reading caused by the monitor's shielding having fallen off. Then, while touring the plant with a licensee health physicist (both of us wearing anti-contamination clothing), we went up to the Containment wall. I asked about the radiation field we were in. That it was over twice the normal value further confirmed the seriousness of the situation.

The fact that this accident occurred meant that operator practices and/or procedures were inadequate. But the plant's design (e.g., the Containment Building) and consultation with company management, the NRC, and industry experts resulted in no radiation harm being done to workers or to the public.

The subsequent corrective actions mandated by the Nuclear Regulatory Commission and taken by the nuclear industry were clearly appropriate. (A few may have been overkill.) One with particular value was simulators that faithfully model the power plant's characteristics and realistically show the effects of plant casualties. Properly used to train operators, those are a potent safeguard against over-confidence in design safety features.

Nonetheless, complacency will always lurk in the wings. Its worst potential was described by the gunnery sergeant who gave me an ammunition safety lesson by saying that, if an accident is possible, it's eventually going to happen. That was reinforced by the boatswain's mate who told me that salt water and sailors will f..k up anything. But my training in and experience with diesel and nuclear submarines, nuclear weapons, and commercial nuclear power plant safety tell me that **vigilant**, knowledgeable, and careful management and operation can nonetheless produce a stellar personnel safety record.

My initial participation in the on-scene TMI-2 response included being in a trailer on licensee property outside the plant, along with several other NRC responders. A media horde had descended on the area, and about a dozen of them were outside our trailer. I felt that somebody should be talking to them. No one volunteered, so I tried to explain to them what was happening. Then a health physicist came up and said there had been a radiation release because we were in a radiation field. The reporters overheard. One asked if they were safe. I said that, if it became dangerous, they (and we) would be moved. In a few minutes, the radiation levels returned to normal, showing that the release of radioactivity had ended.

A short time later, I heard that Pennsylvania's Governor had recommended a voluntary evacuation of pregnant women and pre-school children from within five miles of TMI. (That distance was later expanded to 20 miles.) Like some other onsite responders, I thought evacuation was unnecessary. But we were focused on the radiation hazard, which we considered well-contained. The Governor also had to consider public fear. And, though far more people evacuated than the Governor specified, his action was a safeguard against escalation of the public reaction to mass, panic flight.

My lack of awareness of how the media would contribute to public fear changed when I saw a newspaper with a front page photo of a TMI Cooling Tower. Its caption noted the "evil steam" rolling down its side. (That water vapor was neither radioactive nor evil, and I felt that a responsible reporter would have checked that out before reporting it sensationally.) But a few reporters did try to avoid contributing to the danger of panic.

Licensee, NRC, and nuclear industry brainstorming identified some accident responses that weren't yet practicable. One was putting a TV-carrying robot into the Containment to permit visual inspection. Another short-lived idea was drilling a hole in the top of the Containment and, through it, drilling a hole in the top of the reactor vessel to vent off the gas/steam in its upper volume. But the venting was accomplished by using the system ordinarily used to remove air while the primary system was being filled.

Also, one of my inspectors expressed concern about a potential explosion of hydrogen in the primary system. Hot zirconium (in fuel element cladding) and steam produce zirconium oxide and hydrogen ($Zr + 2H_2O \rightarrow ZrO_2 + 2H_2$). But that makes no oxygen available to the hydrogen. So the inspector went back to his (unnamed) source, found no oxygen source, and we returned to more appropriate inspection considerations.

Onsite activity settled down as the reactor vessel temperature slowly decreased. An inspector brought a *Newsweek* reporter's request to accompany me around the site. Hoping that would increase the likelihood of accurate reporting, I agreed.

The reporter and I were onsite, in view of the Containment Building, when a thud came from it. The reporter asked if that was a hydrogen explosion. I responded that it was consistent with one. But neither of us got excited. (The thud was later assessed as the sound of an explosion of the hydrogen vented from the primary system to the Containment. It didn't affect Containment integrity.)

On the last day of the accompaniment, the reporter asked how much the accident would cost. I gave the standard answer: the NRC monitors safety, not cost. Then came an off the mark question: *Will it cost thousands of dollars, or tens of thousands, or what?* I said: *It'll cost millions.* The reporter said: *MILLIONS!* I said: *We're not talking about hiring a couple of cleaning ladies.*

The next issue of *Newsweek* had a long article on TMI. Much of the information I provided was stated. The only statement attributed to me was about the cost. My Regional Administrator soon phoned, noted that I hadn't said anything inaccurate, and reiterated the mantra that we monitor safety, not cost.

I heard no more about my cost pronouncement from my management. But my NRC colleagues had a field day with it. (Months later, one gleefully popped into my office to ask if I had watched the Saturday Night Live skit about the cleaning ladies going in to clean up the containment.)

As the cleanup costs soared, the references to my gaffe diminished. That didn't change the lesson that reporters may be skilled in putting information they can't state in other mouths.

Many months later, when I was on a train on the way to a meeting at NRC Headquarters, I noticed that the man sitting next to me was editing a write-up on home kerosene heaters. We discussed their characteristics and dangers, and he said he was a writer for a national telejournalist. Then I asked him what he thought about my TMI cost comments. He said that was something that the public needed to hear because it quickly presented a picture that a huge pile of books couldn't. His viewpoint was valid. But that didn't change the fact that a simple ploy had suckered me into saying something I shouldn't have.

After my initial TMI tour and reassignment to my normal duties, I returned to TMI for another stint several months later. By then, almost all evacuees had returned, and the area restaurants had reopened. But the licensee was still feeding the event responders in an emergency restaurant in an onsite tent. Concluding that our inspection now could be restored to normal (eating in local restaurants), I ordered the Regional NRC Inspection staff onsite to do that. Within the hour, an NRC Licensing official was in my office vehemently opining that, if I thought any of the NRC Licensing staff had been influenced by being fed by the licensee, I was out of my bleeping mind (or words to that effect). We each discussed the matter with our own boss, and the NRC stopped eating the licensee's food.

After my tours at TMI, I periodically updated my perspective by discussions with health physicists with current knowledge. One aspect was a farmer's claim that TMI radiation was killing his cows. Another farmer claimed that the radiation was making his goats infertile. The hearsay feedback I got was that the University of Pennsylvania Veterinary School had assessed the cattle deaths as due to unsatisfactory hygiene and the goat infertility as due to excessive inbreeding. A perhaps overstated additional comment was that goats, being mountain creatures, have long lived in a higher radiation field than sea level creatures and a radiation dose that would adversely affect their reproduction would kill them.

The Three Mile Island accident was reviewed by the Kemeny Presidential Commission. It concluded that there will either be no case of cancer or the number of cases will be so small that it will never be possible to detect them, and the same conclusion applies to other health effects. Also, epidemiological studies concluded that radiation from the plant had no perceptible effect on cancer incidence in nearby residents. Anti-nuclear forces disputed the Kemeny Report and the studies that support it. But, to my knowledge, no scientifically credible data shows that this accident did radiation harm to anyone.

Several years after the TMI accident, I attended a training course on presenting information to the media. The instructor had been a media responder to TMI and still considered the event to have been very dangerous. Phone calls from plant personnel about the dangers they were reportedly being exposed to were identified as playing a substantial role in that perception. I tried to point out that observation of the workers going to and from the plant would have shown the actual lack of danger, but concluded I was wasting my breath. (Gullibility, self-aggrandizement, profiteering, the appeal of sensationalism, and malice can play roles in hoaxes besides the ones that lend artificial credulity to the existence of Bigfoot, Nessie, and Supernatural Crop Circles. So sensible minds discount bald assertion that's inconsistent with what is readily observable.)

Radiation safety training and having been at sea on submarines for months within 300 feet of an operating nuclear power reactor gave me a different perspective than people without comparable experience. What was invisible and frightening to the media and the public was measurable and acceptable to me. And, although my onsite time after the TMI accident involved short periods in above normal radiation fields, my measured radiation dose showed no cause for concern. (After my post-accident duty at TMI, I confirmed that my total recorded dose there had been below the measurable minimum.) And post-accident duty at TMI didn't cause me, or anyone I know about, any known health problem.

The TMI accident was assigned a Level Five classification on the International Nuclear Event Scale of One to Seven, with Seven being the most severe.

SL-1

In 1961, about 18 years before the TMI accident, there was a fatal nuclear accident at SL-1, a U.S. Army Stationary Low Power (3 megawatt) reactor at the U.S. National Reactor Testing Station in Idaho. An operator manually withdrew the shutdown reactor's only control rod well past the point at which the reactor would become critical (a self-sustaining nuclear fission rate). That took the reactor from well below the power range to a power level over 6000 times rated power in about a hundredth of a second. The resulting steam explosion ejected the control rod. It impaled and killed the operator. Two other operators also died.

An SL-1 staff member described (many years later) the recovery operations to me as involving monitored entries into the reactor area to perform a task such as operating a valve, and exiting with a stay time of less than a minute. And, to his knowledge, other than the three operator fatalities, no adverse health effects resulted. Nonetheless, the three SL-1 deaths exceeded the zero deaths from the subsequent Three Mile Island Unit 2 accident, which is considered the worst U.S. nuclear reactor accident. (It cost the most, but there's no dollar value on human life and the three SL-1 deaths are a more severe consequence than the zero deaths caused by the TMI-2 nuclear accident.)

The Chernobyl Accident

On April 26, 1986, seven years after the TMI accident, a Severity Level Seven nuclear power reactor accident occurred at Chernobyl in the Ukraine. Like the SL-1 accident, this event resulted from far too fast addition of reactivity to a shutdown reactor. The Chernobyl power excursion caused steam explosions and reactor vessel rupture, and blew the roof off the building housing the power plant. Unlike U.S. water-moderated nuclear plants, the Chernobyl plant was graphite moderated. And it didn't have a pressure-retaining Containment. The accident exposed the graphite and the reactor fuel. Graphite ignition sent a highly radioactive plume into the atmosphere. That produced radioactive fallout onto the western Soviet Union and Europe.

A serious safety inadequacy was shown by the Chernobyl accident. But the Russian responders put water and concrete on the radioactive materials at great personal risk. The official Russian tabulation of the deaths thereby caused was 31 plant workers and emergency responders. Third party assessment put the number of near-term deaths due to radiation overdoses at about 50, while UNSCEAR (the United Nations Scientific Committee on the Effects of Atomic Radiation) placed the near-term deaths of plant workers and emergency responders at 30.

UNSCEAR also noted that, in 1986, about 115,000 people were relocated from areas near Chernobyl. About 220,000 people were later relocated from Belarus, the Russian Federation, and Ukraine. And, up until 2005, over 4000 thyroid cancers were reported among nearby residents who were under the age of 18 at the time of the accident.

> Note: Iodine concentrates in the thyroid. Radioactive I-131 can cause thyroid cancer. That risk is increased by low dietary iodine. Professional medical assessment is needed to determine whether there should be additional iodine intake.

UNSCEAR concluded that the great majority of the population is unlikely to have serious health problems due to Chernobyl radiation. Anti-nuclear organizations disagreed. For example, the Union of Concerned Scientists estimated the Chernobyl results as 50,000 excess cancer cases, half of them fatal, among the hundreds of millions of people living in areas broader than those identified. (If there were 500 million such individuals, that would be one death among every 100,000 people, a 99.995% survival rate.) And a book by the founder of the Russian Chapter of Greenpeace claimed that the billions of people exposed to Chernobyl-produced contamination will experience nearly a million premature cancer deaths. (That's more than a 99.9% survival rate.) As far as I know, no credible proof of those alleged cancer deaths has been provided.

A TV presentation of the post-accident status of the area around Chernobyl showed an abundance of wildlife. Also shown was an animal litter with a deformed offspring, with the concern expressed that that might be due to radiation. Having, as a farm boy, attended the birthing of our dog's litter and seeing her gently push aside and refuse to feed a deformed pup, I saw that as specious speculation. (The implied normal health of wild litters seems to be a prejudice about the unknown.)

International Assessment of Chernobyl

From 2003-2005, over 100 experts in related matters took part in the Chernobyl Forum. Those included representatives of the governments of Belarus, the Russian Federation, Ukraine, and eight specialized United Nations (UN) agencies, including:

- FAO (The Food and Agriculture Organization)
- IAEA (The International Atomic Energy Agency)

- The World Bank
- UNDP (The United Nations Development Programme)
- UNEP (The United Nations Environment Program)
- UN-OCHA (The UN Office for the Coordination of Humanitarian Affairs)
- UNSCEAR (The United Nations Scientific Committee on the Effects of Atomic Radiation)
- WHO (The World Health Organization)

The Forum produced a 3 volume, 600 page scientific report on the accident, as determined about 20 years later. That eliminated speculation. {Speculators can, for example, *Appeal to Ignorance* by claiming that orange juice causes cancer because it hasn't been shown not to. But the absence of proof is not proof of absence (e.g., the absence of proof of God's existence is not proof that God does not exist.)}

At the 2005-2006 session of the UN General Assembly, the Chernobyl Forum's Report was recognized as providing the highest international consensus on the Chernobyl accident.

The Chernobyl Forum's findings included:

- Over 4000 children had thyroid cancer as a result of the accident. Nine of those so afflicted (0.225%) died.
- Most of the over 600,000 emergency workers (Liquidators) and five million contaminated area residents received radiation doses comparable to natural background, with no observable radiation-induced health effects.
- Other than the thyroid cancers, no substantial increase in radiation-induced somatic morbidity (deaths) is forecast.
- The accident cost hundreds of billions of dollars.
- The most significant effects are severe economic and social depression of affected Belarusian, Russian, and Ukrainian regions and associated serious psychological problems.
- Plants and animals were adversely affected up to 18.6 miles from the release point. Recovery from that took several years. But the evacuation of humans produced a unique sanctuary for biodiversity (e.g., the rare white tailed eagle).

- High Cesium-137 (Cs-137) levels will exist in area game, mushrooms, and berries for several decades. (Cs-137's radioactive half-life is 30.17 years. Its 70 day biological half-life can be reduced to 30 days by oral administration of Prussian Blue, a heavy metal poisoning antidote.)

WHO's summary of the Chernobyl Forum's findings includes:

- In 19 years, less than 50 radiation-induced deaths occurred, but the estimated eventual total could be 4000. (Previous estimates numbered in the tens of thousands.)
- Except for radiation workers and thyroid cancer victims, no profound negative health impact was found, nor was dangerous contamination found outside the restricted area.
- Overall, the Chernobyl Forum's findings are reassuring (per Dr. Michael Repacholi, WHO's Radiation Protection Program Manager).
- Zoning of areas under "strict control" needs to be relaxed.
- There's no evidence or likelihood of decreased fertility, and no evidence of congenital malformation.
- Poverty, "lifestyle" diseases rampant in the former Soviet Union, and mental health problems pose a far greater threat to local communities than radiation exposure.
- Other than the radiation-induced deaths/diseases, the largest public health problem is the adverse mental health impact, which is in part due to a lack of accurate information. That problem manifests as "negative self-assessments of health, belief in a shortened life expectancy, lack of initiative, and dependency on assistance from the state."
- Relocation was deeply traumatic. After relocation of 116,000 from the most impacted area, the rest of the 350,000 relocations did little to reduce radiation exposures.
- Persistent radiation myths and misperceptions resulted in "paralyzing fatalism" among affected area residents.
- There's no comprehensive plan for disposing of tons of high-level radioactive waste.
- In most areas the "problems are economic and psychological, not health or environmental." (per Dr. Mikhail Balonov, IAEA

radiation expert, Chernobyl Forum Scientific Secretary, and involved with Chernobyl recovery since the disaster occurred)

WHO also noted that the accident trauma included:

- Disruption of social networks.
- No possibility of returning "home."
- The stigma of not being considered survivors but victims.
- Initial lack of reliable information.
- Widespread mistrust of official information.
- False attribution of most health problems to radiation.

WHO further noted that some of us live in over 2 rem background radiation a year, with no evidence of that being a health risk. Also noted was that one whole body computer tomography (CT) scan is about equal to 20 years of radiation exposure in the low contamination areas around Chernobyl.

WHO assessed the Chernobyl accident thyroid cancers as due to radioiodine-contaminated milk compounded by a general dietary iodine deficiency that caused greater thyroid uptake of radioiodine. Also stated was that, if local (contaminated) milk had not been given to children for a few months after the accident, it's likely that most of the thyroid cancers would have been avoided.

WHO concluded that, of 626,000 Liquidators (post-accident radiation workers), evacuees, and residents, 120,000 (19.2%) would normally be expected to die of cancer, and that the accident "may" cause up to 4000 additional cancer deaths among them. (An additional 4000 deaths changes the overall cancer deaths from 120,000 to 124,000. That's a 0.64% (4000/626,000) increase in the overall cancer rate. WHO stated the increase as between 3%-4% (4000/120,000=3.33%).

The Chernobyl findings raise the following questions:

- Less than 50 total deaths resulted in the 19 years following the accident. What's the scientific basis for predicting up to 4000 total deaths—80 times that number?
- If the major health impact on the affected populace (other than on high exposure radiation workers and the nine child

deaths from thyroid cancer) is on mental health, how many deaths are projected from the psychological impact, and on what basis?

Until those questions are clearly answered, the public will lack adequate information. Nonetheless, the Chernobyl Forum's findings are the most scientifically credible ones available. And they provide a basis for:

- Those involved in the design, approval, and operation of nuclear power plants to safeguard against the identified design and operating inadequacies.
- Those who portray the effects of nuclear radiation to consider the harm of overstating the danger.

In 2009, the World Nuclear Association categorized the 31 near-term Chernobyl accident deaths as two killed by the explosions, one death from a heart attack, and 28 deaths in 1986 from Acute Radiation Syndrome. Nineteen additional deaths from 1987-2004 were stated to be from other causes. The survival rate from thyroid cancer was stated to be 98.8%. Also noted was that no increase in leukemia, which is known to appear 2-3 years after exposure, was identified for more than 10 years after the accident. The conclusion was that lives were disrupted by the accident, but generally positive prospects for the future health of most individuals should prevail.

UNSCEAR concluded that it's very unlikely that statistically detectable radiation-induced cancers will be identified outside the three countries around Chernobyl (Belarus, the Russian Federation, and Ukraine). UNSCEAR also noted that an increase in area cancer occurred before the accident and found a general increase in mortality in most areas of the former Soviet Union in recent decades, with such factors having to be considered in interpreting the Chernobyl accident results.

WHO noted that studies found no cancer increases (other than thyroid) that can be clearly attributed to Chernobyl radiation. But WHO also noted that well developed epidemiological studies are needed to assess indications of leukemia among the Liquidators and a small increase in premenopausal breast cancers in the most contaminated areas.

Economic/ Psychological Fatalities

Deaths from non-radiological effects of the Chernobyl accident were not quantified by the Chernobyl Forum. But the feasibility of such quantification was documented in relation to the austerity measures imposed in Greece. Time Magazine's July 20, 2015 article on that noted that those measures were imposed to prevent national bankruptcy in 2010. They were expected to shrink the economy by less than 6%, but the national output collapsed by a quarter and the suicide rate jumped by over a third.

Greece's population on January 1, 2010 was 11,305,118, and its suicide rate in 2009 was 0.0035%. At that rate, the population should have suffered 396 suicides in 2010. A one-third increase would have added another 132 deaths. A related, Frances Martel June 25, 2015 Breitbart article cited a University of Thessaly finding of a 35% increase in suicides in Greece in 2010 and 2012 due to the debt crisis and unemployment, and a 0.19/100,000 population rise in suicide for every 1% decrease in employment in the 20-59 year age group. That's 21 Greek deaths per 1% rise in unemployment. (The validity of that has to be limited to an economic disruption very close to that involved in the about 25% decrease experienced in Greece's economy.)

Normally, Greece had about one-fifth the suicides that the area around Chernobyl did before the accident. And the Greek suicide deaths may have been understated by suicides (e.g., car crashes) being "charitably" classified as accidents. So the Greek data doesn't directly correlate to Chernobyl. But many of the psychological problems associated with the Greek suicides are the same as those of the Chernobyl survivors, who have the added problem of false fear of serious health effects. That indicates that economic woes plus overstatement of the health effects of the Chernobyl Accident killed more people than the accident did. Moreover, that shows that, if nuclear power is economically beneficial, it's beneficial to human life.

Dr. Jaworoski's Views on Chernobyl

Appendix 2 to the World Nuclear Association Chernobyl Accident Health Impact study includes a Lessons of Chernobyl article by Dr. Zbigniew Jaworoski (1927-2011), MD (a cancer radiotherapist), PhD, D.Sc. (Natural Science), and a Professor of Atomic Radiation. He was a former Chairman of the Central Laboratory for Radiological Protection (CLOR), Warsaw, Poland, and the UNSCEAR Chairman from 1981-82. He also stated that bad science is the basis for overstatement of man's contribution to global warming (saying that *Not man, but nature, rules the climate*). But my interest in Jaworoski involves his disputing of the Linear No Threshold model of radiation damage and related considerations, including his following assertions:

- Chernobyl changed the views of many radiological protection people about the "holy mantra" of the Linear No Threshold (LNT) "assumption" that even near-zero radiation doses may cause cancer and genetic harm. Chernobyl "also sheds light on how easily the global community may leave the realm of rationality when facing an imaginary emergency."
- The LNT assumption contradicts a vast sea of data on the beneficial effects of low radiation doses. Dr. Jaworoski tried, for seven years, to get UNSCEAR to assess that data, published in the scientific literature since the 19th Century. But it wasn't until two years after the Chernobyl accident that UNSCEAR decided to study Radiation Hormesis. Its 1994 report started a virtual revolution in radiation protection research, but vested interests and conservatism leave a long way to go to change the regulations.
- Chernobyl was minor in terms of human losses. But it had enormous political, economic, social and psychological impact. Evacuees suffered mass psychotic disturbances, great economic losses, and traumatic social consequences. Cancer "epidemics" "direly predicted" from the Linear No Threshold assumption to reach tens and hundreds of thousands, or even millions, haven't occurred.

- The accident made Poland's air over 500,000 times more radioactive—a terrible psychological shock even though Poland's dose rate on the first day was just three times higher than the previous day. And it was four times lower than Dr. Jaworoski said he got from visiting Norway, where he described the natural background radiation from rocks as being up to 1.13 rem/year. He also described the doses as some 100 times lower than the about 25 rem annual dose in Ramsar, Iran and over 300 times lower than the 79 rem annual dose rate on Brazilian beaches or the 87 rem annual dose rate in South-West France, with no adverse health effects having ever been reported in residents of such high background radiation areas.

NOTE. Webecoist places the background radiation at Ramsar, Iran at up to 26 rem/year and at the Guarapari, Brazil beaches at up to 17.5 rem/year. (Actual doses depend on stay times and are less.) Also, 43,316 Norwegian nurses who graduated between 1914 and 1984 were followed up from 1953 through 2002 through the Norwegian Cancer Registry. The only adverse health effect found was an increased risk of lung cancer among those who smoked.

- In 1986, the increase in atmospheric radioactivity led to serious consequences in Poland, the Soviet Union, throughout Europe, and then everywhere. The decision making wasn't scientific but emotional, political, and mercantile. Intervention levels imposed varied by a factor of up to 50,000.
- Norway limited Cesium-137 concentration in meat to limit the individual radiation dose from its consumption to 0.047 mSv (4.7 millirem) per year at a total cost of over $51 million. (That's about 5.5 days' worth of natural background radiation.)
- The most "nonsensical" action, based on ICRP (International Commission for Radiological Protection) recommendation, was to evacuate 336,000 people in areas where, from 1986-1995, the Chernobyl fallout increased the average radiation

dose about 250 millirem per year. Those evacuees' prior doses were tens to hundreds of times lower than normal background doses in many other countries. And "ICRP will never accept responsibility for the disastrous effects of this dogmatic application of its armchair lucubrations (thought or study) which has caused the present system of radiation protection [to] become a health hazard."

- In Pripyat, Ukraine, where 50,000 were relocated and no one can enter without special permission, a Polish team measured a total external gamma dose rate of 0.9 mSv (90 millirem) per year in 2009. That's the same as the natural dose in Warsaw, Poland and one-fifth the dose in New York City's Grand Central Station.

- The child thyroid cancers in Belarus, Russia, and Ukraine should be viewed in respect to the occult (symptomless) thyroid cancers found elsewhere by autopsy or ultrasound. In Finland, those occur in 2.4% of 0-15 year olds. Near Chernobyl, the greatest incidence in under 15 year olds of thyroid cancers of the same type of occult thyroid cancers was 0.027% in Russia's Bryansk region in 1994, and decreased in subsequent years. That's about one-ninetieth of Finland's corresponding rate and is inconsistent with radiation-induced cancers, which have a five year latency period with a subsequent increase until 15-29 years after exposure. And, in the USA, a 1974-1979 screening program detected a 21 times higher rate of thyroid cancer than was detected before the screening, an increase similar to the post-Chernobyl accident experience. So the Chernobyl thyroid cancers represent a "classical screening effect."

- In the contaminated regions around Chernobyl, total cancer incidence appears to have been lower than it would have been in a similar but unirradiated group. The only real adverse consequence of the Chernobyl catastrophe among about five million people living in the contaminated regions is the epidemic of psychosomatic diseases. Those were caused by radiophobia induced by years of propaganda before and after the accident, and aggravated by improper administrative decisions. As a result, several million people in three countries have been labeled and perceive themselves as actual or potential victims of Chernobyl. That was the main factor behind the economic losses caused by the Chernobyl catastrophe, estimated for Ukraine to reach $148 billion until 2000, and $235 billion until 2016 for Belarus.

- Dr. Jaworoski claimed that he, most of his professional colleagues, the authorities, and the public were pre-conditioned for irrational reactions: "Victims of the LNT dogma, we all wished to protect people even against the lowest, near zero doses of ionizing radiation. The dogma led to mass psychosis and the greatest psychological catastrophe in history, into which the accident in Chernobyl, with the efficient help of media and national and international authorities, quickly evolved. It seems that professionals, international and national institutions, and the system of radiological protection did not meet the challenge of the Chernobyl catastrophe."

- The radiation monitoring systems in all developed countries detected even the tiniest Chernobyl reactor debris. No such system exists for any other potentially harmful environmental agent. That excellence ignited mass anxiety with disastrous consequences in the former Soviet Union and strangulation of nuclear power development elsewhere. Fighting panic and mass hysteria could be the most important countermeasure to protect the public against the effects of a similar accident.

- Chernobyl was the worst possible catastrophe of a badly constructed nuclear reactor. The reactor core completely melted. There was an uncontrolled release of radionuclides into the atmosphere for 10 days. The death toll was about half of that of a weekend's traffic in Poland, tens to hundreds of times lower than many other industrial catastrophes. It is unlikely that there were any radiation-induced fatalities among the public. "In the centuries to come, the Chernobyl catastrophe will be seen as a proof that nuclear power is a safe means of energy production."

Note. Jaworoski's statements differed from the Chernobyl Forum's findings mainly in the outrage expressed. Neither source explicitly acknowledged that the overstated prediction of radiation effects results in fear-induced deaths. And the reaction to the next Severity Level 7 power reactor accident (in Japan) showed that the fear of radiation hasn't abated.

Fukushima Daiichi

Another Severity Level 7 nuclear accident was caused by a gigantic earthquake off the coast of Japan on March 11, 2011. Compared to the 1906 California Magnitude 7.8 Earthquake that was called one of the world's largest earthquakes, the 2011 Japanese Magnitude 9 Earthquake produced 15.8 times the ground shaking amplitude. (Earthquake magnitude is a power of ten, and the 2011 Japanese earthquake magnitude of 10^9 is 15.8 times that of 1906 California earthquake magnitude of $10^{7.8}$)

The 2011 Japanese (Tohoku) Earthquake was the most powerful earthquake ever recorded in Japan. About 18,500 Japanese were killed and about 500,000 were displaced. Over 300,000 homes were lost. The damage exceeds $300 billion.

Japan's nuclear power plants were stressed well beyond their design basis. Flaws were revealed in reactor siting and in the emergency power sources being located so low in the facility that the flooding took them out. The Fukushima Daiichi six-reactor site was particularly hard hit, with reactor vessel ruptures, spent fuel pool water boil-off, and substantial radiation releases. Reportedly, Japan's radiation releases were about 10%-30% of the Chernobyl releases. Containment buildings and the water-moderated reactor design undoubtedly were major factors in the radiation releases in Japan being relatively low. U.S. commercial nuclear power plant conservatism (the Fukushima Daiichi plants were designed by General Electric), radiation dose limits, and lessons learned resulted in restriction of consumption of food from affected areas and no radiation-induced deaths or radiation sickness.

Fatalities have, however, resulted from the response to the Japanese nuclear accident (ref: World Nuclear Association and Wikipedia internet articles). A Wikipedia article cites a survey as calculating that, among the Fukushima Prefecture's 300,000 evacuees, 1600 deaths occurred due to evacuation conditions while 1599 deaths were caused in that prefecture by the earthquake and tsunami. (A Fukushima Prefecture 2014 report placed the evacuation-related deaths at 1656 and the earthquake/tsunami deaths at 1607.) And the last sentence of the Wikipedia article on Fukushima Daiichi nuclear disaster casualties states: "Another cause of death is the increased number of suicides due to mental stress, despair, anxiety and depression caused by media coverage, and through long periods of evacuation." But the Japanese are quantifying, and making public, the fatal non-nuclear consequences of their nuclear accident.

That nuclear accident evoked great opposition to nuclear power in Japan. All 50 of its nuclear power reactors are shut down. There's no indication that the local approval needed (and appropriate) for the startup of any of them is forthcoming.

Our Outlook

Japan's 2011 nuclear accident indicates that, if a gigantic earthquake and/or Tsunami hit U.S. shores, the nuclear power plant damage will be a tiny amount of the total damage and the radiation-induced deaths (if any) will be a miniscule part of the total fatalities. If we overreact to a U.S. radiation hazard in the way that the response to the Chernobyl and Japanese nuclear accidents did, people will die unnecessarily. But the danger of overreaction must be weighed against the danger of fear-induced panic. The limited evacuation around the Three Mile Island site plus the relatively rapid return of the evacuees militated against lethal non-nuclear deaths like those associated with the Chernobyl and Japanese nuclear accidents. The keys to the safest outcome lie in the emergency response knowledge and capabilities of our elected leaders and emergency response organizations—and in the trust the people have in them. But, without objective education of the public about radiation's nature and hazards, there may be no choice but overreaction. The lethal non-nuclear consequences can, however, be minimized by terminating emergency response measures (e.g., evacuation and relocation) as soon as practicable.

Sodium-Cooled Power Reactors

Sodium is a soft alkali metal that melts at 208°F. It has high thermal conductivity and low neutron absorption, characteristics that are desirable in nuclear reactor coolant. Liquid sodium can be used in very low pressure systems. But it's highly reactive, can explode in water, and has to be kept hot to remain liquid. That makes it less desirable in a ship, especially one that needs to be able to withstand battle damage.

The USS Seawolf (SSN-575)

Sodium was used as the reactor coolant in the U.S. Navy's second nuclear submarine, the USS Seawolf (SSN-575). It was pumped by electromagnets external to the coolant piping.

Seawolf's power plant needed only about 60% of the machinery required by Nautilus, our first nuclear submarine. And Seawolf had only one sodium coolant leak—during fitting out. But steam superheater tube sheet weld cracks allowed high pressure steam to leak into the low pressure (15 psi) primary coolant, forming sodium hydroxide and hydrogen gas. Neutron capture transformed some of that gas into mildly radioactive tritium (^3H) gas, which had to be contained.

In 1956, Admiral Rickover decided to convert Seawolf's power plant to a pressurized water reactor because a sodium-cooled reactor was "expensive to build, complex to operate, susceptible to prolonged shutdown as a result of even minor malfunctions, and difficult and time-consuming to repair." But Seawolf was commissioned with her S2G sodium-cooled reactor on March 30, 1957. Superheater inoperability usually prevented her from operating at full power, but she was awarded a Navy Unit Commendation for submerged endurance during a 60 day, 13,700 nautical mile submerged voyage. And she steamed over 20,000 miles before her conversion to Pressurized Water Reactor power.

When Seawolf's sodium cooled reactor was removed, it was sealed in a stainless steel containment vessel, put on a barge, towed about 120 miles east of Maryland, and sunk in 9,100 feet of water. In 1980, 21 years later, the Navy couldn't find the container, but stated that it wouldn't deteriorate before the radioactivity inside it decayed off.

Better prejudgment might have ruled out sodium-cooled reactors on warships without the cost of building S2G. But it appears that the S2G project was handled safely.

The Sodium Reactor Experiment

The Atomic Energy Commission's SRE (Sodium Reactor Experiment) was built on the Santa Susana Field Laboratory (SSFL) site 30 miles northwest of Los Angeles. It could generate 6.5 megawatts of electric power and operated from 1957-1964. On July 12, 1957, it became the first nuclear plant to supply electricity to the U.S. electric power grid.

The SRE reactor building had Wash Cells in which water was used to clean sodium from fuel elements removed from the reactor. Fuel was put into a Wash Cell through a ceiling hole (normally covered with a heavy shield plug), and the sealed off cell was flooded with inert gas to minimize the violence of the sodium-water reaction. The operators worked behind thick shielding walls.

Tetralin (an oil-like hydrocarbon) cooled the SRE's centrifugal coolant pumps' shaft seals and prevented sodium leakage. In July 1959, tetralin began leaking into the low pressure SRE primary system through a pump seal. It decomposed in the sodium. That impeded cooling flow. The fuel began to overheat.

The affected fuel assemblies were cleaned in a Wash Cell. An explosion lifted the cell's ceiling plug and produced high reactor building airborne radioactivity. Subsequent operations produced increases in reactor building airborne activity too.

When the reactor was shut down because of high fuel temperature and unacceptable reactor top-bottom temperature differential, four stuck fuel elements were found. Operation resumed. During the next shut down, some fuel pieces were found to have fallen to the bottom of the reactor and 13 of the reactor's 43 fuel elements had partially melted. It cost $132 million and took almost 14 months to remove the stuck fuel and the damaged fuel pieces, clean the sodium system, and install new fuel. The SRE then operated until February 1964.

SRE site memoranda stated that the radioactive gases were stored in tanks, allowed to decay, and then slowly released into the atmosphere. A landowner summary of releases states that 28 curies of fission gases were released through a stack in a controlled manner that met federal requirements.

The California Department of Toxic Substances Control summarized Cancer Study and Exposure Assessment Activities related to the SSFL Site. Part of that summary covers the Cal EPA investigation (released on June 3, 1999) of the California Department of Health Services handling of health studies at SSFL. That investigation was ordered by California Governor Gray Davis. Cal EPA combined the evidence from three prior studies and concluded:

- The evidence did not indicate an increased rate of cancer.
- The extremely modest cancer incidence increases associated with known radiosensitive tumors (ones treatable with radiation therapy) could easily be explained by uncontrolled confounding (counting cancers caused by other sources) or impression (multiple counting?) in the data.
- The results do not show a major environmental hazard.
- Further studies should only be undertaken if the protocol can improve exposure assessment and control for confounders while substantially improving estimate precision.

In December 2003, the United States Environmental Protection Agency completed an evaluation that concluded that the Santa Susana Field Laboratory site was not eligible for inclusion on the Superfund National Priorities List.

In February 2004 a class action lawsuit was filed against the Santa Susana Field Laboratory landowner. It alleged (in part) that the SRE harmed nearby residents. The plaintiffs produced an analysis **estimating** that the SRE **may** have released up to 260 times more radioactive Iodine-131 than the official estimates for the Three Mile Island (TMI) accident.

The TMI Presidential (Kemeny) Commission found no harm to the public from the TMI accident. So, **if** there was a much larger release from the SRE, no health hazard was thereby shown. The lawsuit therefore appears to have asserted a hazard without actually stating (or showing) one.

In August 2004, ground water under the former SRE was tested for tritium. Reportedly, none was detected.

In October 2006, California legislators responded to community calls for independent health studies by establishing an SSFL Advisory Panel of "independent" experts from the USA (and one from Britain) and community representatives. The panel released consultants' reports that focused on the analysis of the radiological impacts of the July 1959 Sodium Reactor Experiment incident. One, by David Lochbaum, concluded that, "as much as 30% of the most worrisome of the radionuclides, iodine-131 and cesium-137, may have been released, with a best estimate of 15% of each." But 15% of an unspecified amount of radioactive material doesn't identify a health hazard. And an analysis of the quantity and timing of specific gases released wasn't done, supposedly because of scant and disconnected data.

In another report, Jan Beya noted that some meteorological information was withheld by the plant owner. He alleged Iodine-131 releases based on scoping calculations. When interviewed by a local paper, he reportedly reaffirmed his assertion that Iodine-131 was released, but did not consider that a public health issue.

In September 2008, an SSFL Advisory Panel Co-Chair testified to the U.S. Senate Committee on Environment and Public Works. He called the SRE event one of the worst nuclear accidents in nuclear history and testified that the government covered up its seriousness. That testimony followed the Chernobyl accident by over 20 years, and a contrasting viewpoint reportedly was not presented.

In 2009, the Department of Energy (DOE) transferred $38.3 million to the EPA for a complete radiological survey of a 290-acre part of the Santa Susana Field Laboratory, making $41.5 million the total amount of DOE funds provided for site analysis. In 2012, the

EPA released test results showing that over 10% of the 3735 soil samples had above background radioactivity.

The November 12, 2013 EPA Superfund site list contains about 1300 sites. About 100 of those are in California. The Santana Susana Field Laboratory is not one of them.

SRE operations caused no scientifically shown health hazard. But the lack of independent oversight of SRE's activities detracted from the assurance of safety.

Despite the lack of a public health hazard, SRE's problems are, at least to me, confirmation of the basic unsuitability that led Admiral Rickover to reject sodium-cooled nuclear power reactors.

Fermi-1

Fermi-1 was a 69 megawatt electric, sodium-cooled breeder reactor on Lake Erie. It began operating in 1963. In October 1966, a loose zirconium plate blocked coolant channel flow. Two fuel assemblies started to melt. Radiation alarms prompted a plant shutdown. No radioactive releases occurred. Corrective actions took three years and nine months. The song *We Almost Lost Detroit* was written about Fermi-1's "meltdown." Final Fermi-1 shutdown in 1972 was due to lack of funds and aging equipment.

Nuclear Power's Prospects

Nuclear power plants are built for economic benefit. Both Republican and Democratic administrations of our federal government have endorsed nuclear power. A relevant analysis, reportedly from a draft California Energy Commission report, provided the following comparison of comparative power costs in U.S. dollars per megawatt hour.

- Wind Power $60
- Advanced Nuclear Power: $67
- Geothermal $67
- Hydro Power $67
- Coal $74-$81

- Biomass (living matter) $47-$117
- Fuel Cell $86-$111
- Solar $116-$312
- Gas $87-$346
- Wave Power $611

There's an adverse aspect to every power source. Wind Power is a bird killer that's even alleged to represent potential extinction of the endangered Golden Eagle and California Condor. Biomass' potential is only 10% of the world energy demand. Geothermal emits less than half the carbon dioxide that coal does, but also emits hydrogen sulfide, methane, and ammonia, and can cause ground subsidence. Hydro Power dams can keep fish from reaching their spawning grounds. Solar power requires over 10 times the space that Nuclear does. Wind power requires over 8 times the space that Solar does. Solar costs are dropping but have a long way to go. There are some environmentally friendly aspects to Wind and Nuclear power though—they don't involve significant carbon dioxide generation, and considering carbon costs (not included in the above) makes them more desirable.

Homeowners can choose "green" power (at a higher cost), and can install solar power that pays for itself in about 20 years. Few homeowners seem to be exercising those options, but solar power is beginning to be employed on structures housing commercial enterprises. (Solar could provide all our power needs if it were economically advantageous and environmentally suitable.)

The consequence of unfulfilled demand for power is higher energy costs. An alleviating measure is lowering energy use (and expense). That includes replacing incandescent lights with more energy-efficient CFLs (compact fluorescent lights) or LEDs (Light Emitting Diodes). Another effort to reduce energy consumption is more fuel efficient motor vehicles. Such initiatives advocate conservation, which is contrary to the common practice of selling as much of a product as possible. But few of us link the lowered quality of life that higher costs produce to inefficient power use, gas-guzzling cars, or eliminating nuclear power plants.

Also, we're NIMBYs (Not In My Back Yarders). We don't want power plants near our homes. NIMBY considerations also put nuclear power plants far from the locales that use most of the energy they produce. That makes the lower population areas near the plants the primary victims of their undesirable aspects and provides the advantage of the electricity generated to the population centers. And that won't change.

Nuclear power is a contender in the electric power sweepstakes because of cost. Its opponents claim that alternative power sources can take up the slack of its loss, but the touted competitive costs of doing that haven't been realized. And higher power costs not only affect every electric bill but the cost of everything that requires electric power to be used in the manufacturing or handling processes.

Small Modular Reactors

New reactor designs are being developed. Those include Small Modular Reactors (SMRs) intended to serve small populations and reduce the up-front cost of providing new power generation. The pressurized water reactor SMRs are designed with natural coolant circulation. That makes power loss shutdowns safer. And underground installation should provide for less atmospheric dispersion of radioactive materials if an accident occurs. But, as Kennette Benedict pointed out in a January 29, 2014 *Bulletin of the Atomic Scientists* article, potential problems include a higher likelihood of ground water contamination and more difficult cleanup. She also noted that the improved safety features could be applied to a large power plant.

Other factors in building about 20 small reactors instead of one large one could include a greater overall cost for the same total amount of electricity, maintenance accessibility problems, a larger number of total operating and maintenance staff, higher total training costs due to a greater number of training facilities and staff, and higher overall industry and regulatory oversight costs. Also, for the same total power, SMRs require about four times as much space as large nuclear power reactors do. They also may have a significantly greater total decommissioning cost. And the nuclear waste storage problem could result in 20 small local waste storage sites for each replaced large power reactor site.

If SMRs turn out to be safe and economically feasible, the necessary authorizations and producing operational prototypes and then commercial versions put the potential time for providing SMR power a decade or more away.

Operating (human) inadequacies were a root cause of the SL-1, TMI, and Chernobyl accidents. And developing new and safer designs without also taking particular pains to better assure human performance is begging history to repeat itself. (The ability to screw up isn't limited to salt water and sailors.)

Anti-Nuclear Tactics

Radiation safety conservatism isn't credited by the anti-nukes. They predict radiation-induced deaths without credible scientific proof. (That doesn't mean they're insincere.)

There have also been cases of using scare tactics to foster fear of nuclear power. My second wife described being asked to sign a petition against nearby nuclear power plants. The sales pitch was that, if the plants were allowed to operate, the clouds from the cooling towers would block out the sun. Those plants have operated for decades with no such effect, but that hadn't happened at other plants, and knowledgeable anti-nukes knew it.

Another misleading instance was the use of a zoom camera lens from a seaward viewpoint to falsely depict a near seacoast nuclear power plant as being much closer to the beach. That image was used to buttress the view that a nuclear accident at the plant would involve inability to evacuate the densely populated beach area. I saw that as end-justifies-the-means distortion of the location of the plant. (False depiction is inimical to the ability to make a valid case that evacuation is not practicable.)

These cases are examples of the use of common political tactics (instead of scientific data) to discredit nuclear power.

Nuclear Safety Allegations

Valid nuclear power plant safety concerns have resulted in strengthening of safety controls. An example was confirmation of the allegation that the operators at a nuclear power plant were sleeping on watch. The action taken to prevent recurrence was a notable step toward assuring properly vigilant plant monitoring. But false allegations tend to degrade the allegation process. In one case, a large compilation of allegations was submitted shortly before an operating license was scheduled to be granted to a nuclear power plant. That, to me, looked like the allegations had been stacked up for political advantage, rather than being submitted when identified in order to facilitate timely analysis.

Among the batch, the allegation that I considered least valid was extensive documentation of one side of the utility's radio communications with its staff in the field. (The other, unmonitored side of the communication was on a different frequency.) A local establishment (a strip joint) was mentioned on the monitored communication. The allegation was that that showed licensee misbehavior and/or irresponsibility. Follow-up showed that the establishment was referred to as a landmark, a common practice that also was evident in State Police radio communications. I felt that knowledgeable citizens should have known that. Among that batch of allegations, none sticks in my mind as having had any safety significance. No downgrading of the NRC allegation response effort occurred, but sending NRC inspectors on wild goose chases inhibits their addressal of safety considerations.

A different allegation about another power plant came to me in a phone call from a concerned citizen. He had been told that the very smelly, rotting seaweed that had washed up on a nearby shore was caused by radiation from nearby nuclear power plants. It didn't take long for the NRC regional health physics staff to tell me that plant radiation couldn't have caused that, and I told the distraught citizen that he had been misinformed (or disinformed).

The anti-nuclear inputs that I encountered convinced me that anti-nuclear efforts included tactics aimed solely at increasing the fear of nuclear power and ones that employed delay as the deadliest form of denial. The real control over such tactics is public opinion. That's dominated by fear of nuclear energy, so any loss of credence and reputability that anti-nuclear irresponsibility may merit awaits the judgment of history, which also may be biased.

Concern about nuclear safety is nonetheless beneficial. An example was proposed construction of a nuclear waste incinerator. A public meeting was held in the community, with attendance by the NRC and an anti-nuclear activist. Incinerators weren't my bailiwick, but I was designated, along with an NRC Licensing representative and a Health Physicist, to represent the Nuclear Regulatory Commission. The activist, in his field, was considered a respected scientist. We didn't know why he was anti-nuclear.

The meeting was in a large, Quonset hut style building. We three NRC representatives entered at one end and walked through a packed house to get to our seats on stage at the other. Part of the way through the boisterous crowd was the anti-nuclear activist. He was half sitting on a table, smiling broadly. During the meeting, his inputs were applauded. The NRC position that, if the incinerator met federal requirements, we were obliged to approve it was resoundingly disputed by the irate attendees. (Afterwards, a few of them apologized to us for the crowd's behavior.)

Photos of the meeting were shown in the local paper. The one printed of the NRC representatives showed the three of us caught wide-eyed in the glare of a bright light, and the one of the anti-nuclear activist showed a broad smile.

I haven't since been involved in a forum involving that anti-nuclear activist, and can't draw a conclusion about the rationale behind his anti-nuclear posture. Nor have I had any more exposure to nuclear waste incineration. But the event further alerted the NRC to the depth of public concern about incineration of radioactive wastes. And that was beneficial.

Anti-Nuclear Bias

There is strong, articulate anti-nuclear war, anti-nuclear power advocacy. And there's a vital need to heed intelligent critical inputs about our nuclear policies and practices. But too much unsupported bias also is evident.

Dr. Helen Caldicott is a dedicated and highly respected anti-nuclear activist. She gave up her work as a pediatrician to devote herself to her personal 30 year war on nuclear power and nuclear weapons, and was nominated for the Nobel Peace Prize by Dr. Linus Pauling, who won that prize in 1962—for his campaign against nuclear weapons testing.

Dr. Caldicott's (and other) inputs can be a valuable safeguard against overconfidence, malpractice, and complacency. But her website also contains a fear-projecting assertion that Artificial Intelligence (AI) can start a nuclear war because the military cannot keep from employing it in its computers and giving it the power to start a nuclear war based on misinformation. In another part, the presentation deplores our inability to rule out the possibility that things will get worse. Such statements *appeal to ignorance*. And they have a potential for mushrooming into unjustified adverse consequences (bringing to mind the growth of the McCarthyism of the 1950s into unwarranted, prejudice-based firings, blacklists, and imprisonments.)

Criticism of Dr. Caldicott has included the assertion that she doesn't have a sound basis for some of her statements. An example of that concern was the following statement that was attributed to her: *It takes only one radioactive atom, one cell, and one gene to initiate a cancer.*

One cell with DNA damage that causes its uncontrolled replication is the birth of a cancer. Such DNA damage can be caused by decay of a radioactive atom in the body, by external radiation, by a carcinogen, by genetic fault, etc., etc. The DNA damage might kill the cell, and normal body processes would remove it. Or the body might kill the cell (apoptosis) and rid itself of it. Or the cell might not replicate (become senescent). Or its damaged DNA might be repaired by normal body processes. Or the tumor it develops into might be benign. Moreover, most radiation exits or passes entirely through the body without causing DNA damage. So the one cell, one radioactive atom picture tells only part of the story.

The attribution (rerowland.com/BodyActivity.htm) of the one radioactive atom, one cell, one gene statement to Dr. Caldicott tried to add perspective by listing the major radioactive elements that occur naturally in the body (Potassium-40, Carbon-14, Rubidium-87, Lead-210, Tritium, Uranium-238, Radium-228, Radium-226, and Radon-222). Together, these produce 8054 radioactive disintegrations per second (perhaps more—the Health Physics Society lists the Potassium-40 body load as producing 5000 radioactive disintegrations per second versus the 4000 that Rowland cited.) But, even if the lower potassium value is used, radioactive isotope decay produces over 283 billion radioactive disintegrations a year in an average person's body.

The Nuclear Regulatory Commission's (NRC's) personal radiation dose calculator shows that radiation in the average human body provides that body 240 millirem (0.24 rem) of radiation dose each year. That's about 75% of an average background radiation dose of 320 millirem. And the NRC has also stated that the dose of background radiation that we get has not been shown to cause humans any harm. {Nor, for that matter, has the 5000 millirem (5 rem) annual dose limit for radiation workers.} So, while a cancerous tumor starts with a DNA problem in a single cell, it takes a lot more than 283 billion radioactive disintegrations within the human body to provide a good chance of causing a cancer. So stating that one radioactive atom, one cell, and one gene is **all** that's needed to cause cancer ignores the big picture by stating a truth out of context—as would stating that one puff on a cigarette (or one contact with any carcinogen), one cell, and one gene is **all** that's needed to cause cancer.

As far as accidental initiation of nuclear war is concerned, that concern increased when ballistic missiles carrying atomic weapons replaced aircraft that might be called back. (Whether the aircraft could be recalled is a form of the same concern.)

The first U.S. Intercontinental Ballistic Missiles (ICBMs) were deployed in 1961, 55 years ago. None of them has been launched in error. And, unless Dr. Caldicott is privy to the launch protocol, which is no doubt kept from her (as well as from you and me) as classified information that we have no need to know, her conclusion that the military is unable to assure that Artificial Intelligence will not start a nuclear war is beyond her ability to judge. It's also contrary to my belief that the exceptional safeguards that I once knew something about have been made even better.

Besides, there's a sound basis for the nuclear deterrent. We who served in fleet ballistic missile submarines (SSBNs) in the Cold War were certain that a launch would only be ordered if that were necessary to save the United States from a nuclear holocaust. (I still see those submarines as the world's greatest deterrent to nuclear war.) Nuclear weapons have proliferated since then, and that's continuing. But as long as we have our SSBNs on station, attacking the United States with nuclear weapons is suicide for the nation that does so. So, our sane enemies will reserve their nuclear weapons for defensive use unless and until we abandon our nuclear weapons and thereby make our enemies more powerful than we are.

The specter of Mutually Assured Destruction (MAD) arose when both the United States and Soviet Russia stockpiled and made operational enough nuclear warheads to destroy each other many times over. There have been doomsday projections that an onslaught by either major nuclear power would plunge the world into a lethally frozen (or overheated) disaster that would destroy mankind. But the result has been Mutually Assured Survival. Unless we disarm, that will continue until an aggressor stupid or crazy or fanatic enough to initiate a nuclear holocaust can do that.

It's also true that the Cold War was not without alleged near initiations of nuclear war. Probably the most notorious of these was the September 26, 1983 Soviet satellite-based detection facility that generated an alarm that five ICBMs (Intercontinental Ballistic Missiles) had been launched by the United States at Russia. Lt.Col Stanislaw Petrov, the officer in charge at the detecting station, knew that, if the United States was starting a nuclear war against Russia, there would have been hundreds of incoming missiles and bombers. So he recognized and reported the alarm as false, and over-reaction was prevented.

Another infamous reputed close call involved NORAD, the North American Aerospace Defense Command. Technicians there received an urgent alert that Russia had launched a barrage of missiles at North America. Ten interceptors were scrambled. The president's "doomsday" plane (from which retaliation could be initiated) took off. But NORAD satellite data showed the alert to be false, and that falsity was recognized.

There also were reports of Cuban Missile Crisis incidents. One happened when a U.S. destroyer gained sonar contact on an unidentified submarine. In accordance with information previously provided by the United States to Russia, the destroyer reportedly dropped Practice Depth Charges to signal the submarine to surface. {Having been the Gunnery Officer on a similar destroyer, I credit the charges with being signaling PDCs (Point Detonating Charges), about the size of a hand grenade and no danger to a submarine, and not "Practice Depth Charges."}

The submarine was Russian diesel-electric submarine B-59. She had one nuclear-armed torpedo, had long been out of communication with her Russian commanders, and had the authority to fire that torpedo if attacked—if her Captain, second-in-command, and Political Officer concurred. The Captain and Political Officer concurred. The second-in-command (Second Captain) convinced them to surface B-59 and request instructions from Moscow—though the nature of B-59's operations reportedly prevented her from being informed of the U.S. protocol for signaling a submarine to surface. It has also been reported that the Captain and the Political Officer had considered the dropping of the signaling charges to be an act of war and advocated using their nuclear torpedo on the USS Randolph (CVS-15), the antisubmarine warfare (ASW) Essex class carrier commanding 11 U.S. destroyers.

That the detonation of signaling charges would be mistaken for the explosion of depth charges that each contained the equivalent of 300 pounds of TNT is highly suspect. Also, the fact that B-59 considered surfacing feasible (thereby making herself more vulnerable to attack) is inconsistent with the premise that she saw the signaling to be an act of war. (Truthfulness of the report that B-59 was "pummeled" by explosives from the destroyers seems even more unlikely.) What does seem likely is that B-59 (like several other Russian submarines) correctly decided that she could safely surface and contact Moscow. That doesn't decrease the danger of the Cuban Missile Crisis. But mutual determination enabled direct negotiations between President Kennedy and Russia's Nikita Khrushchev to turn it into a Win-Win outcome. And, despite the decreased danger of initiation of war that accompanied their negotiations, reports about the near initiation of such a war during the Cuban Missile Crisis seem to be becoming more unrealistically sensational.

Yet another reputed Cold War near disaster was the dropping of two nuclear weapons on North Carolina due to weather causing them to be ripped from the plane carrying them. In this case, the assertion was that one low voltage safety switch was all that prevented their explosion. I have no knowledge of the safety circuitry involved, and believe in the need to keep that a secret (as a safeguard against action being taken to cause premature explosion). Besides, Defense In Depth safeguards and Fail-Safe design practices make the conclusion that only one switch prevented a nuclear explosion likely to be erroneous fear-based conjecture, or sensationalism. (Just arming a nuclear weapon while still flying over one's own country would, I think, result in career-ending repercussions for those involved.)

All in all, the reputed near initiations of nuclear war or disaster seem to me to be overblown, as were the dangers of the Three Mile Island and Chernobyl accidents.

Dr. Caldicott's views have been well received in New Zealand. Its 1987 Nuclear Free Zone, Disarmament, and Arms Control Act rejects the atomic bomb and prohibits nuclear powered or nuclear-armed ships within 12 miles of the country. New Zealand also hopes to use wind, solar, geothermal and hydroelectric sources to provide 90% of its power. That country may well have decided that without Dr. Caldicott's input, and may well have been unfazed by being informed in 1984 by our Secretary of State that the U.S. would no longer maintain its security guarantee for the country. But both New Zealand and Dr. Caldicott's native Australia have no intent to have nuclear power or nuclear weapons, and accept the military vulnerability and economic adversity that may entail.

Still, despite the apparent overreaction and sensationalism, anti-nuclear activists spur those they affect into beneficial caution—as long we don't endanger the ability to execute a valid nuclear attack order or prevent a beneficial use of nuclear power.

Dr. Caldicott alternates her time primarily between the United States and Australia. So her anti-nuclear efforts primarily affect English-speaking peoples but not the citizenry of nuclear-armed nations like Russia, China, India, Pakistan, North Korea, and (soon) Iran. Who makes similar inputs to their nuclear programs?

Advocacy and Human Nature

Advocacy's one-sided lack of objectivity was illustrated to me many decades ago when I discussed war with an intelligent lady at a social function. She deplored war—as I did and do. But she also stated that war would end if we unilaterally disarmed—because everyone else would too. When I think of her vision of peace, I also think of Adolph Hitler and the Nazis, Joseph Stalin and the tens of millions of Russians he killed, and Idi Amin and his minions—and of how dangerous unrealistic advocacy can be.

Many peaceful people don't treat evils like genocides as being an inherent part of human nature—as are murders, rapes, robberies, and the crimes that riots enable. But that arbitrarily rejects reality. And war and criminality are fostered when the military and the police are weakened. Moreover, rejecting certain weapons or tactics without evaluating the specific circumstances and alternative(s) weakens a country's ability to defend itself.

Restricting Weaponry

Every new weapon of war has been seriously deplored as making the world more dangerous (including the English longbow). But, except for the so far successful rejection of use of the atomic bomb after it ended WWII, prohibiting the use of specific weapons hasn't worked well.

A prime example is chemical warfare. Opposition to it was evident at the Hague Convention of 1899, which prohibited projectiles used solely for the diffusion of asphyxiating or deleterious gases. Then, after Germany used Mustard Gas against the British, Canadians, and French in 1917 during WWI, and Britain retaliated with its own version during the breach of the Hindenburg line in 1918, the 1925 Geneva Protocol prohibited chemical and biological weapon use in international armed conflicts. But that didn't stop chemical warfare.

A recent example occurred on March 16, 1988, when the Iraqi Air Force dropped reputed nerve gas cocktails on Halabja, a Kurdish city in Iraq, near the Iranian border. Most victims exhibited Mustard Gas symptoms. There were 3000-5000 deaths and 7,000-10,000 were injured. Also, in 1995, a Sarin nerve gas attack on a Tokyo subway killed 12, severely injured 50, and temporarily impaired the vision of 984. (Aum Shinrikyo, the culpable religious group of domestic terrorist culprits, has 13 members under death sentence. Five others have been imprisoned for life, and 80 more were given prison terms.)

In the Syrian civil war that began in 2011, the U.N. found evidence of four chemical weapon attacks by Shi'a government forces against the Sunni rebels. (90% of the U.N. samples taken reportedly detected Sarin.) CBS News described an August 2013 rocket-delivered nerve gas attack on rebel-held Damascus, including ugly deaths caused by respiratory paralysis. There was heart-rending footage of affected children.

The 1997 Chemical Weapons Convention (CWC) treaty bans chemical weapons and monitors their destruction. (It became effective in Syria on October 14, 2013.) All United Nations members are parties except Angola, nuclear-armed North Korea, Egypt, and South Sudan. (Israel and Myanmar have signed but not ratified the treaty.) But the Tokyo subway attack proved that chemical weapons are feasible without government support. And countries at war don't often keep treaty obligations to their enemies. So the CWC treaty is a step toward resolving this more than a century old problem, but diplomacy alone can't solve it.

Nuclear weapons are complex and expensive enough to make their production a national project. The primary atomic bomb danger now may be the potential for Muslim Terrorists to get some and retry a 9/11/01 attack using them. If that happens, the likelihood that the atomic bomb(s) will have come from the U.S. or its allies seems remote.

There's a lot to do vigilantly, every day, to keep nuclear weapons and nuclear power safe. But nuclear weapons are a deterrent that has made the world safer, and economical electric power can make the world more prosperous. A big obstacle to rational decision-making on these considerations is the world's associated lack of objective, balanced education and assessment of all aspects of the issues.

The Media

The media continually seems to embrace antinuclear propaganda. An example is the assertion that: *most scientists agree that all radiation is harmful.* A great deal of expertise is needed to assert that. Moreover, even if a poll were taken and concluded that all radiation is harmful, it would just be unscientific and incorrect opinion.

A February 1982 *Scientific American* article by Arthur C. Upton on *The Biological Effects of Low-Level Ionizing Radiation* reflected a scientific approach. But *The Swallows of Fukushima*, a February 2015 *Scientific American* article, set its basic tone by stating that: *Most scientists agree that there is no such thing as a "safe" dose of radiation.* It also states: *Although scientists have not determined a "safe" dose of radiation...* Such statements not only disregard sunshine and oncology, they contradict the sound basis of radiation dose limits.

The 2015 *Scientific American* article also proclaimed that, until the Chernobyl explosion spread the equivalent of 400 Hiroshima bombs of fallout across the Northern Hemisphere, scientists knew next to nothing about the effects of radiation on vegetation and wild animals. Radiation research has been highly directed toward the effects on mankind, but its results are generally applicable to other mammals. Also, irradiation of food has received significant study. So the "next to nothing" characterization of knowledge of radiation's effect on animals and vegetation is an overstatement. More significant, (see Zidbits), when fission products have been airborne for a few weeks, their most dangerous radioactivity has decayed. The Chernobyl Forum found that the health risks they pose are negligible and generally indistinguishable from the low-level radiation everyone receives simply by living. So correlating the Chernobyl accident's less than 50 radiation-induced deaths to 400 atomic bomb explosions (when two such explosions killed 200,000 Japanese) is alarmist sensationalism.

It would have been educational if the Fukushima barn swallow article included: if and how the defects had been determined to be radiation-induced (and if and how abandoned property effects had been ruled out); why male barn swallows are more defective; if other birds (e.g., barn owls, who have a different diet) have similar problems; the difference in bird and mammal radiation tolerance; whether barn swallows had changed their Fukushima migration endpoint to locales with more food (flying insects); whether substantive peer review had endorsed the findings (some dispute was noted), etc. But the article didn't address those aspects.

That the February 2015 *Scientific American* article didn't display a higher scientific standard was especially disappointing in a magazine that prides itself on the Nobel laureates who have graced its pages.

EPA Guidance

The EPA (Environmental Protection Agency) issues a PAG (Protective Action Guideline) manual to assist in determining protective actions for environmental radioactivity. Examples include evacuations, sheltering, using potassium iodide to protect against radioactive iodine, obtaining an alternate drinking water source, and interdicting food and milk. The manual issued in March 2013, is a draft for interim use and public comment.

That EPA guidance has been disputed. Some of the contentions (per nextgov.com) involve the new threshold for water contaminated with Iodine-131 of 2,700 picocuries per liter being 900 times higher than the previous 3 picocurie value. A counter was that, had the three picocurie value been imposed after the Fukushima accident, protective action would have been imposed for rainwater contaminated by radioactive fallout that crossed the Pacific Ocean. Neither of these postures quantifies the effects on people of the old or the new limit.

Weart's Appeal to Reason

In the Preface to his book *The Rise of Nuclear Fear,* Spencer Weart identifies Pavlovian conditioning and even a single traumatic experience as providing visceral fear and disgust. He also states that our brains scarcely distinguish between direct experiences and vivid imaginary ones seen, for example, in movies. His goal is to point out the power of imagery, to make it easier to resist manipulation by propagandists and by our own unconscious biases, and to make reason, not imagery, our guide.

Weart's dream that reason will control human nature depends on the slowness of cultural evolution and the infinitesimally slow progress of human evolution. (For at least all of recorded human history, Old Blood and Guts George S. Patton's statement that *weapons change but man who uses them changes not at all* is true for all of human nature.)

My Views about Nuclear Energy

My personal view is that nuclear energy has been maligned based on exaggerated fear. My views also include:

- **About 20 years elapsed between WWI and WWII. Since then, 70 years have elapsed without WWIII. The atomic bomb is a major reason why.**
- **If we could again save millions of lives by killing one enemy for every 25-100 lives saved, not doing so would be monstrously inhumane.**
- **If nuclear power weren't needed, it would disappear.**
- **Nuclear accident costs mandate superior preventive and protective measures.**
- **Requirements for new reactors should enhance operator training (e.g., in simulators) as much as design safety.**
- **New reactor Containments should withstand stresses beyond those the reactor plants can, and contain both power plant and fuel storage accident products. (The Nuclear Regulatory Commission is addressing that.)**
- **SL-1 and Chernobyl affirmed that stringent reactivity control over shutdown nuclear reactors is essential.**
- **U.S. radiation dose limits provide a safety margin that should be retained at least until its magnitude is known.**

- Definitive proof of the radiation safety margin will not halt anti-nuclear advocacy.
- Radiation is a manageable hazard.
- Low level radiation is not a killer.
- The Linear No Threshold model of radiation effects is a pig-in-a-poke that no one should still be buying. It provides a low level radiation safety margin, but the overblown risk projections it engenders are lethal. Unwarranted fear of low level radiation has killed a lot more people than nuclear power reactor accidents.
- The Nuclear Boogeyman's unnecessarily lethal trail shows that reason (Science) is no match for overblown fear.

Part V

Ruminations

V-1 The Workplace

Character

We weren't born civilized. Nurture, example, and personal choice put that thin veneer on us. And the people we work with or for typically are sufficiently nurturing and a good example. But some individuals use others to serve their personal agenda(s) without regard for the individuals used.

Examples include the denigrating treatment of others by Fleet Admiral King and by Admiral Rickover. Fortunately, no one with whom I have been closely associated has exhibited their infamous behaviors. (They achieved in spite of their character.)

Power and Corruption

Power over others is necessary to accomplish goals beyond one's ability to achieve alone, and that brings the corruptive effect of power into play. Awareness that the person wearing the face that stares back at you from the mirror is susceptible to being corrupted by power is Step One in avoiding that.

Admiral King's reputed destruction of the career of any officer who disagreed with him was immoral and unethical. It also denied him the knowledge and experience of his subordinates.

Admiral Rickover remained abrasive and untouchable for a long time. Then the Secretary of the Navy censured him for taking $67,628 in gratuities from General Dynamics, the Navy's primary submarine builder, and forced his retirement because of his negative impact on the Navy. He's still credited with nuclear power's gigantic advancement in Naval Warfare and an awesome nuclear safety record, but his career ended with a dose of punishment for his misbehavior. (The only humane act of his that I recall was giving a little bronze desk plaque of the Breton Fisherman's Prayer to President Kennedy and to each nuclear submarine Commanding Officer. It stated: O, GOD, THY SEA IS SO GREAT AND MY BOAT IS SO SMALL.)

Morality

The Service Academies took strong action against inherently immoral acts. That didn't, for example, prevent occasional cheating scandals, but it removed the culprits and strengthened the avoidance of moral turpitude. Still, being human, a few midshipmen lobbied better students to try less because the Academy graded on the curve and those who did well made it harder on their classmates. But those lobbyists did the best they could in areas where they excelled for the same reason that those they lobbied continued to try their best. (The times that I didn't apply myself properly were due to my inadequacies, not to trying to make anyone else's road easier.)

In the post-graduation workplace, it's easier for the immoral to take credit for others' achievements and evade accountability for their own failings. Good management encourages those who do that to seek other employment. And individuals seeking to avoid personal corruption should seek work where individual accomplishment is clearly credited, and should take special care to openly credit others' accomplishments.

It's unwise to associate with those who seek personal advantage by denigrating others (Birds of a feather...). The slings and arrows they aim at you will do less harm than being a part of a chicanery practitioners' circle.

Good people compensate for the rest. So, Illegitimi non carborundum. (Don't let the bastards grind you down.)

Blake-Mouton

The business world has given considerable thought to the tendency to advance oneself at the expense of others. In an industrial engineering course, an aspect of that was depicted as a graphic representation of the Blake-Mouton Management Grid. Its horizontal (X) axis represented concern for the job; its vertical (Y) axis represented concern for people. Each axis was numbered from one to nine. (A 9.1 rating reflected maximum concern for the job and minimum concern for its performers. A 1.9 dating was the opposite.) My recollection is that the two numbers added together couldn't exceed 10 and a 5.5 rating showed equal consideration for the job and people. (A current version of the grid rates the ideal manager as a 9.9 to show maximum concern for both the people and the work.)

The class I was in disputed the grid because concern for people and concern for the job are inter-related to the degree that better treatment of people produces better work. The instructor then identified the purpose of the grid as to provide insights into relationship between people priorities and job priorities.

The insight the grid fosters is important because the people you work with are likely to contribute more to your success if they see you as considerate of them.

Attitude

There are some situations in which the *Kick ass and take names* approach is necessary. But that generally makes the workplace less productive than a positive, constructive attitude.

I once saw belligerence proclaimed on an office door. It had a big poster portraying a large, ugly buzzard perched on a scraggly tree. The caption stated: Yea, though I walk through the Valley of Death, I will Fear no Evil, for I am the Meanest S.O.B. in the Valley. The occupant of the office didn't seem to contribute anything to the organization. But he cast a negative aura which probably lasted until it was overwhelmed by one cast by an S.O.B. so mean that advertising wasn't necessary.

Damaging Behavior

I also once saw a manager split his subordinates into groups, assign a "Lead" in each group, and pass on his duties to them. They then could do less of their work because they were doing his. When the manager's boss assessed the situation, the manager's job was eliminated.

Individuals who jump from job to job without a significant increase in pay or responsibility are suspect. Where no valid reason is evident, the shifts may have been due to mediocre performance. (Management has been known to alter job conditions so that an individual will move on without the company risking any consequent liability.)

It's good practice to adopt one's supervisor's goals as one's own. But a supervisor can take advantage of that by requiring a subordinate to formally proclaim the supervisor's agenda as the subordinate's. That makes it easier for the supervisor to take credit for his or her agenda's successes and blame the subordinate for its failures. Eventually, however, what goes around comes around.

I've also seen managers try to deny their part in unsuccessful outcomes. They thereby tried to shift the blame to someone else. That didn't work consistently, and the esteem for those culprits decreased in the eyes of those in the know.

Vigilance

Despite its inequities, the workplace, by and large, is a Win-Win-Win relationship between supervisors, subordinates, and customers. Still, it's wise to tried to heed an exhortation I recall from a Harry Belafonte concert: *Don't turn your back on the masses, Man!* It's also wise to keep your eyes wide open around "good" people.

V-2 Marriage

The Expectation

Lucky people learn about marriage while growing up in a secure, happy family with both a mother and a father. They, and others, typically expect to marry and live happily ever after—like the fairy tale about Prince Charming and his beautiful bride.

My Own Failures

My two marriages, like many other ones, failed. Neither bride became a dedicated supporter of and significant contributor to the way of life that I had chosen. But they each soon realized that I wasn't Prince Charming. And the compatibility that each marriage began with decreased and became alienation that destroyed each relationship long before it ended.

Knowledge

One should learn more from failure than success, so I should know a lot about marriage. I don't. But I do know that, while there are some lifelong happy matings of couples who wed soon after meeting, that's usually not a good foundation for marriage. Comprehensive knowledge about each other is a sounder base.

Success

Spouses who have common mutual goals and proven compatible characteristics, and who become partners who grow and change together, have a sound basis for marital success. Those who each do his and/or her "own thing" are far more likely to fail at marriage, whether or not they divorce.

Some marriages between unsuited persons endure. But the overall marital success rate rises or falls with the degree of mutual compatibility, partnership, and commitment. The best odds lie in making marriage a partnership that works toward common goals.

Go Slowly

There are many examples of the lasting emotional and financial trauma on the divorced and their children. Living together until long-term suitability and commitment are assured is sound groundwork for a successful marriage. Not starting a family before there's such assurance is eminently sensible.

Divorce Consequences

Sooner or later, about half the marriages end in divorce. Tales abound about the associated unfairness, and especially about the ability of one spouse to be supported by the other one—without being required to earn even part of his or her own living. Those even include being supported in the manner to which one has become accustomed (rather than in the manner one has earned). Fairer divorce laws have been enacted (slowly). But old practices and values often prejudice judgments, and the disadvantages of divorce still can outweigh the down side of marital incompatibility. Knowledge of that has sometimes been expressed as: *I can't divorce the (bleep) because I'll get taken to the cleaners.* Assurances (and laws) that proclaim otherwise notwithstanding, that too often happens. The following factors may play a role:

- The longer the duration of a marriage, the greater the long term financial and other cost of divorce. (The longer you stay, the more you pay.)
- The longer the divorce process, the higher its cost. That can worsen the Lose-Lose-Win-Win aspect. (Both parties pay more, both lawyers gain more.) Courts can make that substantially worse by countenancing delays.

Vindictiveness

All too often, divorcing spouses exhibit vindictive hatred. That can exacerbate the punitive tenor of their associated behavior by, for example, delaying divorce completion. But its worst aspect shows up in parents who teach their children that the other parent is "bad." That may bolster a parent's self-esteem, but it inevitably lowers the self-esteem of the children involved, perhaps seriously and perhaps permanently. Sacrificing one's children on that altar of hate also can happen in failed marriages that are maintained for the sake of the children's well-being.

V-3 Intoxicants

Alcohol

I had a boyhood encounter with alcoholism when my father's best friend visited. For days afterwards, we found half pint bottles of whiskey hidden around our house, and he died relatively young. Also, a favorite uncle died from cirrhosis of the liver, after becoming a derelict whose siblings stopped helping him out because he spent everything on booze.

In the Navy, one of our petty officers dropped dead on the way to work. (The XO expressed appreciation that it had happened on the pier because the paperwork load for death cases was incredible, the Naval Base was better staffed to handle it, and he would have been mired in administrative detail for months if the death had occurred aboard.) Shipboard scuttlebutt was that the deceased was a highly competent sailor who stayed on sea duty to minimize the ravages of alcoholism.

A sailor I counseled about his drinking told me that he didn't care about the hazards, he just wanted to drink. (He was sent off for treatment and didn't return.) Also, I knew a sailor whose drinking had alienated him from his family. He stayed aboard ship for several years without ever going ashore. Then he arranged to see his wife, took leave to do so, got a few blocks ashore, went into a bar, got falling down drunk, and never made the trip. (I don't know how he ended up.)

Another tale was the story told about an officer who had been relieved and sent for treatment for alcoholism. His friends extolled his professional competence and attributed his drinking to his family's successful opposition to his planned marriage. That reminded me of my mother's blaming of her brother's drinking on the woman he would have married if alcohol hadn't ruined his life. Crediting adversity as a cause of substance abuse doesn't help. Substance Abusers who don't accept personal responsibility for their situation aren't likely to recover. Their likely outcome is career and family loss, personal debasement, and early death.

Marijuana

Marijuana is now legal in several states, and some claim that it's no worse than alcohol. That indicates that marijuana abuse is as serious as alcoholism. And smoking pot might have carcinogenic consequences similar to those that cigarette smoking causes.

My first exposure to marijuana use came while I was the Acting Commanding Officer of a fleet ballistic missile submarine and we received a report of marijuana use by a sailor. The Navy had a strong stance against use of unauthorized drugs. LSD use, with flashbacks to the attendant highs long after usage and the associated inability to perform, were a prime concern. But all unauthorized drugs were considered unsafe. On submarines, that was even more important because of the dogma that any one person could sink the boat. Also of concern was a (discontinued) NWIP (Naval Warfare Information Publication) that stated that disregarding some rules encourages disregard of other ones. That pointed out that ignoring the prohibited use of marijuana fostered disregard of other requirements. Moreover, ours was a nuclear powered ship that carried nuclear missiles, and that made illegal drug use on our part particularly unacceptable.

Note. Milder intoxicants can lead to use of ones with more serious addictive effects, especially by the more reckless young. And the unauthorized use of drugs or intoxicants is unjustified. But the overriding consideration with marijuana could be that its prohibition may turn out to be as unwise and corruptive as the prohibition of alcohol was.

This sailor had previously been busted (reduced in rank) from second class petty officer to third class petty officer at Captain's

Mast for a different offense. Implementation of the bust had been withheld. If good behavior was shown, the bust would be voided. In the meantime, the sailor had passed the advancement exam and was scheduled to become a first class petty officer.

I held Captain's mast. The sailor admitted, without remorse, to knowingly using a prohibited, illegal substance. Also, shipboard training had emphasized the prohibition, and the typical supervisory attestation of good performance was absent. So the time to hold him accountable had come. I rescinded the recommendation for advancement to first class petty officer, imposed the withheld bust to third class petty officer, busted him in rate to seaman for this infraction, and disqualified him from submarine duty. The Navy transferred him to Vietnam.

Upon his return, the Captain assembled and addressed the crew. He stated that marijuana was regarded by some as not being a problem but, even if a crew member felt that way, the prohibition was a lawful order and the enlistment contract required compliance with it.

Separately, the Captain said that I should have court martialed the sailor. But that would have severely impeded our training cycle, and a Court Martial conviction would have carried a bigger stigma. Also, redemption would be easier outside a command carrying nuclear weapons. Moreover, a court martial would have taken much longer, and the closer a consequence comes to the act prompting it, the greater its effect.

This incident was an example of the reality that violating rules or expectations can be expected, sooner or later, to produce adverse consequences. The mechanics involved differ in different environments, but that premise is valid in them all.

V-4 Learning

Agendas

What we learn reflects the societal agendas of our teachers. (That's less true in scientific and technical subjects.) When I learned American history in school, George Washington was a quintessentially truthful hero from boyhood on. (*I cannot tell a lie, father. It was I who chopped down the cherry tree.*) We also were mistakenly taught that the United States spread across North America as the virtuous expansion of the American Dream, with no mention of the greed-based conquest that was central to building our and every other country. And we were taught about the balance of power between the Executive, Legislative, and Judicial branches of government, but not about the reality that partisanship in each branch makes that putative balance far from characteristic.

Human nature hasn't changed, but history is now the projection of a different political agenda. That doesn't invalidate education. But it means that a great deal of it isn't reality but an input that opens the door to learning what the reality is.

Generational Impact

Every generation sees itself as different. Genetically, that's nonsense. But it's true because we inherit the intelligence and versatility that enable mankind to adapt to the changes that Science, Culture, and Nature wreak. Unfortunately, our adaptability peaks and then wanes. So we go from teaching current technology to our elders to having a younger generation do that for us.

Aging makes learning harder, and unused skills deteriorate. But application can minimize that—Nuclear Power School did a lot to correct my waning academic skill.

Some believe that the ability to contribute substantially passes as we age. A cited example is Einstein's 1905 publication of five landmark papers when he was 26, with no repeat of such productivity. But, 10 years later, he followed up his special relativity theory (the interrelationship of space and time, or space-time) with general relativity (which recast gravity as the distortion of space-time by mass). His subsequent efforts to develop a unified theory to encompass general relativity and the quantum physics that defines subatomic relationships failed, but so did those of many other geniuses who tried to develop a unified theory in the over 100 years that have elapsed since then.

Gregor Mendel was 42 when he created modern genetic science by presenting its laws of segregation and independent assortment. Charles Darwin's seminal work on the origin of species wasn't completed until he was 49, and his last major work was published in 1881, the year before he died at the age of 73.

Too many people learn too little after the age of 30. But, while the young have more stamina and learn faster, aging enables a cumulative increase in knowledge and wisdom. So always be a student. That makes you smarter. But be aware that human nature tends to make us overestimate our capabilities. I saw that recently in an assertion that we do our best work in our 70s and 80s. In ways involving overall wisdom and the big picture, that can be true. But one has to take that proficiency very far out of context and the realm of reality to generalize (extrapolate) it to situations dependent upon the mental and physical strength, quickness, and stamina that the young are typically superior at.

V-5 Capitalism and Socialism

Propaganda

We've been heavily exposed to propaganda about the marvels of Democracy and Capitalism. They have been justifiably touted as enabling people to prosper regardless of their origins, and justifiably condemned because they concentrate wealth at the top.

Communism (Socialism), which owns all property and industry, has been reviled for being repressive, with kangaroo courts and no redress for wrongs, and for enslaving its people. A primary basis for that was the Soviet Union, the communist state that kept its people impoverished and virtually enslaved.

Socialist Aspects

Soviet Russia slaughtered tens of millions of its dissidents, and fell apart in 74 years. {Tsarist Russia owned its people (serfs) too, but their quality of life may have been better than under Communism under Joseph Stalin.}

Russia's impoverishment may be why WWII UK Prime Minister Winston Churchill described Socialism as the equal sharing of misery. (He also called it a philosophy of failure, the creed of ignorance, and the gospel of envy.)

Socialist values lead to things like Lowest Common Denominator standards, more poorly educated graduates, and an overall lowering of the standard of living.

We're borrowing money to pay for socialistic aspects of our present society, and Socialists promise more freebies. One is free college tuition, which would be terrific if that didn't also mean that entrance standards would be lowered and the Lowest Common Denominator effect increased, or that more government control of the purse strings would increase its control over curricula.

Socialism has had and does have devoted followers. Some of them even recognize the need to ensure that people work and develop their abilities. Nobel Prize winning playwright George Bernard Shaw, a devout Socialist, showed recognition of the difficulty of achieving that when he said that a government that robs Peter to pay Paul has the support of Paul.

Governments perform only as well as the people in power, and Socialism's relative lack of safeguards against abuse is why it doesn't last as long as Democracy does.

Democracy

A key premise of our Democracy is that we are all created equal and have an equal opportunity to advance ourselves. That's aptly called the American Dream because, mentally, physically, and otherwise, we're not created equal. Nurture, education, and experience increase the inequalities. But, insofar as the dream is reasonably achievable, it's wonderful.

Even though the few at the top of the money tree are exorbitantly rich, our Democracy generally rewards incentive and work. But our astronomical national debt gives credence to the assertion that, when the voters realize that they can raid the public treasury, they vote in those who give them more—and in about 200 years that tomfoolery produces a dictatorship. Democracy also suffers from many other ignoble traits. As John Adams, our second President, wrote in 1814:

...democracy never lasts long. It soon wastes, exhausts, and murders itself. There never was a democracy yet that did not commit suicide. It is in vain to say that democracy is less vain, less proud, less selfish, less ambitious, or less avaricious than aristocracy or monarchy. It is not true, in fact, and nowhere appears in history. Those passions are the same in all men, under all forms of simple government, and when unchecked, produce the same effects of

fraud, violence, and cruelty. When clear prospects are opened before vanity, pride, avarice, or ambition, for their easy gratification, it is hard for the most considerate philosophers and the most conscientious moralists to resist the temptation... Individuals have conquered themselves. Nations and large bodies of men, never.

Adams' realism was expressed about 10 years after he lost his bid for reelection to Thomas Jefferson, a defeat that made him bitter. But it's still an unusually harsh statement about the government he did so much to bring about as a highly influential founding father and political theorist. UK Prime Minister Winston Churchill was kinder after being deposed after WWII. He stated: *Democracy is the worst form of government,* except for *all those other forms that have been tried from time to time.*

Aversion to Socialism

Many Americans have a well-conditioned aversion to Socialism. An example was widely expressed outrage when a high school graduating class made its Yearbook motto a dream adopted by Revolutionary Socialist Karl Marx: *From each according to his ability; to each according to his need.* But that was just utopian idealism on the part of the immature—and a wish for people to help each other (and especially them).

Humaneness

Our democracy has done much to pursue humaneness. When our stock market crashed in 1929, the great depression that followed cut the country's wealth in half in three years. By 1934 over half of our elderly population was unable to support itself. And, in 1935, the Social Security Act was enacted with bipartisan support (House: Democrats 19:1 Yeas: Nays, Republicans 5:1 Yeas: Nays. Senate: Democrats 60:1 Yeas: Nays, Republicans 3:1 Yeas: Nays). So the USA became the 35th country to adopt Social "Insurance." We now pay an involuntary, employer-matched 6.2% FICA tax on earnings for Social Security and Medicare, and must earn 40 credits at a maximum of 4/year to be eligible for Social Security retirement. But those who have paid their FICA tax and become disabled before retirement age, and their dependent survivors, are eligible for Social Security disability.

Our Socialism and Profligacy

To the extent that Social Security taxation is based on ability to pay and its benefits are based on need, it's Socialism. Moreover, it's here to stay because most of us live from payday to payday, and are either unable or unwilling to save up for retirement or economic adversity.

Social security is not only socialistic, some see it as a Ponzi scheme because FICA tax revenue is put in the country's general fund, the entire general fund (and more) is spent each year, and government trusts that the economy will provide enough tax revenue tomorrow to pay the social security benefits that today's FICA tax payers have earned. That and borrowing to pay other commitments today with no provision for paying back the borrowed money is called *kicking the can down the road.*

Our federal income tax is Socialistic too. It takes a higher percentage of higher earners' incomes (ability to pay). But, except for dastardly loopholes that enable the wealthy to avoid taxation, and for misuses of the treasury, taxes sustain our Democracy. That's harder each year because the interest payments grow on the ever-increasing, incredible national debt caused by our representative government's profligacy.

Barriers to Socialism

We're not yet a Socialist country because we have private ownership of property and business, and our courts can overrule our government. But judges, including Supreme Court Justices, are typically Liberals (Democrats) or Conservatives (Republicans). They're also noted for making Law as well as for applying it. (An exception is Conservative Supreme Court Justice Clarence Thomas, who came into his office under a cloud but credibly applies the Constitution's literal meaning and original intent.) Partisan election of judges and appointment of sycophantic ones aids a like-minded government's ability to deviate from the Constitution and its implementing Laws. Were it not for the unpredictability of such selections, putting partisans and sycophants in the judiciary instead of jurists (which too few become) would have further degraded, and perhaps ended, the independence of the judiciary.

Dictatorial Democracy

Rule by presidential mandate is undemocratic. My initial exposure to that came when a college instructor told us about President Theodore Roosevelt sending the Great White Fleet (the post-Civil War, steel ship, modern Navy he had caused to be developed) around the world to show off America's power, especially to China and Japan. According to the instructor, Congress refused to appropriate the funds for that 13 month circumnavigation of the world. But the President found that budgeted funds could send the fleet to the Orient and used that fact to coerce the Congress into appropriating the money to bring it home. Being Naval Officers in training, that sounded good to us. But Presidents who disregard or circumvent Constitutional safeguards practice dictatorship.

Government's Great Flaw

The main fault of government is the failings of its governors. A long known serious one was stated by Lord Acton in 1887: *Power tends to corrupt, and absolute power corrupts absolutely. Great men are almost always bad men.* And corruption destroys both Democracy and Socialism (faster).

Core Differences

The criticism that, under Democracy and Capitalism, the rich few have more "rights" is generally (but not always) true. Under Socialism, it's the people in power who occupy that niche (and live highest on the hog). But the main difference is that, under real Democracy with fair elections, people own the government (except the courts) and, under real Socialism, the government owns the people (and everything else, including the courts).

Options

Individually, we can't change our government. But we can scrutinize our own use of power to safeguard against abusing it. And those who can vote need to do so with an eye to their descendants' well-being as well as to their own. The best choice my grandsons have is to be self-supporting in order to have a better chance of surviving the collapse that ends every Democracy—should it happen during their lifetimes.

V-6 Equality

Blacks and Whites

At the Naval Academy, one of the Black midshipmen in my class was in my company. During our plebe year, there also was one Black upperclassman in our company. I saw no difference between the Black and the White midshipmen, and no indication that anyone else did either.

My first wife said that Whites and Blacks are alike because the Black girl she grew up with was just like the White ones. But, after a year on the east coast, she feared Black people.

The Blacks who worked for me and those I worked with were as competent as the Whites. More recently, I've found the Blacks I've purchased furniture and appliances from to be superior to their White counterparts—and I ask for them when I shop in their stores. Moreover, a very competent Black repairman recently solved the problems that had long plagued my telephone service.

My experience therefore indicates that antipathy between Blacks and Whites should be decreasing. But my perception is that the opposite is true. (Perception **is** reality to the perceiver.) I attribute that to the unfair discrimination Blacks perceive in their treatment by Whites and the favoritism that Whites perceive in the treatment accorded to Blacks.

Affirmative Action

Affirmative Action was instituted to compensate for the inequities visited upon minorities and women. It mandates preferential treatment in hiring and in acceptance for higher education opportunities. Supporters proclaim diversity as its virtue. But some States (California, Michigan, and Washington) ban Affirmative Action in public institutions, including schools. And some countries ban it because it treats different races differently.

The argument against Affirmative Action is that preferential treatment of a person or group constitutes unfair discrimination against other persons or groups. The argument for Affirmative Action is that it counters unfair discrimination against minorities and women. Both arguments are valid.

In my experience, the difficulty of finding qualified minority applicants and the emphasis on hiring minorities caused the search for and pursuit of minority applicants to take precedence over selection based on qualification. Comments by other Whites have showed the same perception. As a wag put it, *We're all equal, but some are more equal than others.*

An example told to me involved the competition for some government hires. The top Black applicants scored lower than the top White applicants on the tests given. On a competitive basis, the White applicants would have been given all the jobs. So the jobs weren't filled. Many months later, Black applicants filled them without another open selection process being conducted. I cannot avow that the selections happened that way, but the White applicant I know strongly felt that.

That Whites see Affirmative Action as favoring the lesser qualified is affirmed by other sources. One, reportedly, is Supreme Court Justice Clarence Thomas's perception that, when he graduated from Yale, potential employers considered his degree to have been awarded based on Affirmative Action rather than on being earned.

I've also seen an assertion that Blacks make up 14% of the population and have 18% of the government jobs. That's contradicted by assertions that Black employment falls far short of being consistent with the black proportion of our population. At least one of these assertions is false. And, because end-justifies-the-means politics is so pervasive, both may be far from the truth. The only aspect of these contradictions that we can be sure of is that harmony isn't being fostered.

Core Absurdities

Discrimination between Whites and Blacks based on skin color is ridiculous. Dark skin color evolved in Africa because the increase in melanin in darker skin provides better protection against the tropical sun. Lighter skin is healthier in northern climes where there's less sunshine and where cold weather clothing further cuts back on solar radiation.

The fact that Eskimos don't have the white skin, blond hair, and blue eyes relatively prevalent in Scandinavia indicates that white skin developed over a much shorter period than gradual evolution would produce. One or a few white skin mutations in Northern Europe could have provided a reproductive advantage that propagated widely. So could the appropriation of the few genes we gained by intermixing with Neanderthals. In either case, white skin is a minute alteration of the genome of the about 5000 (or fewer) Blacks who left Africa and become the ancestors of the Caucasian and Mongolian variants of humanity.

Human "races" have always intermixed. And the separation between the White and Black cultures in the U.S. has diminished substantially. In addition to association with those of similar appearance, we're strongly influenced by our preference for association with people we admire and for those with behavior, beliefs, education, and status similar to our own. We also generally admire merit and have low regard for those perceived to have gained unearned benefits. So our cultural differences primarily separate people by a combination of their appearance, character, education, erudition, ethnicity, and wealth.

Unfortunately, there's still far too much unfair discrimination based on color. In too many minds, all Blacks and all offspring and descendants of White and Black intermixing are arbitrarily categorized as Black. That has fostered discrimination based on cultural prejudice instead of on individual character.

The young typically are more tolerant than the older populace, and more likely to assess people on their character. They're the greatest influence on lessening unfair cultural discrimination—at least until ethnic discrimination (including Affirmative Action) adversely affects them. Nonetheless, because feelings and attitudes aren't as mortal as their holders, unless we all let go of the wrongs done to us and/ or our ancestors, we'll pass on the anger those engender—and thereby increase the danger of violence in our descendants' world. (Separate groups who work together to meet common goals have a far better chance of achieving them than groups that work apart from each other.)

Resolution

Since the Civil War, efforts to resolve the Black vs. White issue have produced a lot of change—too much of which is superficial. Correcting the root cause(s) could substantially improve that. An example a colleague gave me was from a training course on quality management under the principles taught by Deming, the Quality Guru credited with teaching the Japanese to produce better products (e.g., cars). The (probably theoretical) illustration was a machine that produced sheets of creased stationery. In America, another machine was added to iron out the creases. In Japan, the faulty machine was redesigned. Five years later, the then lower cost of the Japanese product put its competition out of business—by correcting the root cause.

Selecting/hiring less than the best qualified doesn't fix the root cause of failure to make the disadvantaged as well qualified as their competition. Correcting that root cause requires correcting educational inadequacies and assuring parental emphasis on and support of their children's education. Where there are different male and female work ethics and/or cultures, those too must be changed. Until we accomplish those Herculean tasks, Band-Aids like Affirmative Action will foster increasing discontent.

People of Hebrew, Oriental, and Indian ethnicity are often cited as being successful because their cultures place great value on education and on a strong work ethic. They reputedly don't share the widespread Black and White belief that we are all entitled to the necessities of life, and to luxuries, by virtue of being alive. That false premise leads to people being willing to live off the labor of others without earning their own way. (If and when enough people embrace that belief, there won't be enough labor done for them to live on.)

V-7 Slavery

The Civil War

The perception that White people imposed slavery on Black people is a half-truth. Even a lot of Southern Whites opposed slavery. And many rebels mistakenly thought they were fighting for Southern self-determination, rather than to defend the slavery that the South's economy was based upon. Moreover, slavery is a form of human dominance, which is independent of "race."

When slavery was legal in the United States, Blacks and their mixed race descendants were wrongly treated as subhuman, denied educational and economic opportunity, and their family culture was destroyed. That was worse in the South, but it happened in the North too.

In the 1860 election that made Abraham Lincoln our first Republican President, a key element of the Republican platform was prohibition of Slavery in the western territories. That didn't directly threaten slavery in the Southern States, but Lincoln's election prompted seven of them to secede.

The Civil War began on April 12, 1861 when the South fired on Fort Sumpter. About 750,000 people died in that war. Over 700,000 of them were White, making that war a lethal conflict between Southern and Northern Whites. (Based on figures updated by Professor J. David Hacker, a historian, the death total was 388,500 Union White soldiers, 48,500 Union Black soldiers, and 313,000 Confederate soldiers.) That the war killed 2.4% of the country's population, about eight times the 0.3% of deaths that we experienced in World War II, and that it didn't end until the North defeated the South on the battlefield show how deeply slavery divided the U.S.

Abolition

Slavery's abolition produced but little change in the former slaves' social and economic status. Whites (in both the North and the South) actively maintained the societal conditions that kept Blacks economically and culturally disadvantaged.

The assassination of Abraham Lincoln made post-war oppression of the South harsher. And that strengthened the South's resistance to making the former slaves' lot better. In too many cases, the former slaves' descendants' family values and cohesiveness still suffer from the consequences of that war and the cultural disadvantages that abolition didn't correct.

Mandela's Way

Another example of combatting unfair domination is the non-violent route taken by Nelson Mandela. Even after being jailed for 24 years for his political activity, he stuck to non-violent advocacy of a free and democratic South Africa. He then became its first democratically elected President, and became known worldwide for his humility and spirit of forgiveness. South Africa is still far from free of interracial tension, and its Blacks are still disadvantaged. But, if its Black and its White leaders remain intolerant of interracial animosity and/or maltreatment, and if an effective program is instituted to raise the capabilities of the disadvantaged majority, Mandela's dream can come true without massive fatalities. (Considering that South Africa's population is about 80% Black and the country has about 4.5 million people, a genocidal civil war could jeopardize up to about a million members of its minorities and a corresponding number of its Black majority. That could produce a lot more deaths than the U.S. Civil War did.)

Martin Luther King

Martin Luther King also led a non-violent campaign against unfair discrimination. That cost him his life. His murder furthered his cause but also increased Black anger.

The Generic Issue

We tend to focus on the White vs. Black issue that Slavery made into a horrendous mess. But man has always practiced dominance, using violence if lesser coercion wasn't enough. An example was Rome's conquests and its enslavement of conquered peoples. (Most of Rome's gladiators were slaves, prisoners of war, or convicted criminals.) And the peoples of the British Isles were subjected to brutal warfare until the English conquered and absorbed the Scots, the Welsh and the Picts. (The Irish were conquered and re-conquered but not subdued.) Civilization combats the centuries-old animosities that persist between these Celts but cannot change basic human nature. Violence spawns more violence. Its victims, their families, their descendants and the families and descendants of those who somehow escaped it don't forget—and they don't forgive. If Laws could solve this problem, nobody would speed on our highways. Culture is the key. As long as we hang on to the sins of yesteryear, we perpetuate "racial" and other rifts.

The destructive predilections of large groups of mankind are as intractable as ever. But the fact that our country fought a Civil War shows that there also is a strong basic human perception of fairness and we can be much better. If we don't manage to do that we may once again learn that, to the families of the dead, even successful warfare isn't worth the cost.

The Individual Issue

Human nature makes us all potential victims of unfair discrimination. But we can turn the tables on individual oppressors by making ourselves so capable that those who try to unfairly discriminate against us discredit themselves. And we can present a clear example (the best way of teaching) of the American Dream by treating others based on their character and capability.

Nobility

Human Evil took the lives of Abraham Lincoln and Martin Luther King. And the long imprisonment it imposed on Nelson Mandela had to have shortened his. But the altruism those men showed represents the power behind the persistent dream that the noble Good (God) in all of mankind will someday overwhelm the Evil (Devil) in us.

V-8 Humane-ity

Core Aspects

Biologically, man is a mammal (one that the Sociobiologist author Desmond Morris termed *The Naked Ape).* Like other animals, we inherit natural instincts and emotions. Those include love, nurture, and teaching of offspring, and using violence for self-preservation and/or dominance. We also naturally compete for reproductive advantage, for property and other resources, for wealth, and for social status.

Man's cultures evolved to fit the experiences, education and training, and environments of geographically and/or ethnically separated parts of our world. And there's a mutual protection and support similarity in the clannishness that unites members of the same family, tribe, community, ethnicity, etc. That can produce rejection of outsiders but also provides a unified front against the dangers that others too often present.

Among mankind's complex traits are three intertwined characteristics: inherited emotions and instincts; learned behavior; and a belief in doing good. Properly blended, they produce behavior that transcends the support and protection of individuals and their groups by supporting Good (God) regardless of individual or group self-interest. Religion is at the core of that.

Abraham

The Prophet Abraham advanced his belief in one Almighty God about 1900 BC. Judaism, Christianity, and Islam, religions practiced by over half of mankind, trace their origin to him.

Moses

The Prophet Moses, about 1300 BC, presented a set of God's laws to the Israelites. Its Ten Commandments' three "do's" require honoring Almighty God by having no other God(s) before him, by keeping the Sabbath holy, and by honoring one's father and mother. The Commandments' seven "don'ts" prohibit making or worshiping idols, blasphemy, murder, adultery, stealing, bearing false witness, and coveting.

The Law of Moses was harsh. Death by stoning was the punishment for: taking accursed things; blasphemy; adultery (including urban rape victims who didn't scream loud enough); a woman who was not a virgin on her wedding night; worshipping other Gods; preaching the wrong religion; disobeying one's parents; being a witch or a wizard; breaking the Sabbath; cursing the King; and giving one's child in sacrifice to appease Molech (a Caananite God). Also, the Fifth Book of the Law of Moses states (Deuteronomy 19:21): *thine eye shall not pity: but life shall go for life, eye for eye, tooth for tooth, hand for hand, foot for foot.* It has been speculated that this was a non-obligatory limit on the punishment, but prescribing the death penalty for breaking the Sabbath as well as for murder shows that the concept of making the punishment fit the crime wasn't part of the Law of Moses.

More Humane Justice

A gentler aspect of justice is described in Christianity's New Testament's Book of John, Chapter 8. It states that the Scribes and Pharisees (who opposed Jesus) brought a woman caught in the act of adultery to him and said that the Law of Moses required that she be stoned. His response, *Let he who is without sin cast the first stone*, resulted in there being no accuser(s). And Jesus sent the now unaccused woman on her way with the admonition that she *Sin no More.*

Bart D. Ehrman's Fifth Edition of *The New Testament, A Historical Introduction to the Early Christian Writings,* states (Box 2.4) that the adulteress event was not in the earliest and best manuscripts of John and did not start showing up regularly in Greek Manuscripts until about the 9th Century. St. Jerome (see Vulgate.org) compiled/ translated earlier text(s) into the Latin Vulgate Bible from 382-384 AD but, if Ehrman is correct, the adulteress tale wasn't in St. Jerome's Vulgate Bible. It is, however, in John Wycliffe's 1382 Middle English translation of St Jerome's Vulgate Bible (available on the internet). And it is in the 1534 William Tyndale Late Middle English translation of the New Testament from Greek texts (see the 1989 modern spelling edition of the 1534 *Tyndale's New Testament* by David Daniel).

Current scholars have access to some 5700 parts/fragments of biblical script. But they cannot know all the written and oral history available over a thousand years ago (when a great majority of Christians were illiterate), and even Tyndale's New Testament may have benefitted from records that haven't survived. Moreover, absence of early written confirmation that this event occurred cannot show that it did not. And whether modern scholars are right in disputing the adulteress tale or are revising history to suit their generation's agenda, the story is a valid representation of the non-judgmental forgiveness taught in the Christian religion for over 1200 years. And it's compatible with the Mathew 7:1-3 injunction that the Tyndale-Daniel New Testament states as: *Judge not, that ye be not judged. For as ye judge so shall ye be judged. And with what measure ye mete, with the same shall it be measured to you again.* (That also gives the saying that what goes around comes around biblical support.)

Cruelty's Persistence

The slowness of integrating the fundamental nature of the teachings of Jesus was shown by European Christianity's attacks on Islam (the

Crusades) from the late 11th Century to the late 13th Century. That involved wholesale Crusader slaughter of Muslims, Christians and Jews, with Muslim retaliation in kind.

Joan of Arc was a subsequent infamous example of inhumane "Christianity." In 1431, the 19 year old Joan was denied a papal hearing and convicted of heresy for claiming to hear divine voices. She was burned at the stake. Reportedly, her last word before losing consciousness was "Jesus." Joan was declared innocent by the Pope 25 years later, and was declared a Saint in 1920.

From 1478-1834, Spain tried to purge itself of heresy by forcing Jews, Muslims, and Protestants to convert to Roman Catholicism. That Spanish Inquisition was carried out by torture so painful that death was a merciful outcome.

In 1536, William Tyndale was found guilty of heresy for translating the New Testament into English so that it could be accessed without the help of the clergy. He also partly translated the Old Testament before "Christian" justice killed him. The nature of that justice was evident in Tyndale so convincing his judges of his remarkable scholarship and character that they mercifully had him killed by strangulation before burning his body at the stake.

Such cruelty persists outside Christianity too. The "peaceful" breakup that split part of the British Empire into India and Muslim Pakistan in 1947 produced religious violence that killed half a million Hindus, Muslims, and Sikhs in 1948. And Mohandas Gandhi, the great, nonviolent, Hindu Father of India's democracy, was killed in 1948 by a militant Hindu motivated by the mistreatment of Hindus and Sikhs in Pakistan.

Unfortunately, our culture still incorporates some values that are inconsistent with our aspirations to be Good (Godly) in the way that Jesus taught. An example I saw as a youth was the assertion by older males that a man who found his wife in bed with another man was justified in killing them. And, when my cousin secretly married a sailor during World War II, her Kashubian (Polish) mother sent her to live with us several states away when she became pregnant—because she feared that her husband would kill his daughter when he found out—so my equally Kashubian mother took her in.

Other Unchristian Behavior

A case of what I considered to be decidedly unchristian behavior occurred in the church I attended as a teenager. I received a letter from its new pastor as my first year at the Naval Academy was nearing its end. That letter stated that I had not contributed anything to my church over the past year and, unless I corrected that, my name would be removed from the church rolls. Having, at the time, a monthly spendable income of $3.00 and being required to go to church every Sunday, where the collection plate was passed among the midshipmen, I thought that letter reflected pastoral ignorance as well as the placing of a monetary price on being a church member. (My brother, when he was in the Coast Guard a couple of years later, got a similar letter.) A high school classmate who has a deep, simple Christian faith correctly told me that I shouldn't let that minister's misbehavior govern my assessment of his church. But I don't regret not having ever been inside that church again, or having made no financial contribution to it except for a donation made in the memory of a recently deceased high school classmate. And I mistrust churches.

Judaism vs. Christianity

Judaism is, by definition, not a Christian religion. But the Judeo-Christian ethic makes that a matter of what the hereafter holds and not a matter of Good (Godly) behavior by the living. Individual Christians and Jews deserve respect based on their conformance to Good (Godly) behavior, and disrespecting either religion is not Godly (Good). But the epithetical connotations of the terms Kike and Goyem show that some members of both ethnic groups fall short of Good (Godly) behavior in the esteem they show for each other—and there are much worse indicators.

Islam

The Muslim culture began, as did Judaism and Christianity, in the House of Abraham. Ishmael, Abraham's firstborn son, had 12 sons who fathered the nomadic Arab tribes. The warrior prophet Muhammad, who was born in 570 AD, converted the Arab world to his Islamic faith before he died in 632 AD.

Islam is growing and counts at least one-fifth of the world as its believers. It also considers Jesus Christ to be the immaculately conceived son of Allah and destined to return to guide Islam. But we need to assess the Muslim culture based on its behavior, and not on what we hear to the contrary.

Militant Islamic Fundamentalists (radicals) are at War with infidels (non-believers in Islam). They revere spreading the Islamic religion by warfare. An illustration is the statement by the Iranian Grand Ayotollah Khomeine that: *The purest joy in Islam is to kill and be killed for Allah* (as cited on www.giveshare.org/islam from page 287 of David Lamb's "The Arabs, Journey Beyond the Mirage").

Christians, Jews, atheists, and agnostics are all infidels to Muslims. And Radical Muslims' willingness to die to kill infidels is made easier for them by the Islamic belief that they don't really die but go immediately to the highest level of Islam's Heaven (Jannah).

Jannah

In addition to the spiritual haven for the soul that Christians anticipate, Jannah is Islam's paradise of sensual pleasure.

Jannah has lush gardens. Its rivers flow with milk, and with honey, and with wine (forbidden on Earth but not in Jannah). The houses in Jannah are built of alternating bricks of gold and silver, and the food is served on plates of gold and silver.

Jannah provides voluptuous, beautiful, virgin Houris for the sexual pleasure of the men. Women also are honored with endless happiness in Jannah. But, because they long for jewels and adornment more than for men, their reward is different. Every woman in Jannah is restored to virgin status and made young and more beautiful than the Houris, and has a fully compatible husband. (Everyone in Jannah is married.)

Because there are more women than men on Earth, there are more women in Jannah than men—until the women serve their time in Hell for their sins and then enter Jannah.

The Holy Quran

The Quran is Islam's prime directive. Muslims believe that it is the exact word of Allah and a complete, perfect record of Allah's revelation to his Messenger, the Prophet Muhammad, through the Archangel Gabriel. Additional aspects of Islam are identified by Hadiths, the records of the Prophet Muhammad's life, statements, and actions that many Muslims consider a verbatim record of what Muhammad said and did. (Muhammad is credited with memorizing the Quran as it was revealed to him, and with dictating it to scribes. Those who witnessed his deeds and heard his statements handed them down orally for about 200 years before they were recorded as Hadiths.)

Quran Surah (Chapter) 1 (Dar-us-Salam translation) states:

1. In the Name of Allah, the Most Beneficent, the Most Merciful.
2. All the praises and thanks be to Allah, the Lord of the *'Alamin* (mankind, jinns and all that exists).
3. The Most Beneficent, the Most Merciful.
4. The Only Owner (and the Only Ruling Judge) of the Day of Recompense (i.e. the Day of Resurrection)
5. You (Alone) we worship, and You (Alone) we ask for help (for each and everything).
6. Guide us to the Straight Way
7. The Way of those on whom You have bestowed Your Grace, not (the way) of those who earned Your Anger (such as the Jews), nor of those who went astray (such as the Christians).

Subsequent Quran Chapters (except for Surah 9, Repentance) begin with: In the name of Allah, the Gracious, the Merciful.

Surah 4:74 promises great reward for those who die in Islam's cause. There's no conflict between that and its extolling of forgiveness (e.g., Surah 42:36-37 states that Allah has a better and more lasting reward than exists in this life for those who shun great sins and indecencies, and forgive when they are angry). Muslims can follow Islam's five foundations without committing sins under Christian doctrine. But, in addition to the Quran and Hadiths, Muslim behavior is driven by cultural values.

An Eye for an Eye

Surah 5:45 states: *And We wrote for them in it* (the Torah/Old Testament), *a life for a life, an eye for an eye, a nose for a nose, an ear for an ear, a tooth for a tooth, an equal wound for a wound. But whoever forgoes it in charity, it will serve as atonement for him. Those who do not rule according to what God revealed are the evildoers.* The forgiveness aspect of that is consistent with the Christian rejection of vengeance stated in the New Testament (Romans 12:19 of the King James Bible) as: *Dearly beloved, avenge not yourselves, but give place unto wrath: for it is written, Vengeance is mine; I will repay, saith the Lord.*

Sharia Law

Unlike our Democracy's (imperfect) separation of Church and State, Islamic societies integrate their religion into their laws and their government. Islamic religious law (Sharia) is the primary law of Muslim nations. Muslims consider Sharia Law to be derived from the Quran and the Hadiths, and timeless and perfect. They have tried to apply it in countries to which they have emigrated.

Sharia Law's Character

Sharia Law favors Muslims over non-Muslims, credits the testimony of women half as much as that of men, awards daughters half the inheritance of their brothers, and supersedes civil law. Its harsh punishments include:

- Adultery: 100 lashes, or death by stoning
- Theft: Amputation of a hand
- Consuming alcohol: 40 lashes
- Highway Robbery: imprisonment, amputation, death by crucifixion
- Apostasy (renouncing Islam): death by decapitation, burning, strangling, impaling, or flaying

An example of Sharia Law in the February 23, 2016 issue of the *National Review* is the Saudi Arabian case of Raif Badawi. His crime was starting the *Free Saudi Liberals* website. His bank accounts were frozen and he was forbidden to travel. Then charges were levied against him for Insulting Islam through Electronic Channels; and for Going beyond the Realm of Obedience. He was sentenced to 10 years, with 1000 lashes to be imposed 50 at a time every Friday for 20 weeks. The first flogging occurred on January 9, 2015, reportedly with hundreds of Saudis present and cheering *Allahu Akbar!* (*God is Great!*). Reportedly, no subsequent lashings have occurred yet because Raif Badawi hasn't recovered sufficiently from the first 50 lashes.

Perspective on Living

Christians and Jews regard life as a blessing to be enjoyed, with Good (Godly) behavior a basic duty. Muslims regard life's pleasures as petty and consider living a tribulation with its purpose being to transit toward eternal life.

Muhammad was both a religious leader and a warrior. And the Quran's endorsement of reconciliation and forgiving is consistent with the way Muhammad treated conquered Jews and Christians. But the Muslim culture condones killing infidels based on their beliefs instead of their deeds, and thereby carries endorsed Muslim practice to a plane that the Judeo-Christian ethic does not countenance.

Nonetheless, Islam and Christianity/Judaism are not inherently incompatible. Muslims view the second coming of Christ as being to lead Islam. And Jesus of Nazareth was a messenger of peace, not violence. So Christ's (or equivalent) leadership of Islam should (albeit slowly) make Muslim behavior more consistent with the traditional Muslim greeting of *Peace be unto you.* Until such a transformation overwhelms the Muslim culture, however, it will be a lethal enemy of our own. That's because, while a large number of Muslims practice essentially the same Goodness that the western world endorses, Islam also honors those who kill infidels who have done no harm to any Muslim. And, of the world's 1.5 billion Muslims, each 1% who are Militant Islamic Fundamentalists constitutes a body of 15 million potential Muslim murderers of Christians, Jews, and other infidels. Moreover, each 1% of non-radical Muslims who support their "radical" brethren is 15 million enablers of the murders done.

Honor Killings

Honor killings, though not sanctioned by the Quran, also are a part of the Muslim culture (and of much of South Asia). Their purpose is to erase the dishonor of misbehavior or violation of the community's or religion's principles. The threat they pose is used to control women's behavior. (Female virginity is a family responsibility, and is a gift to the husband upon marriage.)

Honor killing is typically the result of a collective family decision. Causes include extramarital sex, refusing an arranged marriage, having a boyfriend disapproved by the family, being raped (and losing virginity), homosexual acts, western dress, and seeking a divorce. Where honor killings are punished by law, forced suicide has been used to avoid retribution.

We've had Muslim honor killings (murders) in the United States. For example, on January 1, 2008, Yasser Abdel Said, an Egyptian, shot his 17 year old daughter Sarah and his 18 year old daughter Amina dead in Irving, Texas. The reasons involved dating non-Muslims. Yasser is on the FBI's 10 Most Wanted list but hasn't been found. And, in October 2009, Faleh Hassan Almaleki, a Palestinian, killed his 20 year old daughter Noor Almaleki in a Phoenix, Arizona parking lot by running her over with a jeep. Her dishonor was being too westernized, and refusing an arranged marriage. He was sentenced to 34 years in jail for 2nd degree (unpremeditated) murder.

Basically, honor killings show, as did and does Sharia Law, 9/11/01, the Muslim slaughter of Armenian Christians, and Muslim terrorism, that lethal cruelty is an accepted characteristic of Muslim religious practice.

Female Genital Mutilation

Female Genital Mutilation (FGM) predates Islam and its practitioners have included Christians, Jews, and animists. Its purpose is preventing unproscribed sexual activity by eliminating female sexual pleasure. That involves partial or total clitoris and labia removal. (A rationale is that removing these "male" features makes women totally female.) Surgically closing the vagina is sometimes accomplished instead or in addition. But FGM is not endorsed by the Quran and most Muslims do not practice it.

Islamic Terrorist Events

The Quran, the Hadiths, and the teachings of Imams provide precepts. Those can produce different behaviors, and we can be misled by propaganda about the Muslim culture. But actual events show its nature. An historic example was the Muslim Turks' disarming and slaughter of over a million Armenian Christians during WWI. More recently, about 3000 deaths resulted from the 9/11/2001 crashing of hijacked commercial airliners into New York's World Trade Center Towers and into the Pentagon in Washington—in the name of Islam.

In 2009, U.S. Army Major Nidal Hassan, a psychiatrist and a practicing Muslim, shot and killed 13 and wounded 30 in Fort Hood, Texas. In 2013, detonation of two bombs home-made by Russian Muslim brothers killed three and injured 264 (with 14 amputations) near the Boston Marathon finish line. In November 2015, Muslim Terrorist attacks in Paris killed 30 and injured 368. And on June 13, 2016, an American-born Muslim slaughtered 49 customers of a gay bar in Orlando, Florida.

The Orlando massacre affirmed a great deal about our response to the massacres by Muslims. This killer, Omar Mateen, proclaimed his allegiance to the Islamic State during his murder spree. But our government quickly spun the massacre as the work of the man and not of his religion. And gun control advocates leaped on Mateen's use of an assault rifle as an example of the need for gun control, ignoring the fact that our millions of illegal aliens and the prevalence of illegal drugs prove that making guns illegal won't prevent their ready availability. Also, a big to-do was made over whether the term Radical Islam applied. (How would this "rose" smell differently with a different name?) And, in contrast to the contravening of the Constitutional right to bear arms advocated by the gun control ideologists, blind support of the Constitutional right to freedom of religion (i.e., Islam) was evident—without consideration of Islam's honoring of the killing of infidels. Also, much was made of the unproven possibility that Mateen's homophobia (and/or implied latent homosexuality), and not his Islamic faith, could have been the cause. But, lip service to the contrary notwithstanding, this murder spree was, like its predecessors, not only condoned but honored by the Muslim culture, and we have not effectively addressed Islam's obvious central role in Muslim murders and massacres of non-Muslims.

Immigration

Another lesson in the primacy of emotions and prejudice came up in 2016 in regard to bringing Syrian (Muslim) refugees to the U.S. with no protection against their being Islamic Terrorists.

A Republican presidential candidate stated that Muslim immigration into the U.S. should be halted until the immigrants were vetted. The other Republican candidates and the leading Democratic candidate vehemently disagreed because that was not what the U.S. stands for. (A reported past restriction of Iranian Muslim immigration by President Carter wasn't addressed.)

Halting all Muslim immigration is a strong reaction to a serious potential danger, and the American politicians' responses were ideological knee jerks. Rational evaluation wasn't evident. My scoring of the exchange was: Grandstanding-100; Reason-0.

This issue is a consequence of the U.S. government's lawlessness that has resulted in our already having about 11 million illegal alien residents, including a reputedly large number of jailed criminals. We have long needed to take responsible action to assure that we legally admit those we should allow to enter and reject those who will do us harm. (If, for example, a religion were to require its adherents to practice cannibalism, we should not allow its practitioners to immigrate into the U.S.)

Because the Muslim culture integrates church and state and endorses killing non-Muslims, peaceful Muslims are Islamic Terrorists' cultural and religious colleagues. And some "peaceful"

Muslims' endorsement of killing infidels has been stated during interviews by telejournalists.

In addition to honoring the killing of infidels, the Muslim culture violates the tenets of our democracy by incorporating Sharia Law and honor killing (and forbidding the building of Christian churches). Such incompatibilities with our Constitution and culture need to be objectively addressed, with safeguards established against bringing in individuals who will be a danger to us.

Hopefully, my grandsons (and their ilk) will oppose the immigration of those whose religious or other beliefs or practices transgress the right to life, liberty, and the pursuit of happiness (and/or our own freedom of religion).

The Bigger Picture

Militant Islam seeks world domination. It considers non-Muslims inferior and militant Muslims repeatedly slaughter them. Peaceful Muslims seem to generally support or defer to their militant brethren, perhaps because contesting their behavior with more than lip service may bring lethal repercussions. When Muslims slaughtered a million Armenian Christians, the western world postured about taking action but did nothing. Consistent with that, I see our response to Militant Islam today as tokenism that disregards, without realistic assessment of, Militant Islam's actions and its potential to become a bigger scourge than Naziism. That's more significant in view of the Pew Research Center data showing that Europe's Muslim population is increasing 47% faster than its non-Muslim population and that, from 2010-2050, the Muslim population of the world will increase 73% while the non-Muslim population will increase 35%.

V-9 War

Man is inferior to several competing species in fang, claw, and strength. We're also physically inferior to some extinct human species. Homo erectus had a sturdier skull cap and eyebrow ridges, safer temporal blood flow, a stronger jaw, and a more robust body. Homo neanderthalensis was huskier, thicker boned, stronger muscled, and had a bigger brain—but went extinct soon after we invaded his colder world and appropriated some of his genes. (Including some for fair skin, blond hair and/or blue eyes?) The aggressiveness, selective cooperation, and intelligence that then made our species dominant worldwide also made us our own worst enemy.

Weapons were, and are, key to our survival. Man's early ones were made of wood, animal bones, stone, and obsidian. We added fire, swords, spears, and the bow and arrow. The wheel and domestication of horses brought us war chariots and cavalry. The Bronze Age brought better sharp edged weapons. We also poisoned water, and catapulted dead horses into besieged cities to spread disease. Guns further extended our lethal power. Warships, warplanes, bombs, missiles, etc., increased it more.

Some 100-1000 years after the Law of Moses, Sun Tzu, a late 6th Century BC Chinese tactician, wrote *The Art of War* about skills developed over the previous 2000 years. (He was studied by warriors like General Douglas MacArthur and Chairman Mao Zedong, the founder of the Republic of China.) Among Sun Tzu's teachings were defeating enemies before their threats became real, and the value of deception. (Hitler's early WWII successes were aided by those stratagems.)

Few, if any, of man's weapons have gone unused. And warfare is still practiced to gain wealth, power, resources, and/or procreative advantage. An example is the ongoing Syrian Civil War. It started in 2011 and has so far taken over 300,000 lives.

As civilization developed, our emphasis on honesty, altruism, and compassion did too. But those who will not use violence to protect themselves and their people, and who are not protected by people who will do that, end up enslaved or killed. (That doesn't change the dedicated pacifists among us. Some of them have chosen, and will choose, to die rather than go to war.)

There's a related credo derived from comments by football Coach "Red" Sanders and repeated by Coach Vince Lombardi: *Winning isn't everything, it's the only thing.* Even more succinct is one derived from a comment by baseball manager Leo Durocher: *Nice guys finish last.* These show how we place dominance (winning) over other values. Taken to lethal extremes, that's war.

War is so prevalent, and so horrible, that mankind's greatest dream is "Peace on Earth." And those who have practiced or been affected by war hold peace particularly dear. But our competitive nature makes warfare more and more inevitable as populations and disparities in wealth and opportunity increase.

Aggression and war have been the way nations form, grow, and sustain themselves. But after our bloody Civil War ended in 1865, we have followed the principle expressed by the North's greatest general in that war, Ulysses Simpson Grant (who later became President) when he claimed to have never advocated war except as a means of achieving peace. The United States has not since fought a war for conquest. And our subsequent battlefields weren't on our homeland—until 9/11/01, when Muslim (al-Qaeda) terrorists crashed hijacked commercial aircraft into the World Trade Center in New York City and into the Pentagon in Washington, DC. They killed over 2900 people and did $10 billion in damage. In retribution, we killed a lot of al-Qaeda's followers and (on 5/2/2011) its founder Osama bin Laden. But, although we haven't conducted a war for conquest since our Civil War, Islamic leaders still falsely teach that we (and Israel) are set on destroying them, and also teach that the United States is *The Great Satan*—while their ongoing Islamic jihad (Holy War) against non-Muslims endorses beheading them and burning them alive.

Dr. David Perry, Santa Clara University, pointed out that the "proper" translation of *Thou shalt not kill* is *Do not commit murder* and that other biblical passages detail reasons for capital punishment. That's consistent with our culture. We also have religious and ethical constraints on ways of fighting war and on ways of treating the vanquished. But our enemies typically have not shown a similar regard for life. {Dr. Perry also pointed out that Muslim terrorists kill captured soldiers and civilian men, and foreign women and children (whose deaths they blame on us).}

War has always been brutal. For example, during 1500-1200 B.C., Hittites drove tularemia (rabbit fever) victims onto enemy land to cause an epidemic. In 184 BC, Hannibal of Carthage had clay pots filled with venomous snakes and instructed his sailors to throw them onto enemy ships. And in 184 A.D. the City of Hadra (near Mosul, Iraq) repulsed the Roman Army by hurling clay pots filled with live scorpions at them.

America's settlers weren't ethical either. In 1622, to take over property near Jamestown, Virginia, they practiced chicanery on the Powhatan Indians (who were initially well disposed toward them). That triggered retaliation that killed about 350 settlers. Then, during negotiations for the release of prisoners held by the Indians, the settlers' doctor poisoned the liquor (sack) given the Indians for a ceremonial toast. About 200 Indians died, or were incapacitated and then killed.

During the 1763 Pontiac uprising, the Indians burned homes near Fort Pitt. The resulting crowding of the fort spread smallpox. Two Indian Chiefs who went to the fort and unsuccessfully urged the British to give up were given two blankets from the Smallpox Hospital. The fort commander wrote that he hoped the blankets would have the desired effect. (A smallpox outbreak devastated the Indians but no link to the blankets was established.) Britain's Commander in North America also advocated introducing smallpox among the "savages" and trying *every other method that can serve to Extirpate this Execrable Race*. And, during the Revolutionary War, British attempts to inflict smallpox on our soldiers were repeatedly documented.

Pontiac's Indians killed some 2000 civilian settlers and 400 soldiers. They also took women captive, something they didn't do until the White Man slaughtered women and children in the Indian villages they attacked. But the Native Americans were as unethical as their White cousins, and the conflict became no holds barred warfare.

Basically, the initial Native American acceptance of the white man was negated by treachery. Then the Whites and the Natives practiced the same hatred and according of subhuman status to each other that Japan and the United States later did in WWII. Superior weapons and numbers gave the Whites victory.

Realism also requires that we consider the values of those who have been responsible for their country's defense. One unrestrained related input is cited on the Colonial Williamsburg Official History website. It's from Admiral Sir Richard Bacon's book on Britain's WWI Admiral of the Fleet John Arbuthnot "Jacky" Fisher. He proclaimed: *The humanizing of War! You might as well talk of the humanizing of Hell...As if war could be civilized! If I'm in command when war breaks out I shall issue my order—"The essence of war is violence. Moderation in war is imbecility. Hit first, hit hard, and hit everywhere!"*

Admiral Fisher's career involved preparing for the wars that religions, ethicists, and other "good" people have never been able to eliminate. Winning those wars has enabled those "good" people to live free and condemn all war.

The lives of pragmatists like Fisher and other warriors are too often risked and too often lost because their "good" countrymen have "better" agendas than making it prohibitively costly to wage war on their country. Rarely is it acknowledged that doing so contributes to evil's triumphs and the sacrifice of so many lives of their country's youth and inadequately protected citizens.

Had we and our "peaceful" allies not been so militarily and politically weak before World War II, its 60-85 million deaths might have been avoided. Can any Religion or Ethicist (or Pacifist) credibly claim that the "peaceful" nations that were so weak that the Axis dared to attack them have none of the blood spilled in that war on their hands? Can they also credibly deny that the only thing evil needs to triumph is for good people to do nothing?

Wars and lesser conflicts are typically considered individually. That's out of context. That they are so repeated in history and myth shows they are part of all of mankind. Examples abound. The Romans killed or enslaved those they conquered. Black men sold black men, women, and children into slavery. Hitler's Nazis slaughtered Jews and many others. The Japanese defeated the Ainu, assassinated their Generals after plying them with sake at the peace celebration, and enslaved the Ainu people. Pict King Kenneth MacAlpin replaced the Pict's matrilineal inheritance with patrilineal inheritance (the King's son becomes King) by assassinating the other royal Pict families at a banquet.

Typically, victors have laid waste to countries they conquered. The United States broke that mold. For example, after WWII, we helped restore war-ravaged Europe. That didn't stop the "good" former Archbishop of Canterbury from, in 2003, politely castigating us for imperialism by questioning whether we had paid due attention to soft power (assertion of moral values) rather than hard power (war). Our Secretary of State Colin Powell responded that some situations can only be dealt with by hard power, which freed Europe, that soft power followed in the Marshall Plan, and that we did the same thing in Japan. He also stated that in the past hundred years we have put many of our wonderful young men and women at risk overseas, that many of them lost their lives, that the only thing we have asked in return is for enough ground to bury them in, and that we returned home to seek to live in peace.

Note. The overseas cemeteries for our war dead have been well kept by the countries that provided them.

Know Thine Enemy

Colleagues of the lady who believed that universal disarmament would bring peace became evident when a friend said that his wife's book club was reading Machiavelli's *The Prince*. I asked if that club's members would, if it were possible to travel back in time and kill Hitler soon enough to stop WWII, do that. They all claimed they would not. That was a unanimous vote against one killing to save millions of lives.

Peace and love and the Judeo-Christian ethic are taught at home, in church, and (especially) by example. But we also need to learn how to combat evil. A relevant statement from Sun Tzu's work is: Know thyself, know thy enemy; a thousand battles, a thousand victories. It's wise to know what to expect from our enemies and competition. Some of Machiavelli's related assessments follow.

- **Cruelty that brings peace and loyalty is not cruel.**
- **Cruelty that increases over time is bad.**
- **Cruelty is valid only to avoid greater wrongs.**
- **Mercy that makes the majority suffer is not merciful.**
- **Armed men do not obey the unarmed.**
- **Rulers who don't study war lose their states.**
- **Controlled cruelty to a few can avert widespread lawlessness and violence.**
- **People forgive the loss of a loved one faster than the confiscation of their property.**
- **People love by choice but fear punishment. Govern by using what you can control.**
- **Rulers can trust only those dependent upon them.**
- **The world isn't trustworthy, generous, and merciful. Nations must act in their own interest regardless.**
- **Satisfy the people, who are more powerful than armies.**
- **Choose wise advisors over flatterers.**
- **Reward beneficial behavior. Punish its opposite.**
- **War can be postponed but not avoided.**
- **Violence is unavoidable. Efficiently control it.**
- **Don't do unnecessary harm. Do necessary harm so severely that your victims cannot exact revenge.**
- **Be humane only when there's a tangible benefit.**
- **Armed prophets succeed. Unarmed ones fail.**
- **Empowering others weakens yourself.**
- **Break promises that don't serve your purpose.**
- **Colonize, but don't occupy; that brings hatred.**
- **Strength unused is wasted. Without strength, opportunity is wasted.**
- **A ruler who cannot trust his subjects is not safe.**
- **Do not act to be moral but to achieve results. (i.e., the end justifies the means.)**
- **Nations need good laws and good armies.**
- **Depending on others for your defense makes you their subordinate.**
- **Virtue is for imaginary rulers of perfect worlds.**

- **Wise advisors are wasted on unwise rulers, who cannot understand their advice.**
- **One cannot avoid all vices. Avoid those that lower your reputation, because they decrease your power.**

Sun Tzu and Machiavelli treated war as innate human behavior. The following table shows how valid that is. Compiled from several sources (e.g., Wikipedia, history.com), it has errors and approximations. But the nearly 300 million deaths it tabulates are far less than the total that violence has caused. And, as man's populations have increased, war has taken a greater toll. WWII killed about one-quarter of all the people recorded to have died in war. If we had invaded Japan, that one-fourth could have become one-third. WWIII will be worse.

WHEN	WARFARE		DEATHS
	KILLED	**KILLERS**	
58-50BC	Gauls	Caesar's Rome	1,000,000
184-280	China's 3-Kingdom War		37,000,000
755-763	China's An-Shi Rebellion		21,000,000
1095-1291	The Crusades		1,700,000
1206-1368	Xi-Xia	Mongols	35,000,000
1298-1303	Jews	Germany	100,000
1306-1405	Eurasians	Mongols	17,000,000
1337-1453	Europe's 100 Years War		2,800,000
1492-1900	Americans	Europeans	14,000,000
1562-1598	French Protestant-Catholic Wars		2,800,000
1616-1662	China Ming/Quing Dynasty War		25,000,000
1618-48	Europe's Protestant Rebellion		5,900,000
1665-60	Swedish Deluge of Polish-Lithuanian Commonwealth		240,000
1755-58	Zunghars	Quing Dynasty	500,000
1803-15	Napoleonic Wars		4,900,000
1816-28	Shaka Zulu's Conquest		1,700,000
1817-67	Circassians	Tsarist Russia	1,000,000

WHEN	WARFARE		DEATHS
	KILLED	KILLERS	
1851-65	China's Taiping Rebellion		32,000,000
1856-73	China's Panthay Rebellion		900,000
1861-65	United States Civil War		750,000
1864-67	Circassian Genocide		500,000
1864-76	Paraguayan War		600,000
1885-1908	Congolese	Belgium	6,500,000
1904-08	Namibians	Germany	50,000
1914-18	World War I		30,000,000
1915-23	Armenians	Turks	1,250,000
1917-21	Ukrainian-Soviet War		6,700,00
1919-20	Cossacks	Bolsheviks	400,000
1921-22	Russians	Bolshevism	7,500,000
1922-23	Ukrainians	Stalin	3,900,000
1927-49	Chinese Civil War		8,000,000
1932-33	Ukrainians	Stalin	4,500,000
1933-45	Jews	Germans	7,000,000
1936-39	Spanish Civil War		500,000
1937-38	Kurds	Turks	40,000
1937-38	Chinese	Japan	350,000
1937-38	USSR Poles	USSR	180,000
1939-45	World War II		75,000,000
1943-44	Poles	Ukrainians	130,000
1945-50	Germans	Europeans	1,750,000
1950-53	Korean War		1,340,000
1955-75	Vietnam War		1,500,000
1962-96	Maya	Guatemala	150,000
1965-66	Communists	Indonesia	300,000
1966-70	Nigerian Civil War		2,000,000
1969-79	Bubi	Eq. Guinea	50,000
1971	Hindu Minority	Pakistan	1,500,000
1972	Hutu	Tutsi	75,000

WHEN	WARFARE		DEATHS
	KILLED	KILLERS	
1975-79	Cambodian Genocide		1,700,000
1977-78	Ethiopians	Communists	265,000
1980-88	Soviet-Afghan War		1,000,000
1983-2005	2nd Sudanese Civil War		1,400,000
1986-89	Iraqi Kurds	Iraq	125,000
1994	Tutsi	Hutu	750,000
1995	Bosnians	Serbs	8,000
1996-97	1st Congo War		15,000
1998-2008	2nd Congo War		5,400,000
1999-2015	Falun Gong	China	35,000
2000-2013	Reported Murders in U.S.		221,563
2003-10	Non-Arabs	Sudan	400,000
2001-13	U.S. War on Terrorism		585,000
2008-15	Mexican Drug Cartel Killings		120,000
2011-15	Sudanese Civil War		300,000
2012	Murders in Columbia		14,700
2012	Murders in Nigeria		34,800
2015	Yazidis	ISIL Terrorists	5,000

V-10 Truth-Seeking

We're gullible. Advocates use that—and the more sincere they seem, the more effective their sales pitches. We develop resistance after a while, but we're still sometimes taken in by false or misleading information.

Debunking misinformation was an interest of the soaring intellect of famous scientist, astronomer, and Pulitzer Prize Winner Carl Sagan. {He advocated nuclear disarmament and introduced the idea that a nuclear holocaust could produce a nuclear winter. A gentle agnostic, Sagan didn't believe in the afterlife but stated that, if God is the physical laws that govern the universe (Einstein's belief), there is such a God. He also considered science a source of spirituality and termed the notion that the two are mutually exclusive a disservice to both.} Sagan considered skepticism necessary to determining truths and described his debunking "tools" in his 1996 book *The Demon-Haunted World* (co-authored by his third wife, novelist Ann Druyan). Its Chapter 12, *The Fine Art of Baloney Detection*, describes the tools in his **Baloney Detection Kit**. (which is available on the internet).

Many of my mistakes could have been avoided by better use of Sagan's tools. So, for my own use as well as my grandsons', I've recast/rephrased Sagan's tools, used some examples that he didn't, and added a caution or two.

Get Independent Confirmation

Findings confirmed by reliable independent sources are more likely to be valid. Unconfirmed results are suspect, irreproducible ones much more so. But even independent confirmation can be invalidated by the same fault(s) (common mode failure).

Check Alternatives

Conclusions are strengthened by critical comparison (including appropriate testing) with the alternatives. That's especially true of one's own hypotheses. (Proprietary interest can foster retention of invalid aspects.)

Seek Substantive Debate

A position becomes stronger if it survives substantive critical debate, especially if the debating is with knowledgeable advocates of all other points of view.

Rejecting Argument from Authority

Sagan's view was that arguments from authority have little weight in science (i.e., that science has experts but no authorities). He also discounted non-scientific authoritarian inputs, citing as an example the statement that: *President Nixon should be re-elected because he has a secret plan to end the war in Southeast Asia.* Sagan saw that as an invalid position because the electorate couldn't evaluate the plan on its merit and it required a (mistaken) trust in the President.

Quantification

Quantify (and specify). Ambiguity makes statements harder to assess. Specificity also provides a truer perspective. For example, compare *Rocky Marciano was undefeated* with: *Rocky Marciano, who retired in 1956 after six defenses of his Word Heavyweight Boxing Championship, had 49 fights and won them all, 43 by knockouts.*

Chain Links

In a chain of argument, every link in that chain, and the premise, must be valid. (A chain is only as strong as its weakest link.)

Use Occam's Razor

Occam's razor states that when there are several ways that something may have happened, the simplest way is the most likely one. (It has been used, for example, to deduce the steps in genetic mutations by selecting the simplest way the DNA could have been altered.)

Check Testability

Propositions that cannot be verified aren't worth much. For example, there's an estimate that the Universe contains 10^{21} (a billion trillion) stars. (Counting that many stars at a million stars counted a second would take over 31 million years.) And the Universe is reputedly 13.7 billion years old and has a diameter of at least 91 billion light years. (Such an expansion from a single point had to be at over three times the speed of light.) So the light from stars over 13.7 billion light years away hasn't reached us yet. Moreover, stars are still being created and destroyed, the light from some far away stars may be too faint to detect, and there may be a lot more than a billion trillion stars. So estimates of how many stars there are aren't worth much. Consequently, estimates of how many Earth-like civilizations there are, if they're based on how many stars there are, aren't worth much either. (That discounts wild speculations like: if there's a one in a trillion chance that a star has a planet with life forms comparable to Earth's, there are at least a billion such planets. But some narrower assertions about the likelihood of there being life elsewhere may have merit. An example is the Drake equation. It provides a probabilistic estimate of the extraterrestrial civilizations in the Milky Way Galaxy.)

Do Controlled Experiments

Controlled experiments are essential elements of proof. An example is that proving that a medicine cures a disease 20% of the time requires a test group that includes individuals who all get the medicine and individuals who all get a dummy pill (with none of them knowing which pill they are getting) to separate the effect of the medicine from the placebo effect.

Attack Arguments

A common tactic is to try to discredit an argument by attacking the person making it. (That's a lot like a defense attorney trying to absolve a client by blaming the victim for the crime.) If an argument's logic and foundations are valid, the character of its proponent(s) is immaterial. Ergo a proper critical assessment attacks the argument, not its arguer(s).

Reject Adverse Consequence Arguments

An argument must not be credited based on the consequences. It's invalid, for example, to credit the statement that, if the accused in a sensational murder trial isn't convicted, others will be encouraged to kill. (The issue is the guilt in that case.)

Seek Proof

An updated (by me) version of an old mantra is: *Absence of proof is not proof of absence.* (I've replaced "evidence" with "proof.") The absence of evidence may establish reasonable doubt, but it falls short of being proof. Sometimes we're stuck with the risk of having to take action based on insufficient or even no evidence, but we need to avoid that if and when we can. (That's a major reason why nations spy on each other.)

Reject Appeals to Ignorance

An appeal to ignorance is a claim that something that hasn't been proven to be true is false, or vice versa. Such claims are inherently false. An example of Sagan's is the false assertion that there's no compelling evidence that UFOs aren't visiting Earth, so they are—and there's intelligent life elsewhere in the Universe. Appeals to ignorance, especially when stated by Gurus, are often mistakenly credited. Those who use them may take advantage of the great difficulty of proving a negative assertion (e.g., finding life on Mars is a daunting task, but it would only require finding one life form there to prove that life exists on Mars, while proving there's no life on Mars would be far harder.)

Reject Special Pleading

A paraphrased example of Sagan's is: *How can God permit Jews, Christians, and Muslims—who are all enjoined to embrace loving kindness and compassion—to have perpetuated such cruelty for so long?* The special plea in response is: *You don't understand free will.* I see that as evading the question about God's permission and the implied one about God's disinterest.

Recognize Non Sequiturs

A non sequitur provides an unsupported conclusion. The term is Latin for "it doesn't follow." (Basically, any fallacious argument is a non sequitur.) A Sagan example is: *Our nation will prevail because God is great.* Nearly every nation pretends that's true, with Germany stating it as *"Gott mit uns."* But that example invites religious hair-splitting, so I prefer one I heard when I was a boy scout on a weekend camping trip. During a clear night with a panorama of brilliant stars, a scoutmaster looked up and proclaimed that the beauty of that sky was proof that there is a God. It wasn't, of course, any more than the destructive rampage of a gigantic hurricane proves that there is no

God. (But I still often think of that sky with a special reverence when I see so few stars in a seemingly clear night sky.)

Reject Propositions That Assume the Answer

A Sagan example of this fault was: *We must have the death penalty to discourage violent crime.* He made the point that whether the death penalty actually reduced the crime rate is the criterion. To that I add is that, unless it is known that the courts will convict and the death penalty will be imposed and carried out, there's no way to tell the death penalty's impact. (Threatened punishments that aren't carried out soon become ineffective.)

Reject Observational Selection

Observational Selection, as Philosopher Francis Bacon put it, is counting the hits and forgetting the misses (tossing out data that doesn't support the desired result.) Sagan's example was that a State boasts of the Presidents it has produced but is silent about its serial killers.

Understanding Statistics

Sagan's example was President Eisenhower's expression of alarm and astonishment upon discovering that fully half of all Americans have below average intelligence. (The other half have to be above average.) But that anecdote masks the need to accompany Whats with Whys. Statistical deviations above and below the "average" may require explanation. And samples may not be representative. Some studies might use wrong reference values. For example, an assumed average IQ of 100 may not be the average IQ for the test(s) used. (It's wiser to explain statistical analyses to us non-mathematicians than to expect us to learn their intricacies.)

Big Picture Consistency

Look at the big picture and assess all of it under the same criteria. A Sagan example of failing to do that was considering the conjecture that the Universe will continue to exist forever (i.e., that it will never end) to be reasonable but the conjecture that it has always existed (i.e., that it had no beginning) to be absurd.

Cast Out Meaningless Questions

Sagan's example was: *What happens when an irresistible force meets an immovable object?* (Neither premise is objectively true, and the presence of either mandates the absence of the other.)

Reject the Excluded Middle

This practice involves considering only the extremes while ignoring the possibilities between them. A Sagan example was: *Either you love your country or you hate it.* {Some situations are either-or ones (binary), but many, like this example, aren't.}

Separate Correlations From Causes

A Sagan example was: *A survey shows that more college graduates are homosexual than those with lesser education, therefore education makes people gay.*

Reject Post Hoc, ergo Propter Hoc

This Latin phrase means: it happened after, so it was caused by. That's a subset of the distinction between correlation and cause. My first lesson in it came when my father quizzically stated that roosters crowing before dawn make the sun come up. A Sagan example of it was: *Before women got the vote, there were no nuclear weapons.*

Don't Credit Straw Men

A Straw Man caricatures an argument to shoot it down. Emotion-charging an issue makes Straw Men more effective. An example was Richard Nixon's 1952 "Checkers" speech (it's available on the internet). During Nixon's campaign for the Republican Vice-Presidential nomination, he was accused of illegally diverting $18,000 in campaign contributions to his personal use. Nixon denied that, described costs that a candidate had that shouldn't be paid by taxpayers, proclaimed his poverty relative to his Democratic Party counterpart, and cited the gift of a black and white cocker spaniel to his young daughters. He said that they loved the dog, had named it Checkers, and no matter what was said about it, we aren't going to give the dog back. His Straw Men depicted his opposition as heartless nitpickers, the fund diversion issue died, he became Eisenhower's running mate, and they won the election in a landslide.

Abjure Half-Truths

A half-truth, by definition, is partially true or mingles truth and falsehood with the intent to deceive. A Sagan example was a TV program prophesizing the assassination attempt on President Reagan. If the program was recorded after the event, it was a statement of history masquerading as a prophecy. My example of a half-truth is White enslavement of Blacks in America. It's a true statement that provides a false image. Slavery wasn't (and isn't) a White vs. Black issue but a way that man subordinates those he can dominate. And the whole truth also must include the fact that, in America, more Whites died in the fight against slavery than the Whites who died to keep it intact.

Discredit Weasel Wording

Calling one thing another, especially when done from a position of authority, can reduce or eliminate repercussions. An example of such weasel wording was President Truman's bypassing of the Constitutional vesting of the authority to declare war in the Congress by calling the Korean War a Police Action when he started it.

Don't Stand on Slippery Slopes

A Slippery Slope argument states an inevitable consequence without showing that such will be the case (e.g., *If sexually explicit magazines are banned, we'll end up burning books.*)

Another Slippery Slope proposition is: *Guns kill, so banning them will prevent killing.* This emotion-charged issue has proponents and opponents who misstate the facts. Still, one can deduce, from the estimates that 9.9% of Hondurans have guns while 47% of the Swiss do, and Honduras has the world's highest homicide rate while Switzerland has one of the lowest, that the rate of homicides is a function of the cultures and conditions involved, not of their access to guns. That lends credence to the opposing viewpoint that *Guns don't kill people, people kill people* (and will do so with other weapons, like knives or home-made bombs, if they don't have guns).

Lost in the polemics is the consideration that the inability to keep illegal drugs off the streets also shows an inability to eliminate guns, and illegal ones will abound. Another factor is the degree to which the bases of the Constitutional right (and the need) to bear arms are still valid. (How has society and human nature changed since the 18th Century? What has changed to make invalid the 20th Century lesson learned from the disarming of the Armenians and the subsequent slaughter of over a million of them? Why did Hitler insist that conquered peoples be disarmed? Why are the multitude of statements by the founding fathers about the necessity for the people to be armed now invalid?) Yet another consideration is the effect of disarming law-abiding citizens and making them easier targets for the criminal element. Further, Christianity's peaceful founder endorsed being armed. At the Last Supper, during a discourse about how to handle the difficulties to be faced after Christ's impending suffering, Jesus said: *When I sent you without purse, and scrip, and shoes, lacked ye anything? And they said, nothing. Then said he* *unto them, But now, he that hath a purse, let him take it, and likewise his scrip: and he that hath no sword, let him sell his garment, and buy one. (*Luke 22:35-36). (This message is the same in the Vulgate Bible, Tyndale's New Testament, and the King James Bible.)

Arguments for and against gun control need to be objectively weighed, and pitted against each other, with a sound rationale presented and accepted for either the sustaining or rejection of each argument. The actual effect of a gun ban is very relevant to that. Australia tightened its gun controls in 1996, and gun ownership there dropped 28.5% (from 7% to 5%). The fluctuating homicide rate decreased from 354 homicides in 1996 to 282 homicides in 2007. If that oversimplified data were representative, the drop in gun ownership was 71% effective in cutting back on homicides. But a more comprehensive analysis was needed and three were conducted. The 2003 one concluded that some of the decline began before the reform. The 2006 one concluded that the decline was more rapid after the reform. The 2008 one concluded that the reform had no effect on the homicide (or suicide) rate.

Quantification hasn't helped this issue. The claim that gun control reduces the homicide rate is an example of Inconsistency (advocates not giving objective, equal consideration to alternative choices) and of the inability to discriminate between correlation and cause (in this case, Post Hoc, ergo Propter Hoc). And gun control's effect on the murder rate hasn't been separated from cultural and economic effects on it.

Scientific resolution of this issue is highly unlikely. My opinion is that a gun is a tool—and not the only one available—that people use to kill, and is no more the cause of killing than Hemingway's publisher authored *The Old Man and the Sea* or my computer wrote this book. Banning guns may have a temporary effect but cannot correct the root cause(s) of killing. And unless the means chosen really reduce the murder rate enough to clearly outweigh the adverse consequences, those are controlling. {Better means of keeping known dangerous people away from potential victims may better address the root cause(s) than banning guns would.}

Some Slippery Slope arguments might turn out to be correct projections; their fault is that they invalidly presume an outcome. That typically happens when advocacy outweighs objectivity.

Determine Why

(Sagan didn't specifically address this.) We're often confronted with propositions that, at most, only rhetorically address Why and/or Why Not. But propositions that lack well considered, valid answers to both questions aren't justified.

Utilization

The preceding thinking tools and examples better enable their users to avoid, in personal and professional matters, becoming equivalent to Rubes who were sold the Brooklyn Bridge.

V-11 Wrap-Up

My fiancé (whose values, goals, and intellect are more compatible with mine than I had any hope of encountering) opined that I couldn't have written this book much sooner. She was right. Maturation has improved my grasp of the big picture, and I'm less swayed by conventional wisdom.

I hope that man's awesome repository of written knowledge will benefit my grandsons as much as it has me. In spite of the transition toward TV viewing, the written word is still irreplaceable. And the internet (the world's largest library) enables us to surmount many propagandas that polarize us.

Significant parts of our species have come a very long way toward the Goodness (Godliness) and sensibility that are civilization's goals. I hope my grandsons will further that progress with a non-disparaging, "...what fools these (we) mortals be" eye that sees and fosters mankind's potential to be far better.

There's also a need to reject the Pollyannaish view that biases us toward considering man to have better traits than his history shows. That view often prevents realistic assessment of the threat posed by our competition, locally and internationally.

Darwin, in his *Origin of Species,* observed that all life forms proliferate beyond the sustaining ability of their resources. We see that in repetitive pleas to feed starving unfortunates. But, notwithstanding the likes of Albert Schweitzer and Mother Teresa, we do little to better their lot. The lack of resources and the inability to exploit them remain. Unless and until we enable the disadvantaged to compete with the advantaged, our aid to each new generation of the impoverished will contribute to the birth of more offspring under similarly adverse circumstances.

In earlier times, the young were expected to delay marrying until they were well enough established to support a family. That since diminished thrust still exists, but the stronger natural and religious *Go Forth and Multiply* mandate ensures overpopulation, warfare, and genocide.

A population control example exists in China's now doubled one-child per family limit. It has been maligned for abortions and for a high abortion rate of female fetuses (families limited to one child generally prefer males). And there's still no proven way to replace war as a means of matching a population to its resources.

We even support overpopulation—through tax deductions and welfare payments based on the number of children involved. Many deplore having children in order to get more money from the government (or pay less tax). But few of us are hard-hearted enough to deny the funds, however misused, that the children involved need. The overpopulation we thereby foster is an example of why Machiavelli was right when he said that war can be postponed but not avoided.

Our combination of Natural, Societal, and Godly (Good) behavior may evolve to the point where we tailor our reproduction to prevent outstripping our resources. We even may become able to effectively punish and prevent the use of force to further personal and group goals. But until we evolve that far, any culture that isn't strong enough to protect itself is on the road to extinction.

My hope is that my genetic and cultural descendants will contribute to man's cultural evolution by carefully planning the size of their families, living economically, and investing wisely (starting before a family is begun) to better assure the ability to give their children a good education. (That's a big dream. We live in a world in which raising children strains parents' resources. Few of us have the means and self-discipline to prepare for that.)

By being born in America, you've been given a significant advantage, guys. Do your best to enable your offspring and other cultural descendants to be deserving. If they are, try to give them an even greater advantage. In addition to sound planning, economic living, and investment, setting a good example of hard work and honesty, and of a lack of hate, greed, and complacency would be a fine start on doing that.

Unfortunately, I can but wistfully hope that America will sustain the lives and freedoms of its people. Still, I hope for your Good (Godly) behavior and for war's horrors to be kept away from your door. And, in any case, may your goodness earn and God grant you sunbeams to warm you, moonbeams to charm you, laughter to cheer you, good friends near you, a special angel to keep you from harm and, when the time comes, eternal peace.

Appendix

Some Military Terms

ASW: Anti-Submarine Warfare

CNO: Chief of Naval Operations

CO: Commanding Officer, or Captain. Officer in command.

Command Duty Officer: A position whose meaning can have different roles and authority depending on the Command involved. As I encountered it on ballistic missile submarines, it consisted of the designation of either the CO or the XO as the officer to whom the Officer of the Deck (Conning Officer) initially reported maneuvers, contacts, events, occurrences, etc. Typically, the Captain had the Command Duty during the day, and the XO took the Command Duty from after the Wardroom movie in the evening until the Captain relieved him after breakfast. That kept one of the two most senior and experienced officers readily available to the Officer of the Deck

ComSubLant: Commander, Submarine Force, U.S. Atlantic Fleet

ComSubPac: Commander, Submarine Force, U.S. Pacific Fleet

Conn: The task of giving ship control orders (course, speed, etc.)

Deck: The task of being in charge of, and responsible for, the maneuvering of the ship.

DivCom: Division Commander

Enlisted Personnel Ratings. These are the specialties of noncommissioned naval personnel. Abridged descriptions of some follow.

BM: Boatswain's Mate. BMs are the Navy's seamanship rating. They operate boats and operate and maintain deck equipment, lines and rigging, and remove corrosion from and paint exterior surfaces.

GM: Gunners Mate. GMs maintain weapons.

ET: Electronics Technician. ETs maintain electronic equipment.

EM: Electrician's Mate. EMs maintain generators, batteries, wiring, etc.

EN: Engineman. ENs maintain engines (e.g., diesels).

FT: Fire Control Technician. FTs maintain weapon control systems.

MM: Machinist Mate. MMs maintain propulsion and auxiliary machinery.

TM: Torpedoman: TMs maintain torpedoes.

QM: Quartermaster. QMs maintain navigational equipment and charts, and visual signaling equipment.

YN: Yeoman. YNs type letters and reports, and maintain associated files.

Enlisted Personnel Rating Levels. Levels of seniority/authority. In decreasing level of seniority, they range from E9 to E1 as follows.

E9: Master Chief Petty Officer. (e.g., BMCM, GMCM, QMCM)

E8: Senior Chief Petty Officer. (e.g., BMCS, GMCS)

E7: Chief Petty Officer. (e.g., BMC, GMC, ETC, FTC, QMC.)

E6: First Class Petty Officer. (e.g., BM1, GM1, ET1, QM1)

E5: Second Class Petty Officer. (e.g., BM2, ET2, FT2)

E4: Third Class Petty Officer. (e.g., BM3, TM3.)

E3: Seaman (SN), eligible to advance in deck ratings. Also a designated apprentice (e.g., BMSN, GMSN, etc.)

Fireman (FN), eligible to advance in engineering ratings. Also, a designated apprentice in those ratings (e.g., EMFN, MMFN, etc.)

E2: Seaman Apprentice (SA). Fireman Apprentice (FA).

E1: Seaman Recruit (SR). Fireman Recruit (FR).

Note. Other E1, E2, and E3 ratings include Airman, Hospital Corpsman, etc.

Field Grade Officer: One of the rank of O5 (Commander or Lieutenant Colonel) or above.

JOOD: Junior Officer of the Deck. (A trainee position.)

Knots: Nautical Miles per hour. One knot = ~1.1516 miles per hour. (A nautical mile is one minute of latitude anywhere on the earth's surface, and one minute of longitude at the equator.)

LPO: Leading Petty Officer. Enlisted rating in charge of a group.

<u>Officer Ranks</u>: (In order of decreasing seniority)

O11   Fleet Admiral (wartime use only)
       General of the Army (wartime use only)
       General of the Air Force (wartime use only)

O10   Admiral (ADM) Chief of Naval Operations, or
       Admiral (ADM) Commandant of the Coast Guard, or
       General (Gen) Commandant of the Marine Corps
       General (GEN) Army Chief of Staff
       General (Gen) Air Force Chief of Staff

O9   Vice Admiral (VADM) - Navy, Coast Guard
       Lieutenant General (LtGen) - Marine Corps
       Lieutenant General (LTG) - Army
       Lieutenant General (Lt Gen) - Air Force

O8   Rear Admiral, Upper Half (RADM) - Navy, Coast Guard
       Major General (MajGen) - Marine Corps
       Major General (MG) - Army
       Major General (Maj Gen) - Air Force

O7   Rear Admiral, Lower Half (RADM) - Navy, Coast Guard
       Brigadier General (BGen) - Marine Corps
       Brigadier General (BG) - Army
       Brigadier General (Brig Gen) - Air Force

O6   Captain (CAPT) - Navy, Coast Guard
       Colonel (Col) - Marine Corps & Air Force
       Colonel (COL) - Army

O5   Commander (CDR) - Navy, Coast Guard
       Lieutenant Colonel (LtCol) - Marine Corps
       Lieutenant Colonel (LTCOL) - Army
       Lieutenant Colonel (LT Col) - Air Force

O4   Lieutenant Commander (LCDR) - Navy, Coast Guard
      Major (Maj.) - Marine Corps & Air Force
      Major (MAJ) - Army

O3   Lieutenant (LT) - Navy, Coast Guard
      Captain (Capt) - Marine Corps & Air Force
      Captain (CPT) - Army

O2   Lieutenant Junior Grade (LTJG) - Navy, Coast Guard
      First Lieutenant (1stLt) - Marine Corps
      First Lieutenant (1LT) - Army
      First Lieutenant (1st Lt) - Air Force

O1   Ensign (ENS) - Navy, Coast Guard
      Second Lieutenant (2ndLt) - Marine Corps
      Second Lieutenant (2LT) - Army
      Second Lieutenant (2nd Lt) - Air Force

Note. That different services construct abbreviations for the same rank with the same name differently is a tiny clue to the difficulties of inter-service cooperation.

OOD: Officer of the Deck. The On-Watch Officer in charge of maneuvering the ship.

Super Nuke: A nuclear qualified individual with exceptional expertise in both nuclear and conventional engineering, in both operational and maintenance aspects.

Task Force: A group of ships assigned a specific mission, and typically given a two-digit number and abbreviated to TF. (e.g., Task Force 88 = TF-88.)

XO: Executive Officer. Second in Command. May take the Deck and the Conn (but not from the Captain). Also the ship's personnel and reports administrator.

1MC: Shipboard General Announcing System.

Printed in the United States
By Bookmasters